Designing Your Future

Key Trends, Challenges, and Choices Facing Association and Nonprofit Leaders

Designing Your Future

Key Trends, Challenges, and Choices Facing Association and Nonprofit Leaders

Fast Future

Rohit Talwar

Garry Golden

asae & the center™
for association leadership

ASAE & The Center for Association Leadership
1575 I Street, NW
Washington, DC 20005-1103
Phone: (202) 626-2723; (888) 950-2723 outside the metropolitan Washington, DC area
Fax: (202) 220-6439
E-mail: books@asaecenter.org
We connect great ideas and great people to inspire leadership and achievement in the
association community.

John H. Graham IV, CAE, President and CEO, ASAE
Susan Sarfati, CAE, President and CEO, The Center for Association Leadership and
Executive Vice President, ASAE
Karin I. Croft, Vice President, Strategic & Future Focused Research, ASAE &
The Center for Association Leadership
Keith C. Skillman, CAE, Vice President, Publications, ASAE & The Center for Association Leadership
Baron Williams, CAE, Director of Book Publishing, ASAE & The Center for Association Leadership

Cover design by Beth Lower, Art Director, ASAE & The Center for Association Leadership

This book is available at a special discount when ordered in bulk quantities. For information, contact the
ASAE & The Center for Association Leadership Member Service Center at (202) 371-0940.

A complete catalog of titles is available on the ASAE & The Center for Association Leadership
web site at www.asaecenter.org/bookstore.

Contents

Preface

The Fundamental Challenge for Associations and Nonprofits

Charting a course to adapt to future economic, demographic, social, environmental, and technological changes may be the single greatest challenge and opportunity facing associations and nonprofits. Identifying and analyzing those trends, issues, and events that are likely to have a transformational impact within the association sector is critical if associations are to remain healthy and relevant to their members. This means that they need practical insights and tools to help define their options, assess emerging risks, identify opportunities for future sustainability and growth, and develop and implement responsive strategies. Through consultation with members we established that they needed these tools—and that they wanted them now! ASAE & The Center for Association Leadership's *Association of the Future* research program was established specifically to help support association leaders on this journey toward creating their preferred future.

Designing Your Future

Designing Your Future: Key Trends, Challenges, and Choices Facing Association and Nonprofit Leaders is the first release in a series of planned resources and tools from the *Association of the Future* program. The aim is to provide associations with critical perspectives on the future global environment, including competitive and market issues that will help formulate strategic plans to capture opportunities and prepare for emerging threats.

Getting ahead of change is difficult. It is easier to respond to problems of the day than it is to invest time and resources in what might come to pass. But make no mistake: there are very real existing and emerging threats to the future viability and competitiveness of associations and nonprofits. We fully expect that many will seize the opportunity and overcome the challenges to thrive in a changing world, but we also know that others will fail to take heed of the warning signs and will succumb to the threats.

The widespread assessment among leaders of those governments and industries who are coping best with a changing world is that past success strategies are less valid in a world being shaped by new rules, new players, and fundamental shifts in power and influence. Today, associations and their members must begin repositioning themselves to address these emerging realities. This publication is the first in a series of practical resources and tools designed to help leaders, boards, and staff to design and build their associations of the future. Each new content release will provide different aspects of the resources and knowledge that leaders need to develop future strategies, plans, and innovations. Our goal is to provide insights, tools, and ideas that will help your association stay vibrant and relevant in the face of a changing U.S. and global environment, new operational challenges, and the constantly evolving needs and expectations of your members.

Designing Your Future is the first of these tools, designed to help identify the drivers of change, to surface critical implications for associations, and to set out the key choices and decisions that associations will need to make. This publication addresses three specific objectives:

- *Introduce critical trends, ideas and developments* that could have an impact on associations and their members over the next five to ten years.
- *Identify the key challenges* that these trends create for association leaders as they develop their longer-term strategies.
- *Provide a strategic framework for making key choices and decisions* about the preferred future for your organization, whether an association or other type of nonprofit.

The structure and content of the report are designed to address the very clear needs expressed during the extensive range of member consultation activities we conducted between June 2007 and April 2008.

Subsequent phases of the *Association of the Future* program will deliver a range of publications, case studies, implementation tools, and resources, such as trend updates and industry- and functional-level impact assessments. Through continuous member engagement, ASAE & The Center aim to broaden the reach and value of this program to truly impact the associations of the future.

Program Methodology

Since 1994 ASAE & The Center have conducted a series of standalone environmental scans using a variety of methodologies to provide members with critical insights into the trends and forces shaping our world. The *Association of the Future* program was conceived as a means to deepen and extend the scope of the futures research process. The aim is to deliver an integrated range of outputs to stakeholders within the association community through a dynamic multi-year program having continuous scanning as a core component.

The *Association of the Future* program was formally launched in December 2007. Its foundation is an environmental scan that has resulted in the detailed profiling of 50 key trends, issues, and developments considered of importance to the association community. In addition, we have created shorter profiles of a further 100 trends that could become increasingly important over time. The challenges and guidance presented in this document are based on the analysis of these trends and their implications for the association community. A number of key requirements have driven the design of the *Association of the Future* program, but the primary drivers of the methodology are

- *Iterative design*. We have chosen to adopt a continuously evolving program design adjusted as stakeholder participation yields new insights.
- *Broad consultation and engagement*. The commitment is to involve a broad cross-section of the association community through invitations to participate in survey-based reviews, workshops, and a range of other engagement mechanisms at key stages.
- *Gradual build and piloting*. Each release will deliver manageable levels of information able to be added to over time. The program also seeks to ensure that the methods adopted deliver value to members; hence, we have a strong commitment to regular testing of both the formats and content of deliverables.

These objectives are illustrated in the approach to developing *Designing Your Future*. We began with an initial stage of consultation from June to December 2007 to help scope out both the overall shape of this first phase of research and the key requirements of those it was intended to serve. Key activities included

- Informal interviews with large and small associations, industry experts, and consultants,

- A "focus group" session in October 2007 with members who had already undertaken different forms of environmental scanning in order to understand how they currently do it, how the information is captured, how it is used, and the kind of support that would be required from ASAE & The Center to help with environmental scanning and future planning,
- A workshop session with approximately 60 people at ASAE & The Center's Great Ideas Conference in Orlando in December 2007, and
- A series of small-group breakfasts and lunches at the Great Ideas Conference.

This was followed by a phase of desk research and consultation with experts and stakeholders that yielded a list of approximately 250 trends. These were then whittled down to a long list of 149 trends, issues and developments that could have an impact on associations as soon as within the next five years. For each trend a short description was written and a request to review these descriptions was sent out to 2,050 members and staff of ASAE & The Center and members of the association management company (AMC) community. Respondents were asked to

- Select the trends they felt would have the greatest impact on associations,
- Comment on the trends as appropriate, and
- Identify additional trends that should be considered.

A total of 240 responses were received. The respondent selections produced a ranking of the trends. This ranking was used to short-list key trends considered to be of greatest importance to the association community. In addition, as a result of respondent feedback, some trends were merged, others had their titles changed, and additional trends were added. This resulted in a list of 62 key trends. These were profiled in detail and sent to over 2,300 association community stakeholders and members of the AMC community who provided their views on the potential impact of these trends on the strategies and key functions of associations. Respondents were offered the opportunity to respond electronically or take part in one of eight half-day workshops held in Washington, DC, from April 14 to 17, 2008 (over 100 people participated in these sessions).

At this stage, the entire program and methodology and the 62 key trends were evaluated by a panel of five independent peer reviewers. As a result of the feedback from respondents and peer reviewers, some trends were merged—resulting in a final set of 50 key trends—for which the profiles were then updated. This feedback was also used to help define both the key challenges facing association leaders and the decision making framework presented in this report.

At every opportunity, ASAE & The Center staff and consultants probed to find out how association leaders currently use future-focused information, how they would like to use it, and the delivery formats that would provide greatest value to them. This continuous feedback has had a significant bearing on the design of the overall program, the detailed objectives and activities of the first phase, and the contents of this report.

One report cannot address all the varied needs of the association community. Associations and nonprofits vary along many dimensions, but most obviously in size, resources, and experience with environmental scanning, future thinking, and strategic planning. A desired outcome of the *Association of the Future* project is to help narrow this gap over time, establishing a knowledge base and set of tools supported and expanded upon by a community of members who wish to advance more innovative and sustainable practices for associations.

The first round of outputs are not targeted at the very largest or smallest of organizations: we are focusing on what might be considered the association "middle market"—typically associations with a budget of over $1 million employing at least five permanent staff. We believe many larger associations may already have well-established environmental scanning and strategic management processes; those largely run by part-time volunteers, however, may lack the time and resources to devote to this exercise. However, we hope that both groups will still find value in our analysis of trends and challenges and in the questions they raise about the future of associations.

Defining and building the association of the future is not a one-off activity but a journey—one that every association must take to ensure a sustainable future. As you prepare for your journey, we hope that *Designing Your Future* will prove to be a valuable and inspirational resource and a powerful call to action.

ASAE & The Center for Association Leadership
August 2008

Acknowledgments

ASAE & The Center wish to acknowledge and extend our appreciation to the association executives and the consultants and researchers from Fast Future Research who contributed to the development of *Designing Your Future*. This project was unusual in many ways; of particular significance were, first, the emphasis placed on association stakeholder involvement in project design and content development as the project evolved; second, the speed at which the activity was carried out—delivering this publication in five months. The research team from Fast Future Research demonstrated great flexibility, commitment and stamina, working with an evolving project design and an ever-narrowing production timeframe.

We would like to acknowledge and thank Rohit Talwar, lead author and CEO of Fast Future Research, Garry Golden, coauthor and researcher, and their team of researchers: Tim Hancock, George Padgett, and Michele Bowman.

We would also like to extend our gratitude to the members of the Environmental Scan Task Force drawn from ASAE & The Center's Research Committee, who contributed countless hours conceiving, planning, and designing the *Association of the Future* project and overseeing the project as it has proceeded:

Mark N. Dorsey, CAE, Chair, American Snowsports Education Association

Jeff De Cagna, Ed.M., Principled Innovation LLC

Mark T. Engle, CAE, Association Management Center

Suzanne Pine, Fernley & Fernley Inc

Cathlene Williams, Ph.D., CAE, Association of Fundraising Professionals

Additional thanks are due Mark Dorsey, Suzanne Pine, and Mark Engel for their thorough, thoughtful and insightful review of *Designing Your Future* before its publication.

A final word of acknowledgement and our sincere gratitude go to those members, stakeholders, and staff of ASAE & The Center who participated in the various stages of project design and insight development. Our thanks go to all those individuals who participated in the various initial consultation activities that took place between June and December 2007. Our deepest appreciation also goes to the more than 350 members of ASAE & The Center who participated in our trend development process by completing our survey, responding via email or participating in the workshops in Washington, DC.

Section 1
A Call to Action

1.1. Emerging Trends, Inescapable Challenges

As you read the newspapers, scan your favorite blogs, or watch the television news, your senses are assaulted by a constant flow of signals that the world is changing. You are confronted by powerful trends, emerging issues, and new developments. Although individually powerful, when viewed as a whole, they combine to suggest that massive shifts are taking place in the economy, in society, and in our daily lives. The 30,000-foot perspective suggests that we are entering a period of five to ten years during which tumultuous and transformational changes will unfold that will affect us all in fundamental ways.

Figure 1. A Changing Global Landscape

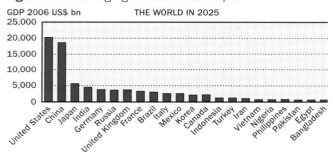

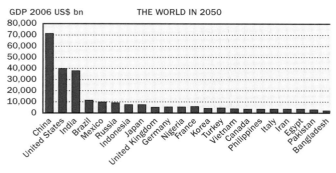

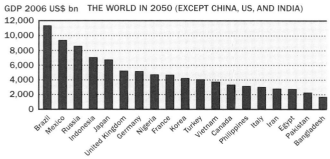

Source: http://www2.goldmansachs.com/ideas/brics/BRICs-and-Beyond.html

1.2. New Choices for Associations and Nonprofits

All of the often unspoken but critical planning assumptions you have traditionally made in your lives and in your associations are being challenged. Western nations can no longer assume uninterrupted growth and global economic leadership as given (Figure 1). Across the globe, developing economies are gaining strength, taking their people out of poverty, increasing their capacity for homegrown innovation, and creating new opportunities for domestic firms and foreign partners. Globally, concerns about sustainability and the environment are exerting greater influence on decision making, and advances in the internet and social networks are now transforming how you can innovate, communicate, and build communities.

At home, rising life expectancy means that you can imagine lifespans of 25 years post-retirement, with many working on into their eighth and ninth decades. At the same time, new generations are entering the workforce with very different expectations. How to manage the multi-generational workforce will be one of the critical employer challenges of the next two decades. All of these changes will have a direct influence on your members and their expectations of the associations that serve them.

Clearly these trends, issues, and developments will affect us all in different ways and to different degrees: but the inescapable truth is that we can't ignore them. They are changing industries and professions, influencing incomes and wealth distribution, driving political decision making, and reshaping the social agenda. They are forcing us all to rethink how to manage our careers, where to look for the next opportunity, how to educate our children, and how to ensure the long-term future of ourselves and our families. For associations, the implications will be equally transformational. You are faced with a clear choice: understand and respond to the changes, or ignore them and hope that somehow you'll survive. *Hope is not a strategy.*

In preparing this publication, we consulted association leaders from across America. Those leaders see the convergence of these changes as both an opportunity to transform their associations and as a fundamental threat to their existence. Most recognized that there are no neat solutions, no perfect response strategies, no three-point plans, and no perfect recipes for how to make sense of the changes, and map out a course guaranteeing survival and growth. What they said they needed were solid research-based insights into the trends and forces shaping their worlds, a clear sense of the challenges these will create for associations, and a range of ideas, roadmaps, case studies, tools, and approaches to help them design and implement preferred futures for their associations. That is the role of the *Association of the Future* Project.

1.3. The *Association of the Future* Project

The *Association of the Future* Project is a multi-year research program from ASAE & The Center designed to help associations understand the drivers of future change and use the insights to help envisage, plan, and transform toward their "preferred futures." The program is driven by extensive consultation with members and other key stakeholders and will evolve in line with changing member needs and challenges. It was clear from our consultations that the first of these tools should identify the drivers of change, surface critical implications for associations, and set out the key choices and decisions associations need to make. *Designing Your Future* was created to address those needs.

1.4. Designing Your Future: Key Trends, Challenges and Choices Facing Association and Nonprofit Leaders

Designing Your Future has three specific objectives:

- *Introduce critical trends, ideas and developments* that could have an impact on associations and their members over the next five to ten years.
- *Identify the key challenges* that these trends create for association leaders as they develop their longer-term strategies.
- *Provide a strategic framework for making key choices and decisions* about the preferred future for organizations, whether an association or other type of nonprofit.

At the heart of the report are a set of 50 key trends, issues, and developments (Appendix 1) that were selected and refined from an initial list of 250 through an extensive process of consultation with members and key stakeholders. The emphasis throughout this "call to action" is on providing practical insights into the implications, opportunities, key challenges, and choices raised by these trends. An explanation of how to use *Designing Your Future* to drive change in your organization is provided at the end of this section.

1.5. Document Structure

The document is broken down into five sections and seven appendices (see page 3).

1.6. Developing a Foresight Culture

Although some associations have a very clear sense of how to shape their future, most are at the start of a new era. You are entering an age of uncertainty in which you cannot assume that the past will be your guide in determining how the trends, issues, and challenges outlined in this report will shape the economic and social landscape. Because uncertainty is one of the few things you can take for granted, perhaps your biggest challenge is developing an organization that can operate effectively with imperfect information. This means developing a tolerance for uncertainty and creating a culture of foresight by constantly

- Exploring your assumptions about the future factors that will affect your current activities, plans, and new projects,
- Asking about what's coming next,
- Analyzing the ways in which emerging trends and developments will affect your members and their expectations of you, and
- Preparing for alternative scenarios of how the future may play out.

1.7. Creating an Innovation Architecture

In an era in which many expect greater pressure on budgets and a heightened focus on returns on investments, a critical success factor will be your organization's resilience, adaptability, and ability to

- Seek out innovative solutions,
- Search for new funding sources,
- Leverage social networks and community,
- Try new business models,

Designing Your Future

• Constantly evolve the design of your organization to respond to changing needs, and

• Look for collaborative opportunities wherever possible.

These are all activities that require skills that may or may not exist within your organization today. Hence, determining the mix of core activities and talents required of tomorrow's organization is now a priority, for it will drive the decisions about the capabilities required in-house and those to be sourced through partners or vendors. These choices will, in turn, shape the profile of the kind of talent you need to recruit, develop, and retain and the organizational structure you need to put around it to enable that talent to perform. In short, you need to develop an "innovation architecture" for your association that facilitates the development and implementation of fresh ideas.

> *Do you have a culture that encourages foresight and an "innovation architecture" that facilitates the development and implementation of fresh ideas?*

1.8. Designing Your Future: A Leadership Call to Action

In order for a foresight culture and innovation architecture to succeed, they must work for members and be supported by the active engagement of executive management, the board, and volunteers. This requires an honest appraisal by these groups of how they spend their time, what they focus on, what demands they make on the organization's resources, and what contributions they make in return. As the competition to associations grows and members place their own spending under the microscope, they may increasingly ask how their membership dues and the association's revenues are spent. This raises the question *"What proportion of income is spent on governance and serving the board? How much are members prepared to spend on these items?"*

> **What proportion of income is spent on governance and serving the board? How much are members prepared to spend on these items?**

For boards in particular, a critical issue is what they choose to focus on—and ensuring that their priority is helping to frame strategic responses to the emerging challenges, and to map out a vision and direction for the association. *Ultimately, the choices you make as leaders in defining your future roadmap will determine whether you are designing an association that will struggle to survive or that is built to thrive.*

> **Ultimately, the choices you make as leaders in defining your future roadmap will determine whether you are designing an association that will struggle to survive or that is built to thrive.**

1.9. The Power of Reflection

We believe that many of the trends and challenges highlighted here will lead to fundamental change in the economy, society, professions, and the workplace. The temptation may be to rush to action and look for quick fixes. We believe there are very few "just add water" recipes. In most cases, in order to understand and address these issues the single most important thing we can do is give ourselves permission to take the time to reflect and discuss the implications with colleagues, members, volunteers, and the board.

Reflection should not be mistaken for procrastination. The former requires a clear head to consider the implications and options, a willingness to experiment, and the ability to execute plans quickly once they are formed. The latter just requires a suitable patch of sand in which to bury our heads and hope the issue goes away.

1.10. How to Use *Designing Your Future*

This report has been designed to be used in a range of flexible ways depending on your organization's current readiness for change:

I Want to Talk Strategy

We know that many leaders believe that as a result of the changes taking place in the world, their organization may require a fundamental rethink of why it exists, what it does, how it does it, and how best to organize. In this case, we would recommend reading through the five main sections and the appendices, sharing them with your colleagues and board and then agreeing on which of the approaches from Section 5 (or variations thereof) you will use to drive forward your response. Typically, this might involve a review of key trends and challenges, a scenario exercise to see how the trends may combine, and then the adoption of a systematic approach to working through the stages of the key choices framework.

I Have Issues

We also know from the consultations that many organizations already have a number of the appropriate strategies in place. In that case, we suggest following a similar path to that outlined above while focusing on those trends and challenges that require the most attention. You can then select those aspects of the key choices framework that you feel need to be addressed.

I Need to Change Mindsets

For some, your organization may just not be ready for any kind of strategic review. In such cases, introducing the trends and challenges may actually be part of the process of shifting mindsets within the organization and among the board. We suggest you read through Sections 1 to 5 and familiarize yourself with the content of the appendices so that you understand the resources and tools provided. You can then use the ideas in Section 5 to help determine how best to introduce the material to your organization. In the first instance it may be more appropriate to encourage a focus on particular trends that you think will have a big impact and will encourage your colleagues to reflect on the implications and opportunities for your organization.

Show Me the Trends

For those who want to focus on the trends and their implications, we recommend reading Sections 2 and 3 and the trend profiles in Appendices 1 and 2.

I Want Action

Whichever category best fits your situation, you may also want to identify some specific ideas you can take early action on. To satisfy your cravings, in Appendix 4 we have provided a set of ideas on actions you can literally move forward on starting tomorrow morning.

1.11. Enjoy the Ride!

This report may inspire you, worry you, or even encourage you to have that health check you've been putting off or to review how your pension is doing! Most important, we hope it catalyzes you and provides you with a very practical sense of how to assess the implications of the changes taking place in the world, mapping out how you want to respond, and starting the process of *Designing Your Future*.

Section 2

Key Trends

The Global Drivers of Change

In this section we introduce the 50 key trends and explore the patterns of global change emerging from the analysis and examining the resulting implications, opportunities, and key challenges arising for associations.

2.1. Environmental Scanning Framework

Through a combination of the scanning and consultation processes described earlier, we identified a total of 50 key trends that our analysis suggests are already having, or could have, an impact over the next five years globally or, more specifically, in the United States. These could have a direct impact either on the association community or on the economy, government, governance, individuals, professions, businesses, and industry sectors in the United States—which could in turn have implications for associations and nonprofits. In addition, a further 100 "emerging" trends were identified that could have an increasing impact on different sections of the association community in the next five to ten years. The trends were categorized according the "origin" (type) of change using the STEEP framework:

- Socio-demographic
- Technological
- Economic
- Environmental
- Political

Table 1 shows a breakdown of these trends (title only) by STEEP category.

Full descriptions of each of these trends are presented in Appendix 1. For each key trend we have provided a one-to-two page profile providing the following information:

- **Description:** an explanation of the trend including supporting data where relevant; where appropriate, a link to the source reference has been included;
- **Timeframe:** the time window over which we believe the trend could have an impact across at least 50 percent of the U.S. population (note that, by its nature, this is very subjective: for some associations and individuals, the trends are already having an impact; for others, it may not come onto their radar screen for many years);
- **Potential Impact:** The *possible* effects of the trend on society as a whole;
- **Implications and Opportunities for Associations:** Examples of *possible* implications for overall policy and strategy, and opportunities for associations to develop new activities;
- **Functional Implications and Opportunities:** Examples of *possible* implications and opportunities related to what is delivered to members and the ways in which associations organize to deliver;
- **Example Industry Implications:** Highlighting possible impacts for specific/all sectors; and
- **Sources and References:** Bibliographical list showing where the underlying data came from.

Table 1. The 50 Key Trends Organized by STEEP Category

Socio-demographic Trends

1. Generation Y (Millennials): digital, "civic," and connected
2. Millennials increasingly seeking overseas experience
3. Rising life expectancy, aging global populations
4. Widening generational gap: values, attitudes, behaviors, technoliteracy
5. Baby Boomer retirement and unretirement; talent shortages
6. Increasing political and economic impact of diversity—minorities one third of the U.S. population
7. Redefining work-life balance
8. Funding and chronic diseases shaping future healthcare challenges
9. Growing popularity of online education relative to that of classroom-based courses
10. Increasing economic power of women
11. Growing role for "social entrepreneurship"
12. Evolving trust: declining trust in government and media
13. Increasing interest in philanthropy and volunteer work
14. Deepening personalization of products, services, communications, and experiences

Technological Trends

15. Internet continues transforming government, governance, and business
16. Social media explosion creating new approaches for engagement, communication, publishing, and marketing
17. Rise in mobile and location-based web services as "smart" phones displace laptops
18. Cybercrime, cyberwar, and cyberterrorism
19. Nanotechnology: the next trillion-dollar market?
20. Energy: increasing demand and rising cost accelerate the search for alternative sources
21. Evolving personal technology "ecosystem": intuitive, visual, and smart

Economic Trends

22. Uneven economic growth
23. Growing financial market risks and uncertainty
24. Rising economic strength of China and India, representing an increasing share of global GDP
25. Rise of the "Next 11" nations on the global stage
26. Future U.S. growth fueled by rising immigration
27. Rising U.S. personal and federal indebtedness
28. Growing challenge of maintaining physical infrastructure
29. Nations competing on science investment to drive economic performance
30. Growing economic importance of global knowledge economy—50 percent of U.S. GDP by 2010
31. Global talent shortages increasing with economic growth
32. Attractiveness of U.S. business environment weakens relative to that of other countries
33. Education falling behind employers' expectations
34. Pay-as-you-go and "freemium" services becoming more prevalent business models

Table 1. *(Continued)*

35.	Global outsourcing market could hit $1.43 trillion-U.S. outsourcing deepening
36.	Global rise in entrepreneurship
37.	Rise in U.S. corporate and individual social responsibility
38.	Evolution of tomorrow's company
39.	Continued shift in global wealth and spending power
40.	Shifting patterns of global inequality and unmet needs
41.	Changing patterns of U.S. income, wealth, and savings

Environmental Trends

42.	U.S. organizations and investors focusing on green issues
43.	Global consumption patterns challenge Earth's resource capacity
44.	Climate change a growing political and economic priority globally
45.	Rises in ecoliteracy, green practices, and ethical consumption

Political Trends

46.	Diminishing U.S. political influence internationally
47.	India and China becoming "spokesnations" of the developing world
48.	Increasing political and economic transparency
49.	Increasing global role for single-party states
50.	Changing patterns of global governance—growing influence of non-state actors

2.2. 10 Key Patterns of Change

Although the trends are important individually, they also converge to form a number of distinct higher-level "patterns of change" that will affect the individual, society, business, nation, and world. Of the many different patterns to focus on, we have selected 10 key patterns of change that we think will capture the important storylines of change for the next five years and beyond, thus having the greatest importance for associations. These 10 patterns are listed in Table 2 below. Table 3 shows the mapping of the 50 key trends to the 10 patterns of change. The numbers in parentheses refer to the relevant trend number in Table 1 and Appendix 1. As might be expected, many of the trends contribute to multiple change patterns.

Each of the 10 patterns of change is explored in more detail below. For each one, we provide a short narrative and identify some of the key underlying data points from the 50 key trends (the source references for each data point are contained within the 50 trend profiles). The key trend number for each data point is included in parentheses. We also highlight some of the key implications and opportunities for associations. Finally, we highlight the key strategic challenges for associations that result from each change pattern. These strategic challenges are discussed in Section 3. As can be seen from the discussion below, all of the change patterns contribute to multiple strategic challenges.

Table 2. 10 Key Patterns of Change

1. ***Economic Power Shifts:*** *Global integration, emerging economic powers, and shifting patterns of wealth*

2. ***Politics Gets Complex:*** *A rising number of domestic issues, increasing pressure on federal funding, and an increasingly complex global political landscape*

3. ***Expanding Business Agenda:*** *Pressure to address the "triple bottom line" of people, planet, and profits; more global competition and ever-widening technology choices*

4. ***Science and Technology Go Mainstream:*** *Nations competing in innovation, science impacting our daily lives, and technology becoming central to middle-class lifestyles*

5. ***Demographic Destinies:*** *Global population growth, increasing life expectancy, aging societies, and a more ethnically diverse population*

6. ***Generational Crossroads:*** *Aging Baby Boomers and the emerging Millennial generation*

7. ***Rethinking Talent, Education, and Training:*** *Growing talent gap, rising concerns over educational performance, and the mainstreaming of online and lifelong learning*

8. ***Global Internet Expansion:*** *More global users, more connected with more functionality*

9. ***A Society in Transition—An Era of Responsibility and Accountability:*** *Evolving societal norms and expectations, pressures to serve the greater good and perform to the highest ethical standards, and declining trust in key institutions*

10. ***Natural Resource Challenges:*** *Growing resource pressures, rising commodity prices, and energy and the environment as dominant agenda items*

Table 3. Mapping of the 50 Key Trends to the 10 Patterns of Change

No.	Patterns of Change	Key Trends
1.	**Economic Power Shifts** *Global integration, emerging economic powers, and shifting patterns of wealth*	Increasing economic power of women (10)
		Internet continues transforming government, governance, and business (15)
		Energy: increasing demand and rising cost accelerate the search for alternative sources (20)
		Uneven economic growth (22)
		Growing financial market risks and uncertainty (23)
		Rising economic strength of China and India, representing an increasing share of global GDP (24)
		Rise of the "Next 11" nations on the global stage (25)
		Future U.S. growth fueled by rising immigration (26)
		Rising U.S. personal and federal indebtedness (27)
		Growing challenge of maintaining physical infrastructure (28)
		Nations competing in science investment to drive economic performance (29)
		Growing economic importance of global knowledge economy—50 percent of U.S. GDP by 2010 (30)
		Global talent shortages increasing with economic growth (31)
		Attractiveness of U.S. business environment weakens relative to that of other countries (32)
		Global rise in entrepreneurship (36)
		Continued shift in global wealth and spending power (39)
		Shifting patterns of global inequality and unmet needs(40)

Table 3. *(Continued)*

No.	Patterns of Change	Key Trends
		Changing patterns of U.S. income, wealth, and savings (41)
		Emergence of India and China as global powers and "spokesnations" of the developing world (47)
		Increasing political and economic transparency (48)
		Increasing global role for single-party states (49)
2.	**Politics Gets Complex** *A rising number of domestic issues, increasing pressure on federal funding, and an increasingly complex global political landscape*	Increasing political and economic impact of diversity—minorities one third of the U.S. population (6)
		Funding and chronic diseases shaping healthcare challenges (8)
		Evolving trust: declining trust in government and media (12)
		Internet continues transforming government, governance, and business (15)
		Growing financial market risks and uncertainty (23)
		Rising economic strength of China and India, representing an increasing share of global GDP (24)
		Future U.S. growth fueled by rising immigration (26)
		Rising U.S. personal and federal indebtedness (27)
		Growing challenge of maintaining physical infrastructure (28)
		Nations competing in science investment to drive economic performance (29)
		Attractiveness of U.S. business environment weakens relative to that of other countries (32)
		Shifting patterns of global inequality and unmet needs(40)
		Changing patterns of U.S. income, wealth, and savings (41)
		Climate change a growing political and economic priority globally (44)
		Diminishing U.S. political influence internationally (46)
		Emergence of India and China as global powers and "spokesnations" of the developing world (47)
		Increasing political and economic transparency (48)
		Increasing global role for single-party states (49)
		Changing patterns of global governance—growing influence of non-state actors (50)
3.	*Expanding Business Agenda* *Pressure to address the "triple bottom line" of people, planet, and profits; more global competition and ever-widening technology choices*	Baby Boomer retirement and unretirement; talent shortages (5)
		Redefining work–life balance (7)
		Increasing economic power of women (10)
		Growing role for "social entrepreneurship" (11)
		Evolving trust: declining trust in government and media (12)
		Deepening personalization of products, services, communications, and experiences (14)
		Internet continues transforming government, governance, and business (15)
		Social media explosion creating new approaches for engagement, communication, publishing, and marketing (16)

Table 3. *(Continued)*

No.	Patterns of Change	Key Trends
		Rise in mobile and location-based web services as "smart" phones displace laptops (17)
		Cybercrime, cyberwar, and cyberterrorism (18)
		Nanotechnology: the next trillion-dollar market? (19)
		Energy: increasing demand and rising cost accelerate the search for alternative sources (20)
		Growing financial market risks and uncertainty (23)
		Rising economic strength of China and India, representing an increasing share of global GDP (24)
		Rise of the "Next 11" nations on the global stage (25)
		Growing challenge of maintaining physical infrastructure (28)
		Growing economic importance of global knowledge economy—50 percent of U.S. GDP by 2010 (30)
		Global talent shortages increasing with economic growth (31)
		Attractiveness of U.S. business environment weakens relative to that of other countries (32)
		Education falling behind employers' expectations (33)
		Pay-as-you-go and "freemium" services becoming more prevalent business models (34)
		Global outsourcing market could hit $1.43 trillion—U.S. outsourcing deepening (35)
		Global rise in entrepreneurship (36)
		Rise in U.S. corporate and individual social responsibility (37)
		Evolution of tomorrow's company (38)
		U.S. organizations and investors focusing on green issues (42)
4.	**Science and Technology Go Mainstream** *Nations competing in innovation, "science" impacting our daily lives, and technology becoming central to middle-class lifestyles*	Deepening personalization of products, services, communications, and experiences (14)
		Internet continues transforming government, governance, and business (15)
		Social media explosion creating new approaches for engagement, communication, publishing, and marketing (16)
		Rise in mobile and location-based web services as "smart" phones displace laptops (17)
		Nanotechnology: the next trillion-dollar market? (19)
		Energy: increasing demand and rising cost accelerate the search for alternative sources (20)
		Evolving personal technology "ecosystem": intuitive, visual, and smart (21)
		Nations competing in science investment to drive economic performance (29)
5.	**Demographic Destinies** *Global population growth, increasing life expectancy, aging societies, and a more ethnically diverse population*	Rising life expectancy, aging global populations (3)
		Increasing political and economic impact of diversity: minorities one third of the U.S. population (6)
		Future U.S. growth fueled by rising immigration (26)

Table 3. *(Continued)*

No.	Patterns of Change	Key Trends
6.	**Generational Crossroads** *Aging Baby Boomers and the emerging "Millennial" generation*	Generation Y (Millennials): digital, "civic," and connected (1) Millennials increasingly seeking overseas experience (2) Rising life expectancy, aging global populations (3) Widening generational gap: values, attitudes, behaviors, technoliteracy (4) Baby Boomer retirement and unretirement; talent shortages (5) Redefining work–life balance (7)
7.	**Rethinking Talent, Education, and Training** *Growing talent gap, rising concerns over educational performance, and the mainstreaming of online and lifelong learning*	Baby Boomer retirement and unretirement; talent shortages (5) Growing popularity of online education relative to that of classroom-based courses (9) Internet continues transforming government, governance, and business (15) Social media explosion creating new approaches for engagement, communication, publishing, and marketing (16) Global talent shortages increasing with economic growth (31) Education falling behind employers' expectations (33)
8.	**Global Internet Expansion** *More global users, more connected with more functionality.*	Deepening personalization of products, services, communications, and experiences (14) Internet continues transforming government, governance, and business (15) Social media explosion creating new approaches for engagement, communication, publishing, and marketing (16) Rise in mobile and location-based web services as "smart" phones displace laptops (17) Cybercrime, cyberwar, and cyberterrorism (18) Pay-as-you-go and "freemium" services becoming more prevalent business models (34)
9.	**A Society in Transition—An Era of Responsibility and Accountability** *Evolving societal norms and expectations, pressures to serve the greater good and perform to the highest ethical standards, and declining trust in key institutions*	Generation Y (Millennials): digital, "civic," and connected (1) Rising life expectancy—aging global populations (3) Redefining work-life balance (7) Funding and chronic diseases shaping healthcare challenges (8) Growing popularity of online education relative to that of classroom-based courses (9) Increased economic power of women (10) Growing role for "social entrepreneurship" (11) Evolving trust: declining trust in government and media (12) Increasing interest in philanthropy and volunteer work (13) Deepening personalization of products, services, communications, and experiences (14) Internet continues transforming government, governance, and business (15) Social media explosion creating new approaches for engagement, communication, publishing, and marketing (16)

Table 3. *(Continued)*

No.	Patterns of Change	Key Trends
		Rise in mobile and location-based web services as "smart" phones displace laptops (17)
		Growing financial market risks and uncertainty (23)
		Future U.S. growth fueled by rising immigration (26)
		Rising U.S. personal and federal indebtedness (27)
		Growing challenge of maintaining physical infrastructure (28)
		Attractiveness of U.S. business environment weakens relative to that of other countries (32)
		Education falling behind employers' expectations (33)
		Rise in U.S. corporate and individual social responsibility (37)
		Continued shift in global wealth and spending power (39)
		Shifting patterns of global inequality and unmet needs(40)
		Changing patterns of U.S. income, wealth, and savings (41)
		Rises in eco-literacy, "green" practices, and ethical consumption (45)
		Increasing political and economic transparency (48)
		Changing patterns of global governance—growing influence of non-state actors (50)
10.	***Natural Resource Challenges*** *Growing resource pressures, rising commodity prices, and energy and the environment as dominant agenda items*	Energy: increasing demand and rising cost accelerate the search for alternative sources (20)
		U.S. organizations and investors focusing on green issues (42)
		Global consumption patterns challenge Earth's resource capacity (43)
		Climate change a growing political and economic priority globally (44)
		Rises in eco-literacy, "green" practices, and ethical consumption (45)

1. Economic Power Shifts

Global integration, emerging economic powers, and shifting patterns of wealth

Leaders must rethink assumptions about global opportunities and risks in the face of a changing economic landscape, new sources of competition, and challenges to waning economic and political leadership of the United States. The trends tell a story of changing patterns of growth across the planet as rapidly developing nations such as the BRIC economies (Brazil, Russia, India, and China) seek to build their industrial base and take their people out of poverty on a long-term basis. These emerging economic powers are themselves influencing the global regulatory landscape, exerting political influence over trade policies, competing for global R&D investments, and increasing domestic consumption—thereby pushing up commodity and energy prices.

In the years ahead, many of the greatest business opportunities will emerge outside the United States. How will this change the focus of associations and their individual and organizational members?

• China could overtake the United States. to become the world's largest economy as early as 2015. (24)
• More than half the growth in the world's GDP over the next 15 years will come from China (27 percent),

the United States (16 percent), and India (12 percent). In comparison, the 25 European Union countries will average 2.1 percent. (24)

• A billion new consumers could enter the global marketplace in the next decade as economic growth in emerging markets pushes individuals beyond the threshold level of $5,000 in annual household income—a point when people generally begin to spend on discretionary goods. (39)

• The pool of potential philanthropic donors is growing. There are now over 1,000 billionaires and nearly 10 million millionaires globally. America has 469 billionaires, followed by Russia with 87, Germany with 59, and India with 53. India has four of the ten richest people on the planet and could have between 700 and 3,000 billionaires by 2020. (40)

• Sovereign wealth funds—often from single-party states—could become an increasingly important source of investment for U.S. businesses. China's sovereign wealth fund is estimated at $200 billion, Abu Dhabi's at over $800 billion, and Singapore's at $300 billion. (49)

• U.S. personal savings have dropped from 10.8 percent of personal disposable income in 1984 to just one percent in 2007 (Figure 2). The U.S. national debt stood at approximately $9.1 trillion at the start of 2008 and is expected to rise to $10 trillion in 2009. (27)

Figure 2. U.S. Saving Rates in Decline.

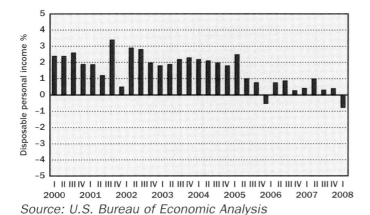

Source: U.S. Bureau of Economic Analysis

Implications and Opportunities

▪ *Direction: Where are you going?* With growing economic uncertainty, associations need to be clear on their purpose, vision, and strategy in order to focus their revenue-generation activities and control internal costs.

▪ *International offering demands clarity on the scope of our global ambitions.* This creates the opportunity to support domestic members going overseas, attract a growing pool of potential members overseas, and assist foreign members coming into the U.S.

▪ *Follow the money.* This drives the need to understand the impact of members' changing financial circumstances and identify where future members and donors may come from.

Strategic Challenges

? What's your leadership paradigm—envisioning tomorrow's association (1)

? What's plan B—adapting to a new economic landscape (2)

? Where's the money—responding to shifting patterns of income and wealth (6)

? How can you exploit new business models—staying responsive and solvent (7)

? How sustainable are you—managing your ethics, transparency, accountability and responsibility (9)

? What's next on the radar—embedding environmental scanning, scenario planning, and what-if thinking (10)

2. Politics Gets Complex

A rising number of domestic issues, increasing pressure on federal funding, and an increasingly complex global political landscape

The political agenda has become increasingly crowded and complex as an ever-diversifying range of issues, interest groups, and challenges compete for government attention and federal funding. The constant rise in healthcare costs, infrastructure demands, and federal debt are demanding a fundamental rethink of budgetary policy and priorities. At the same time, declining savings rates, rising food and energy prices, and continued uncertainty resulting from the subprime loan and global credit crisis are increasing the pressure on the government to find social, economic, and political solutions addressing citizen needs and concerns. The development of new global political alliances, adverse reaction to U.S. foreign policy from several countries, and continual shifts in global power relationships are all contributing to a decline in U.S. influence internationally.

- In 2007, the U.S. minority (non-white) population passed the 100 million mark and now makes up one third of the U.S. population. Some forecasts suggest that the number of Hispanics could rise to one fourth of the U.S. population by 2016. (24)
- The U.S. Congressional Budget Office's projections suggest that in the absence of changes in federal law, total spending on healthcare would rise from 16 percent of gross domestic product (GDP) in 2007 to 25 percent in 2025, 37 percent in 2050 and 49 percent in 2082. (8)
- The International Monetary Fund estimated U.S. subprime-based losses at $945 billion, and Credit Suisse forecast that up to 6.5 million U.S. home loans (nearly 12.7 percent of all U.S. residential borrowers) could be foreclosed by the end of 2012. (23)
- The American Society of Civil Engineers estimates that $1.6 trillion is needed over a five-year period to bring the nation's infrastructure up to a "good condition." (28)
- The CIA/NIC "Mapping the Global Future: Report of the National Intelligence Council's 2020 Project" suggests that the era of American global dominance could end by 2020. (46)

Implications and Opportunities

- *Solutions, Not Problems:* Growing political challenges and pressures on federal budgets create the opportunity for associations to show where they and their members can make a difference.
- *Effective Representation:* This drives the need to assess lobbying and awareness raising strategies to ensure they are effective, taking advantage of the power of the internet and social networks.
- *Navigating Turbulent Waters:* It becomes increasingly important for associations to scan ahead and monitor the political and legislative agenda to ensure that members are forewarned and prepared for potential future changes that could affect them.

Strategic Challenges

? What's your leadership paradigm—envisioning tomorrow's association (1)

? Where's the money—responding to shifting patterns of income and wealth (6)

? How can you exploit new business models—staying responsive and solvent (7)

? What's your consumption footprint—facing up to energy and environmental pressures (8)

? How sustainable are you—managing our ethics, transparency, accountability, and responsibility (9)

? What's next on the radar—embedding environmental scanning, scenario planning, and what-if thinking (10)

---

3. Expanding Business Agenda

Pressure to address the "triple bottom line" of people, planet, and profits; more global competition and ever-widening technology choices

Certainty is the factor that businesses crave most, but it is a commodity in short supply. The rapid rise of emerging economies has created opportunities, but it has also introduced increased risk of new competition and the uncertainty that comes with venturing into unknown territory. The business landscape itself is evolving dramatically with new entrants from home and abroad, a rising number of women-owned businesses, a general growth in entrepreneurship, and the new breed of "social ventures." The rise of the internet has opened up new possibilities for communication, collaboration, and customer engagement and has given rise to a wave of new business models.

At the same time new business management challenges are emerging with the pressure to innovate and create unique intellectual property, uncertainty about the long-term benefits of outsourcing, rapidly rising energy costs, a complex set of views on what constitutes work–life balance and the issues of managing a multi-generational workforce. Businesses also face increasing expectations to display high levels of corporate social responsibility (CSR) and address a growing expectation to behave in an environmentally sustainable manner and drive down their ecological footprints.

- A 2007 Monster.com work–life balance survey found that while 89 percent of employees polled placed importance on work–life balance programs, only 29 percent of workers rated their employer's work–life balance initiatives "good" or "excellent," and 58 percent felt their employer "encourages working too much." (7)
- As of 2006, in the United States there were an estimated 10.4 million privately held firms in which 50 percent or more of the equity was owned by women, or two in five (40.2 percent) of all businesses in the country. (10)
- 52 percent of Fortune 500 companies have corporate blogs. (16)
- With over 3.2 billion mobile phones in circulation globally at the start of 2008 and smart phone sales now exceeding those of laptops, an increasing range of business applications are expected to migrate to the palm of our hands. (17)
- Today, intangible assets such as knowledge and skills account for around 70 percent of the total value of companies in the S&P 500. (30)
- In 2007, America fell to the ninth position in the *Economist's* business environment rankings. (32)

Implications and Opportunities

- *Expanding Opportunities:* Associations could help fill the expanding business need for training, advice, best-practice guidance, industry foresight, and facilitation of collaboration on issues as diverse as work force management, sustainability, international operations, talent management, and developing resilience.
- *New Competitors:* Private-sector providers at home and overseas will increasingly compete to provide the services offered by associations.
- *Partnership:* Effective partnering relationships with private and not-for-profit organizations could help associations extend the range of offerings to members, mitigate competitive threats, and generate new revenue streams.
- *Learning:* As associations come under pressure to generate new revenues, manage costs, leverage the internet, deepen member relationships, and drive efficiency, key lessons and practices can be learned from the for-profit sector and social ventures.

Strategic Challenges

? What's your leadership paradigm—envisioning tomorrow's association (1)

? What's plan B—adapting to a new economic landscape (2)

? Who's driving the talent agenda—recruiting and preparing tomorrow's labor force (3)

? How do you connect your community—tapping the potential of social networks (5)

? Where's the money—responding to shifting patterns of income and wealth (6)

? How can you exploit new business models—staying responsive and solvent (7)

? What's your consumption footprint—facing up to energy and environmental pressures (8)

? How sustainable are you—managing our ethics, transparency, accountability and responsibility (9)

? What's next on the radar—embedding environmental scanning, scenario planning, and what-if thinking (10)

- A start-up auto insurance operation in Dallas aims to make Texas the first state to offer drivers pay-as-you-go insurance policies. (34)
- The global market for shared services and outsourcing is expected to grow to $1.43 trillion by the end of 2009, from $930 billion in 2006. (35)

4. Science and Technology Go Mainstream

Nations competing on innovation, "science" impacting our daily lives, and technology becoming central to middle-class lifestyles

Nations and businesses alike are now recognizing and seeking to compete on the "innovation advantage" that comes from leadership and investment in science and technology. Public awareness of the importance of science is also rising as recognition grows of its contribution in fields as diverse as health, new materials, environmental protection, and food production. Technology is increasingly embedded at the heart of business and is becoming a critical part of daily life for young middle classes, in particular, around the world, offering an ever-increasing array of options for connectivity and personalization.

• Companies across a range of consumer product sectors are experimenting with enabling "mass customization" that allows consumers to choose personal preferences in product design, color, texture, and functionality. (14)

• The National Science Foundation estimates that the global nanotechnology market could be worth $1 trillion by 2015. (19)

• Global sales from clean energy sources such as wind, solar, geothermal power, and biofuels could grow to as much as $1 trillion yearly by 2030. (20)

• R&D spending by the "Global Innovation 1,000" (the leading global spenders on R&D) rose in 2006 by $40 billion to $447 billion, a 10 percent increase. (29)

Implications and Opportunities

• *Horizon Scanning:* The rapid pace of science and technology advances and their critical impact on competitiveness creates a demand and opportunity to monitor and evaluate emerging developments and provide members with regular updates and guidance.

• *Facilitating Collaboration:* Associations can play a key role in helping members leverage their research investments by conducting multi-client "precompetitive" studies on emerging science and technology and monitoring the state of the art in key fields.

• *Best Advice:* Associations may want to appoint specialist "chief scientific advisors" or advisory panels to provide guidance on the impact of new developments for their membership.

Strategic Challenges

? Who's driving the talent agenda—recruiting and preparing tomorrow's labor force (3)

? How can you exploit new business models—staying responsive and solvent (7)

? What's next on the radar—embedding environmental scanning, scenario planning, and what-if thinking (10)

5. Demographic Destinies

Global population growth, increasing life expectancy, aging societies, and a more ethnically diverse population

The main demographic stories of the next two decades are expected to be growth of the global population toward 9.2 billion by 2050, the aging of the world's population, and the rise and increasing influence of a more diverse global middle class. In particular, an aging global population will bring with it tremendous financial liabilities to governments, businesses, and families, testing the robustness of pensions and healthcare systems. Associations will also be tested in terms of their own operations, service delivery, and ability to meet changing member needs and wants.

• The global population is expected to rise from 6.6 billion at the end of 2007 to around 8 billion by 2025 and 9.2 billion by 2050 (Figure 3). (43)

• The American Life Extension Institute believes that average life expectancy in the United States will reach 100 by 2029. (3)

• By 2050, those aged 60 and over could comprise one third of the population in developed regions and 22 percent of the total global population. (3)

The fastest growing segments of middle class both in the United States and globally will come from populations much different than the traditional Western

Figure 3. Three Billion More People in 40 Years.

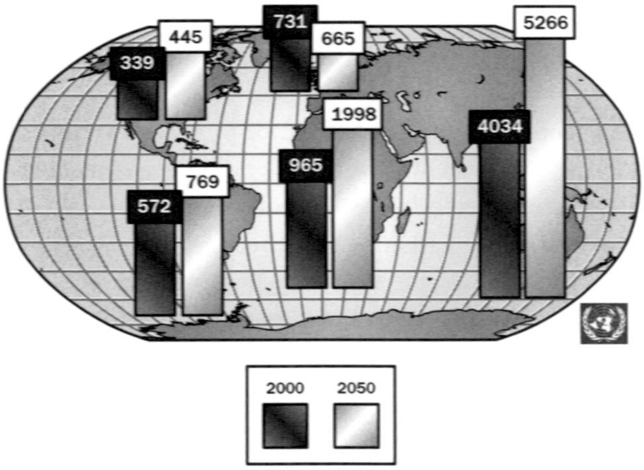

Source: United Nations

Figure 4. Changing Makeup of the U.S. Population.

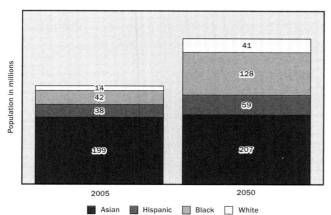

Source: http://pewhispanic.org/datasets/

cultures, testing the ability of businesses to adapt to their changing needs and expectations:

• Hispanics represent around one seventh of the U.S. population; forecasts suggest this could rise to one fourth by 2016. (6)
• Up to 2.2 million people could migrate from poor to rich countries every year from now to 2050. (26)
• The middle class in poor countries is the fastest-growing segment of the world's population. By 2020, the world's middle class could grow by 1.8 billion to 52 percent of the total population, up from 30 percent now. (39)

Implications and Opportunities

• **Who's the Customer?** Demographic shifts, a changing ethnic mix, and evolving patterns of income and wealth are forcing associations to think carefully about whom to target and the cost of servicing those members' needs.

• **Managing Diversity:** This creates the opportunity to provide employers with a range of products and services to help manage and get the best from a multi-generational, multi-ethnic, and geographically dispersed workforce.

• **Internal Capability:** This drives associations to look at how they can manage these challenges within their own staff, while serving the needs of a potentially increasingly diverse membership.

6. Generational Crossroads

Aging Baby Boomers and the emerging "Millennial" generation

Within the United States, the next two decades will see the need for unprecedented levels of intergenerational work collaborations between Baby Boomers (born 1946–1964), generation X (born 1964–1980), the emerging "Millennial" generation (born 1980–1999), and those that follow. These cohorts bring widely differing attitudes to working practices and communications preferences as well as differing attitudes toward the role of technology and work-life balance. The challenge for employers will be creating an environment where each group can feel valued and be effective.

• Around 70–95 million Baby Boomers will retire by 2025, but only 40 million from the generation X (born 1964–1979) and generation Y (born 1980–1999) age groups will enter the workforce. (5)
• More than 60 percent of U.S. employers say they are experiencing tension between employees from different generations. (4)
• Of 260,000 college freshmen surveyed in the fall of 2007, more than 66.3 percent said it is "essential or very important" to help others, the highest percentage to say so in 25 years. (1)
• According to a U.S. State Department annual report, in 2006 the number of students studying abroad reached 205,983—up 144 percent over a decade. (2)

- **Serving Baby Boomers** creates the opportunity to provide a range of services to help members prepare for retirement, enjoy their retirement, and work beyond retirement.
- **Serving Millennials** encourages development of communications methods, technologies, and event designs catering to the different needs and preferences of this generation.
- **Resource Management** raises critical issues about how associations decide the level of resources to allocate to serving different member segments and to maintaining different communication channels.

Strategic Challenges

? What's your leadership paradigm—envisioning tomorrow's association (1)

? What's plan B—adapting to a new economic landscape (2)

? Who's driving the talent agenda—recruiting and preparing tomorrow's labor force (3)

? Who's the customer—serving an aging, multi-generational, and ethnically diverse population (4)

? How do you connect your community—tapping the potential of social networks (5)

? Where's the money—responding to shifting patterns of income and wealth (6)

? What's next on the radar—embedding environmental scanning, scenario planning, and what-if thinking (10)

7. Rethinking Talent, Education, and Training

Growing talent gap, rising concerns over educational performance, and the mainstreaming of online and lifelong learning

The so-called "demographic time bomb," describing the pending retirement wave of aging workers, is creating an impending skills crisis for employers. At the same time, the constantly evolving nature of the business environment, the work undertaken, and the technologies used are driving the demand to update existing skills and learn new ones. Rising life expectancy also implies that our working lives will lengthen and adds further impetus to the need for lifelong learning. Concerns over the standards of graduates emerging from the high school and university system, changes in our working lives, time pressures, cost considerations, and a growing understanding of individual learning preferences are helping to accelerate the growth of new and nontraditional educational delivery methods.

- Over the next three decades the demand for experienced IT professionals between the ages of 35 and 45 is expected to increase by 25 percent even as the supply may decrease by 15 percent. (5)
- A shortage of more than 1 million nurses—amid a workforce of 3 million—is expected by 2012. (5)
- Today more than 96 percent of the very largest institutions (more than 15,000 total enrollments) have online offerings, and some of the fastest-growing online learning populations are based in Asian countries. (9)
- A 2005 survey for the National Association of Manufacturers found that 84 percent of employers say that U.S. K–12 schools are not doing a good job of preparing students for the workplace. (33)

Implications and Opportunities

- **Gap Closure:** Some associations may feel they have a valuable role to play in addressing the perceived shortfall in basic educational standards of high school and college graduates.
- **Accelerated Learning:** With several proven models for delivering rapid improvement in educational standards for adults and children alike, associations could be a vital channel in helping businesses upgrade workforce capability.
- **High-End Capabilities:** This raises the question of what associations should be doing in terms of helping professions and sectors develop advanced skills and expertise.
- **Lifelong Learning:** This encourages a reassessment of the underlying educational model adopted by associations and how to support lifetime learning requirements.
- **Online Solutions:** Time and cost pressures will drive more associations to explore online delivery of education and training and to examine how they can become portals for third-party suppliers to provide "just in time" and highly personalized solutions to members' differing individual needs.

8. Global Internet Expansion

More global users, more connected with more functionality

The internet is increasingly becoming a core tool for business and individuals in Western societies, and the developing world is catching up fast. Social web tools such as blogs, wikis, social networks, virtual worlds, and portable computing devices are becoming more mainstream, evolving into essential tools for marketing, communication, and engagement.

Figure 5. Global Internet Usage Growth. 2000–2007

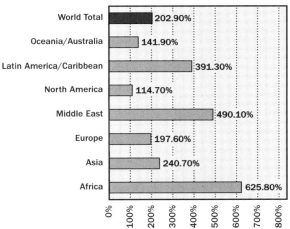

Source: http://www.weboma.com/internetic-world-in-the-year-2015/

- Global internet usage grew 265.6 percent from 2000 to 2007 with close to 1.3 billion worldwide users as of December 2007, and 1.5 billion expected by the end of 2008. (15)
- By 2010, China is expected to have more broadband users than the United States. (15)
- Active usage of social media services such as MySpace, Facebook, YouTube, LinkedIn, and Flickr are expected to rise from 373 million broadband users in 2008 to over 1 billion by 2012, representing 75 percent of all broadband users. (16)
- 120,000 new blogs are created every day. Japanese is the number-one blogging language (37 percent), followed by English (33 percent) and Chinese (8 percent). Ohmynews is a popular South Korean online newspaper/blog written by 60,000 "citizen reporters." (16)
- Up to 80 percent of U.S. internet users could become members of virtual worlds by 2011. (16)
- P&G has created a series of networks with over 3 million external members to help them reach their target of generating half of all new product ideas from outside the organization. (16)

Strategic Challenges
? What's your leadership paradigm—envisioning tomorrow's association (1)
? What's plan B—adapting to a new economic landscape (2)
? How do you connect your community—tapping the potential of social networks (5)
? How can you exploit new business models—staying responsive and solvent (7)
? What's next on the radar—embedding environmental scanning, scenario planning, and what-if thinking (10)

9. A Society in Transition—An Era of Responsibility and Accountability

Evolving societal norms and expectations, pressures to serve the greater good and perform to the highest ethical standards, and declining trust in key institutions

The trends paint a picture of an increasingly diverse, multi-generational, multi-ethnic society with changing family structures and evolving views regarding values and standards of behaviour. At the same time, expectations are increasing globally for greater corporate social responsibility (CSR), more transparency, and higher standards in public life. These are being driven by growing public awareness of the scale of social challenges, environmental pressures, changing consumer values, and a rise in "ethical consumption." Over the next few years, these issues will receive still greater prominence through the communication accelerator effect provided by social media and more widespread adoption of reporting and accountability standards on issues relating to transparency, social justice, and the environment.

Associations and their members might soon need to revisit their vision and mission statements, as well as the implications found within their supply-chain and partnership structures, to align themselves with emerging social-justice and environmental issues. It might usher in an era of unprecedented transparency and stronger trust with their customer base.

• Approximately 89.6 million Americans—34.7 percent under 65 years of age—were uninsured at some point of time during 2006–2007. (8)

• Americans over the age of 16 are volunteering at historically high rates, with 61.2 million giving their time to help others in 2006. (13)

• Over half of the Fortune 100 companies now issue CSR reports. Of the top 100 companies in America, 59 issue CSR reports, compared to nearly 90 percent within Europe and 61 percent in the rest of the world. (37)

Implications and Opportunities
• ***Establishing a Social Role:*** The changing pressures and needs of society force associations to determine what their roles should be in contributing to the future talent, awareness, values, outlook, and aspirations of society.
• ***Building a Responsible Brand:*** Growing societal pressures are encouraging associations to think about what "trust," "accountability," and "responsibility" mean to them and how to embed and reflect them in all their activities.
• ***Social Responsibility:*** Associations need to decide whether they want to coordinate social initiatives on the part of members and adopt particular causes to support.

Strategic Challenges
? What's your leadership paradigm—envisioning tomorrow's association (1)
? Who's the customer—serving an aging, multi-generational, and ethnically diverse population (4)
? How do you connect your community—tapping the potential of social networks (5)
? Where's the money—responding to shifting patterns of income and wealth (6)
? How can you exploit new business models—staying responsive and solvent (7)
? What's your consumption footprint—facing up to energy and environmental pressures (8)
? How sustainable are you—managing our ethics, transparency, accountability, and responsibility (9)
? What's next on the radar—embedding environmental scanning, scenario planning, and what-if thinking (10)

• Business is considered more credible than government or media in 13 of the 18 countries surveyed in Edelman's 2007 Trust Barometer. (12)

10. Natural Resource Challenges

Growing resource pressures, rising commodity prices, and energy and the environment as dominant agenda items

For the last two decades, there have been many voices warning about unsustainable natural resource demands and pressures on the natural environment. However, in reality, it is only in the last two years that issues related to energy and the environment in particular have taken on a true sense of urgency among mainstream audiences, businesses, and political organizations. Both are now seen as critical issues with implications for economic growth, geopolitics, national security, and the conduct of business.

• Total world consumption of energy will increase by 57 percent between 2004 and 2030 with most of the new demand coming from developing countries such as China, India, and Brazil (Figure 6). (20)
• Global warming has the potential to cut worldwide food production by 20 percent by 2020. (44)
• Air pollution is estimated to cost China 3.8 percent of its GDP while water pollution costs another two percent, according to the World Bank. (44)

Figure 6. Estimated Rise in Global Energy Consumption.

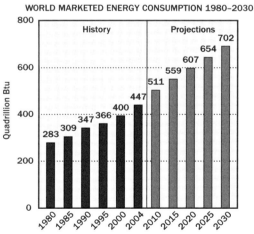

Sources: *Energy Information Administration;*
History: *International Energy Annual 2004 (May–July 2006), www.eia.doe.gov/iea;*
Projections: *System for the Analysis of Global Energy Markets (2007)*

• The economic cost of U.S. catastrophes related to climate change could reach $150 billion annually by 2017 (the U.S. insurance industry's share of the overall cost could be $30–40 billion). (44)
• By 2015, the "green tech" market is forecast to more than quadruple to $167 billion, and the market value for renewable energy consumption worldwide is projected to double to $198.1 billion. (20)
• Today, 1 billion people consume two thirds of the world's raw materials. Some 5.6 billion people consume the other third and are quickly moving up the socioeconomic ladder toward a higher-consumption middle-class status. The industrial revolution involved 300 million people. The emerging nation revolution will involve over 6 billion. (43)

- Paper use in the United States has declined by more than 20 percent over the past decade, and the recycling rate increased by 20 percent in the decade leading up to 2006. (42)

2.3. Responding to Change: Choose Your Strategy

The patterns of change summarized in this section suggest that it will be hard to maintain a business-as-usual stance when fundamental shifts are affecting every aspect of our members' lives. Although you can develop scenarios of how the changes may play out, you cannot predict with any certainty how the cards will fall or how governments, businesses, and citizens will respond and adapt. The scenarios and exercise presented in Appendix 5 could help you explore how these trends can combine into bigger picture macro-economic stories of how the changes may play out over the next five years.

The choice of how you respond will come down to personal preferences of association leaders and boards and the extent to which these trends are already confronting you or are still sitting in the yet-to-be-serious tray. Hence, there is no single strategy or approach that will work for everyone. In the following section we highlight the key challenges these trends and patterns of change create for associations.

It is up to each association to decide whether to focus on individual trends or look at higher-level patterns of change and undertake a systematic appraisal of its future. Either way, it is critical to allocate time and space to understanding the issues, assessing their impact, examining how others are addressing them, and to being willing to consider and experiment with alternative solutions. Developing a culture of active foresight and a willingness to test alternative solutions will be fundamental capabilities for associations of the future.

Section 3
Key Challenges
10 Strategic Priorities Association Leaders Must Address

3.1. 10 Key Strategic Challenges

In Section 2 we explored how the 50 key trends were converging to create 10 important patterns of change that will have an impact on associations and non-profits. For each of the 10 patterns we also identified critical challenges they were creating for leaders to address as part of defining and designing the preferred future for their organization. Each of the change patterns contributed to multiple challenges. In total we identified 10 key challenges that come out of this analysis of the key trends and patterns of change. The 10 key strategic challenges are presented in Table 4 below.

For each challenge, we have presented an example of how an organization is currently addressing it. We have also identified the key questions each challenge raises for the organization's strategy. A strategic framework for addressing those questions is presented in Section 4. The framework looks at four key stages of strategic decision making:

1. *Why are we here?* Purpose, Strategic Direction, and Vision

2. *What will we do?* Core Products and Service Offerings

3. *How will we do it?* Service Delivery Model

4. *How should we organize ourselves?* Organization Model

Section 4 also includes a table showing how the 10 challenges map to the different stages of strategic decision making.

Challenge 1: What's your leadership paradigm—Envisioning tomorrow's association

How you see yourself in the world will ultimately shape your responses to all of the trends and resulting challenges presented here. This prevailing leadership paradigm will determine whether new developments appear to you as yet another problem to overcome or as opportunities to help you grow, evolve, or even reinvent yourself as an association or nonprofit.

From our consultations in preparing this guide, it is clear and unsurprising that there is a full spectrum of governing paradigms across the association community. At one end are those who have adopted a "victim" posture and see their future as a constant struggle for survival in the face of ever-greater challenges. Typically, such associations are caught up in current challenges and are unable or unwilling to confront the issues shaping the future.

At the other end of the spectrum are the optimists, who see the changes in the world as creating opportunities for their association. They see the potential to envision an even bigger role for their members and their association in driving forward the capability, impact, and

---

	Table 4. 10 Key Strategic Challenges
1.	What's your leadership paradigm—envisioning tomorrow's association
2.	What's plan B—adapting to a new economic landscape
3.	Who's driving the talent agenda—recruiting and preparing tomorrow's labor force
4.	Who's the customer—serving an aging, multi-generational, and ethnically diverse population
5.	How do you connect your community—tapping the potential of social networks
6.	Where's the money—responding to shifting patterns of income and wealth
7.	How can you exploit new business models—staying responsive and solvent
8.	What's your consumption footprint—facing up to energy and environmental pressures
9.	How sustainable are you—managing ethics, transparency, accountability, and responsibility
10.	What's next on the radar—embedding environmental scanning, scenario planning, and what-if thinking

strategic contribution of their profession or sector to society, the nation, and the global economy.

Critical to determining your paradigm are the nature, composition, and behavior of your board and volunteer-leadership community. Those associations with a firm focus on defining a bigger role for themselves have often created or are building "low-maintenance" governance structures that are typically lean, responsive, and focused on strategic direction. Such boards are often populated by engaged individuals who see a board position as an opportunity to drive the organization toward an inspiring future in which it can survive and thrive despite the uncertainty of the world in which it operates.

Case Study: The Pacific Asia Travel Association

The Pacific Asia Tourism Association (PATA) determined that it wanted to take a leadership role in helping to ensure the sustainability of the sector in the face of dramatic growth of travel and tourism in the Asia Pacific region. As a first step, PATA's leadership convinced its board of the need to focus on the CEO-level challenges and operate at the most strategic level in the sector. The board approved the strategy, and its first step was to make the bold move of transforming its annual conference from a 2000+ multi-topic gathering into a single-issue "CEO Challenge" forum to address key economic, social, and environmental sustainability issues for the sector. The first event in Bangkok in April 2008 focused on the theme of climate change. The success of the event has led to several countries asking PATA to host similar events for them—when most had previously been reluctant to even discuss climate change or sustainability.

Key Questions

? What do you give yourselves permission to believe you can achieve?

? What is the current health and capability of your association?

? What are your strengths, weaknesses, opportunities, and threats?

? What role should your association play for citizens, society, business, and the nation in the twenty-first century?

? Which other stakeholder groups in society do you wish to connect with, and what impact are you aiming to have?

? What kind of organization do you want to be?

? Where are you trying to take the association over the next 5–10 years?

? What would success look and feel like for your members and staff?

? What is the right managerial structure for the organization going forward to fulfill your purpose and deliver on your vision?

Challenge 2: What's plan B—Adapting to a new economic landscape

The global opportunity landscape for associations is being transformed. Key drivers of change include growth of the global population to potentially 9.2 billion by 2050 and the accompanying rise in the size of the middle class worldwide, as well as the rapid pace of development of the BRIC economies—in particular China and India. A new wave of opportunities is also being presented by emerging groupings such as the N-11,[1] ASEAN,[2] and the increasing influence and ambitions of wealthy resource-backed states such as those in the Middle East. The importance of these developments is heightened by increasing concerns over the potential for an economic slowdown in developed economies.

These changes are forcing associations to think hard about the assumptions that underpin their business plans. Are you basing your goals on what has gone before—when the United States had clear economic leadership and it was safe to assume continued growth?

NOTE 1 The Next Eleven (N–11) list was a term coined by Goldman Sachs to cover the next wave of emerging economies that have promising outlooks for global investors and could become top 20 economies by 2025-namely, Bangladesh, Egypt, Indonesia, Iran, South Korea, Mexico, Nigeria, Pakistan, Philippines, Turkey, and Vietnam. (25)

NOTE 2 The Association of Southeast Asian Nations (ASEAN) has the twin objectives of (1) accelerating economic growth, social progress, and cultural development in the region and (2) promoting regional peace and stability. Its members are Brunei, Cambodia, Indonesia, Laos, Malaysia, Myanmar, Philippines, Singapore, Thailand, and Vietnam.

Is it realistic to hope that past membership and income trends will continue, or do you need to frame new assumptions using insight into how the global economic landscape is changing and where the future challenges, risks, and opportunities may lie? Such analysis typically forces out very clear decisions about how to achieve your goals under different economic circumstances and how to fulfill your international ambitions.

Case Study: The Project Management Institute

The Project Management Institute spotted early on that the global spread of its membership demanded that it become a more global organization. Faced with a rapid rise in demand for membership, content, and events from overseas members, its strategy has been to develop tailored content solutions, events, and support structures for each of the key markets it aims to serve.

Key Questions

? What's your growth strategy? What are plans B and C? How would you respond if there was an economic turndown?

? What is your international strategy? Are you a U.S. association looking for opportunities in key markets internationally, or are you building a truly global association?

? What are the core offerings required to fulfill your international ambitions?

? How do you ensure that your organization can withstand potential shocks in the system, such as an economic downturn, rapid rises and falls in membership numbers, dramatic increases in travel costs, or the loss of key sponsors?

? What are the critical partnerships you will need to deliver your range of member offerings in the most effective and cost-efficient manner?

? What is the right set of performance measures with which to manage your association?

Challenge 3: Who's driving the talent agenda— Recruiting and preparing tomorrow's labor force

However much we automate and however sophisticated our financial models are, we know that people and their talent are still the lifeblood that drives successful organizations forward. Despite short-term concerns, most analysts expect long-term economic growth in the United States. This is driving forecasts of significant increases in demand for skilled workers— particularly in the high-value-added and knowledge-intensive sectors. However, supply-side concerns are rising, fueled by the anticipated retirement of large numbers of the Baby Boomer cohort, coupled with declining birth rates and tougher immigration controls. At the same time, employers' demands are increasing for "just-in-time" learning solutions to rapidly emerging training needs, and their concerns are growing regarding the educational and social capability of the students coming through the system.

Many experts see parts of the education solution coming from the rise of online learning, the emergence of "just-in-time" or accelerated learning and retraining programs, and emerging experiential and behavioral learning approaches. These collectively offer the potential for more personalized, tailored, and adaptive learning solutions that can genuinely address the needs of the individual. Associations need to determine what role they should play in ensuring an adequate supply of talent, addressing the remedial training issues and delivering on the high end skills requirements. This is driving the need for a radical appraisal of how to evolve associations' research focus, professional education, training, and credentialing offerings to serve the needs of the professions and sectors they want to cater to at home and internationally.

Case Study: The Association of Professional Interior Designers

The Association of Professional Interior Designers was formed in the United Arab Emirates as a direct response to a massive construction boom across the region that is driving the demand for interior design skills. They have a twin aim of establishing professional standards for the sector and driving a focused educational agenda by working with all of the relevant learning institutions to ensure they are delivering the capability required by the sector over the short, medium, and longer-term horizons.

Challenge 4: Who's the customer—Serving an aging, multi-generational, and ethnically diverse population

There is a pressing need to understand the different life stage requirements of your membership and how major demographic forces are changing the lifestyles of people in the United States and across the globe. Rising life expectancy, migration, and differing birth rates among America's diverse communities are creating a more ethnically diverse labor force. Associations are faced with the challenges of understanding the changes taking place, assessing their impact on member requirements, and then deciding which potential member demographics to focus on.

Decisions on target membership need to be backed up by tough decisions on how best to target "hard to reach" segments and how to address the diverse service requirements, communication styles and technology preferences of different generations in society. These challenges are encouraging associations to adopt a "cost–benefit analysis" approach to the evaluation of current and potential members. This analysis needs to start by evaluating the benefits to members and the value to society of what the association could offer. These "positives" then need to be compared to the economic returns, costs, and cross-subsidies required to provide services via each segment's preferred channel(s), what it costs to offer lifetime membership, and the investment required to attract hard-to-reach groups. If the numbers don't measure up, hard choices need to be made about who you can afford to serve or how you raise the funds to serve those you want to attract but for whom the cost-benefit isn't there.

Challenge 5: How do you connect your community—Tapping the potential of social networks

Productivity in the knowledge economy depends on high degrees of innovation and collaboration. Fundamental internet-enabled shifts are taking place in how you can use networks to communicate, market your offerings, develop new policies and products, collaborate, innovate, and cocreate. At the heart of these changes are the rapid rise in popularity and improvements in functionality of web-based social networks and their underlying Web 2.0 technologies,

Figure 7. Leading Languages on the Internet.

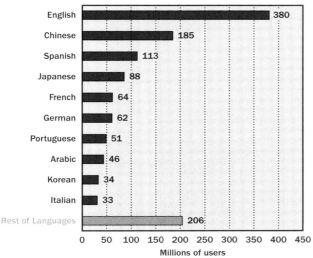

Source: www.internetworldstats.com; copyright ©
2008, Miniwatts Marketing Group

such as wikis, blogs, and personal profiles. The increasingly multilingual nature of the web creates the opportunity, demand, and challenge to serve international members in their own languages (Figure 7).

The association community is recognizing both the threat and the potential of these developments. Some have chosen to recreate their own suites of social networking tools, but others are opting to leverage the investment being made by third-party providers, creating exclusive forums to serve their members within those networks. Many are discovering that such an approach also drives the recruitment of new members and avoids the risk of being caught by rapid changes in what the technology can deliver and the resulting evolution of user requirements.

Case Study: The Association of Professional Futurists

The Association of Professional Futurists (APF) established an APF members–only forum within the Linkedin online networking platform, which claims over 20 million members in 150 industries around the world. The impact has been to raise brand awareness of the APF and generate a steady flow of new membership inquiries from people who see the forum and want to know more about the APF.

Key Questions

? How do you want to develop the face-to-face, virtual community, and networking elements of your association?

? What is the right economically sustainable mix of delivery channels to serve current and target members, in light of the growing multi-generational mix and its members' increasingly broad range of communication and technology preferences?

? How best can you use your available resources to help your members get the maximum possible benefit out of collaboration and social networking?

Challenge 6: Where's the money—Responding to shifting patterns of income, wealth and power

The trend data highlights patterns of fundamental change in the distribution of wealth globally and the rising influence on the political stage of the new middle-class consumers in the marketplace. Domestically we can see limited growth, stagnation, and even decline for different groups toward the middle and bottom of the income and wealth spectrum. This is in stark contrast to rapidly rising incomes and wealth among higher earners and record numbers of billionaires and millionaires at the very top of the range.

This is taking place against a backdrop of dramatic shifts in spending power internationally, driven by a massive leap in the potential size of the super-wealthy and middle classes globally. By 2020 the global middle class could grow by 1.8 billion, 600 million of them in China alone. These shifts raise questions about how to serve members who are struggling, which potential new membership segments to target, and how to access the growing pool of philanthropic funds.

Case Study: The Men's Dress Furnishings Association

The Men's Dress Furnishings Association was set up to promote male fashion accessories such as neckties and dress shirts and to support the development of manufacturers and retailers in the sector. After 60 years, the association had to close in June 2008 as membership had fallen from 120 members in the 1980s to just 25. The association had failed to respond to a significant decline in

---

Key Challenges

the wearing of neckties ("business casual" becoming the norm) and increased foreign competition which have both adversely affected their traditional membership. It had not responded to the warning signals and determined a viable future for itself – which may have come from extending its scope to other areas of men's fashion or seeking a merger with other menswear associations.

Key Questions

? What changes are required to your current propositions, and how they are communicated in order for you to reach attractive but untapped market segments at home and abroad?

? How can you raise the visibility of your impact on the economy and society in order to increase interest and support from donors?

? What role should you play for individual members beyond the information, networking, and professional development services you have traditionally offered?

? Which segments of the membership are facing the greatest financial risk, and what can you do to help protect and enhance their living standards?

Challenge 7: How can you exploit new business models—Staying responsive and solvent

The web has fundamentally changed the nature of how services are delivered. As more people migrate to the web, user expectations of how they'll be served and how they will pay for those services are evolving. The emergence of the internet as a commercial delivery channel has helped drive innovation in business models from pay-per-use to "freemium," which sees core offerings provided free, funded through other streams such as advertising, sponsorship, and sale of additional products and services. These models are moving offline and encouraging customers to examine the value they place on each of the elements of a packaged purchase, such as membership subscriptions.

A number of virtual communities have been formed via the internet, which offers content and networking benefits similar to those offered by traditional associations. Although it is too early to judge whether these networks can all survive, they are forcing associations to think about their own business models. Leaders, staff, and boards are increasingly asking themselves difficult questions about the value delivered, the pricing of membership, the charges for additional products and services, the cost of delivery, the use of cross-subsidies, and the sustainability of current business models in the face of increasing competition.

Case Study: Sermo

Sermo was established as a web-based platform for anonymized MDs to share their views on medical conditions and treatments. Over 50,000 MDs access the site for free; pharmaceutical companies, insurance companies, and healthcare investors pay annual subscriptions to monitor the results of their conversations.

Key Questions

? How should your pricing models evolve as you move more activity to the Web?

? Can you become an effective portal for third-party solutions to the information, education, and support resources your members need?

? What are members' expectations when it comes to the personalization of services?

? What new membership segments and market opportunities could you open up through the provision of personalization facilities?

? What are the right models to support the association going forward over the next five years in a changing environment? What alternative business models should you be evaluating and experimenting with?

? What is the right legal structure to support what you want to do for your members in the way you want to do it?

Challenge 8: What's your consumption footprint— Facing up to energy and environmental pressures

We are entering an era in which governments, organizations, and citizens will be increasingly focused on concerns over the cost and availability of key resources such as energy and the parallel challenge of environmental protection. As this publication went to press, the oil price had reached $139 a barrel, and some analysts were forecasting that it could reach $200 a barrel by year's end. This is forcing every sector to identify ways in which it can drive down its energy consumption. In the aviation sector for example, airlines are reducing the amount of ice and bottled water carried on flights, removing footrests, replacing cookies with chips, and investigating lightweight seat designs—all in attempts to cut their fuel bill and reduce greenhouse gas emissions.

Associations will come under pressure from all sides to drive down resource consumption and improve their environmental footprint in every area, from energy consumption and water use to the choice of event venues. Perhaps more important still will be the need to help members find innovative, effective, and sustainable solutions to these challenges.

Case Study: The International Air Transport Association

In April 2008, the International Air Transport Association took the initiative of bringing together the leaders in airlines, airports, and aircraft manufacture to sign a declaration committing to carbon-free growth and a carbon-neutral future—an unprecedented step for an industry that has been under attack for its environmental impact.

Key Questions

? What is your strategy for reducing your own consumption and providing best-practice support to members in reducing their own environmental footprints?

? What is your strategy for thriving in a world where competition for scarce resources could result in limits to what you may actually be able to afford or consume?

Challenge 9: How sustainable are you—
Managing ethics, transparency, accountability, and responsibility

Most organizations are beginning to acknowledge that their long-term viability comes from addressing the "triple bottom line" of people, planet, and profits, ensuring they are socially, environmentally, and financially sustainable. The challenges described above have

focused on addressing the financial and environmental dimensions. Social sustainability demands that you conduct yourself in an exemplary manner when it comes to business ethics, transparency, accountability, and taking responsibility for your actions. Many associations are now focusing on how these critical drivers of trust can be built into the core brand values of their profession or sector and be used as a powerful differentiator in an increasingly global, complex, confusing, and competitive operating environment.

Case Study: ASAE & the Center for Association Leadership

From April 30 to May 2, 2008, ASAE & The Center hosted a combined live and online Global Summit on Social Responsibility. Over 800 participants came together to explore how to create a new magnitude of socially responsible leadership with associations leading the way and driving the social-responsibility movement forward to help solve some of the world's biggest problems. A total of 23 projects and initiatives resulted from the process.

Key Questions

? What are the sustainability standards, measures and best practices you should be promoting through your membership?

? What kind of organization do you want to be?

? Where are you trying to take the association over the next 5–10 years?

? What would success look and feel like for your members and staff?

? What distinctive and value-adding representation role can associations play on behalf of members?

? How do you ensure that your association and its members will conduct activities in a transparent, ethically sound, environmentally sustainable manner?

? What is your broader societal responsibility?

? Are you operationally, financially, and environmentally sustainable?

? What is the right sustainable-governance model and structure with which to drive the association forward?

Challenge 10: What's next on the radar—Embedding environmental scanning, scenario planning, and what-if thinking

The future is an evolving landscape, and new trends, ideas and developments don't impact us all equally and at the same rate. You need to ensure that however large or small your association, you have active early warning mechanisms that alert you to emerging signs of change that could create new opportunities, challenges, and risks. Ideally, such mechanisms would balance data-gathering with analysis and would engage members, volunteer leaders, boards, and staff. Each key trend or development identified should be assessed to explore its potential impact on who you serve, what you do, and how you do it.

A higher-level analysis is also extremely valuable, looking at how a combination of key trends, issues, and developments could play out into possible future scenarios. These scenarios can be used to rehearse the future and test how robust current plans and contingencies are in the face of a range of possible futures. This kind of what-if thinking needs to become as commonplace as questions such as "What do members want?" To achieve this, it needs to be embedded and become part of the core management approach and "operating system" of the association. An example set of scenarios and an exercise for evaluating them is presented in Appendix 5.

Case Study: The American Society of Mechanical Engineers

The American Society of Mechanical Engineers (ASME) has formalized its environmental scanning process, and it is led by a subcommittee of the board who shape the agenda for scanning activities. Scanning projects are conducted on a regular basis, alternating between broad-based scans of emerging trends and "deep dives" on specific topics. ASME recently conducted a project looking to 2028 to explore the future of the profession, which culminated with a global conference on the theme in Washington in April 2008.

Key Questions

? How can you embed future thinking in the key management processes and tools of the organization?

? How can you encourage a "culture of foresight"—a culture that naturally thinks about the future in every action it takes?

? How can you integrate ongoing "environmental scanning" into your strategic and operational decision-making?

? How can you help members prepare for the future through the provision of best-practice guidance and foresight materials?

? How quickly can you respond to external changes and new member requirements?

3.2. From Strategic Challenges to Strategic Responses

By now, a clear picture may be building of the critical trends, challenges, and priorities for your association. It may be that the imperative is so strong that you want to proceed directly to action because these are "burning platform" issues, and you feel you have to put the fire out. If that's the case, you may want to still scan the next couple of sections and then go straight to investigating the relevant trends in Appendix 1, the choice framework in Appendix 3, and the menu of immediate actions in Appendix 4.

However, you may also feel that responding to individual trends and challenges is not enough and that you have to tackle them strategically as a group. In that case, the following section will provide you with a four-stage strategic framework to guide you through answering the key questions raised by the key challenges.

Section 4
Key Choices
A Strategic Decision Making Framework

4.1. A Strategic Choice Framework

The previous two sections present a picture of fundamental change in our operating environment. They set out the key trends, emerging patterns of change, and critical challenges for associations, their leaders, their boards, staff, and volunteers; and all those involved in helping organizations define and build their preferred futures. The challenges raise a number of critical strategic questions for leaders. This section provides a strategic choice framework to guide you through answering those questions and making key choices and decisions about the future of your association. The feedback from our consultations for this project was clear: *"Don't tell us the answers, but do give us a sense of the issues we need to address and the questions we need to ask ourselves."* In response, we have defined a four-stage framework (Figure 8) that covers the following key areas of decision making when mapping out the future for your association or nonprofit:

1. *Why are we here?* Purpose, Strategic Direction, and Vision
2. *What will we do?* Core Products and Service Offerings
3. *How will we do it?* Service Delivery Model
4. *How should we organize ourselves?* Organization Model

4.2. Mapping the Key Challenges to the Choice Framework

As can be seen from the diagram below, for each stage of the framework, a series of "planning factors" have been defined. For each of these we have identified the key choices and decisions that need to be made. These are presented in Appendix 3. In addition, for each of these planning factors, we have identified the key trends that may have an impact and some of the critical implications and opportunities that arise from those trends. To help you work through these stages, Table 5 (next page) shows how the 10 key challenges from the previous

Figure 8.

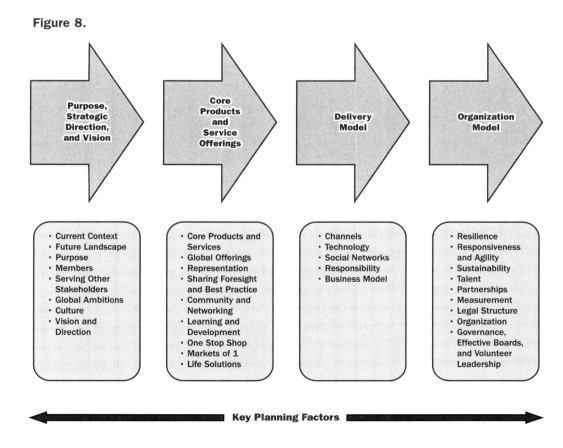

- Current Context
- Future Landscape
- Purpose
- Members
- Serving Other Stakeholders
- Global Ambitions
- Culture
- Vision and Direction

- Core Products and Services
- Global Offerings
- Representation
- Sharing Foresight and Best Practice
- Community and Networking
- Learning and Development
- One Stop Shop
- Markets of 1
- Life Solutions

- Channels
- Technology
- Social Networks
- Responsibility
- Business Model

- Resilience
- Responsiveness and Agility
- Sustainability
- Talent
- Partnerships
- Measurement
- Legal Structure
- Organization
- Governance, Effective Boards, and Volunteer Leadership

Key Planning Factors

Table 5. Mapping of Strategic Challenges to Strategic Choice Framework

	What's your leadership paradigm?	What's plan B?	Who's driving the talent agenda?	Who's the customer?	How do you connect your community?	Where's the money?	How can you exploit new business models?	What's your consumption footprint?	How sustainable are you?	What's next on the radar?
1. Purpose, Strategic Direction and Vision										
1.1. Current Context	X			X		X		X	X	X
1.2. Future Landscape	X	X	X	X	X	X	X	X	X	X
1.3. Purpose	X			X					X	X
1.4. Members	X	X	X	X		X	X			X
1.5. Serving Other Stakeholders	X	X	X	X	X	X			X	X
1.6. Global Ambitions	X	X	X	X	X	X	X			X
1.7. Culture	X	X						X	X	X
1.8. Vision and Direction	X	X	X	X	X	X	X	X	X	X
2. Core Products and Service Offerings										
2.1. Core Products and Services	X	X	X	X	X	X	X			X
2.2. Global Offerings	X	X		X	X	X	X			X
2.3. Representation	X			X	X				X	X
2.4. Sharing Foresight and Best Practices	X	X	X	X	X	X	X	X	X	X
2.5. Community and Networking	X	X	X	X	X	X	X			X
2.6. Learning and Development	X	X	X	X		X	X			X
2.7. One-Stop Shop	X	X	X	X	X	X		X	X	X
2.8. Markets of One	X	X	X	X		X	X		X	X
2.9. Life Solutions	X	X		X		X				X

Table 5. Mapping of Strategic Challenges to Strategic Choice Framework *(Continued)*

	What's your leadership paradigm?	What's plan B?	Who's driving the talent agenda?	Who's the customer?	How do you connect your community?	Where's the money?	How can you exploit new business models?	What's your consumption footprint?	How sustainable are you?	What's next on the radar?
3. Delivery Model										
a. Channels					X		X			
b. Technology					X		X	X	X	X
c. Social Networks					X		X			
d. Responsibility	X								X	
e. Business Model		X		X		X	X			
4. Organization Model										
4.1. Resilience	X	X						X	X	
4.2. Responsiveness and Agility	X	X		X			X		X	
4.3. Sustainability								X	X	
4.4. Talent		X	X						X	
4.5. Partnerships		X			X		X		X	
4.6. Measurement		X		X		X	X	X	X	
4.7. Legal Structure	X	X					X		X	
4.8. Organization	X	X					X		X	
4.9. Governance, Effective Strategic Boards, and Volunteer Leadership	X	X		X	X		X		X	

section map to the key stages and planning factors in the choice framework.

4.3. Using the Framework

The framework has been laid out in a manner that enables you to either work through it from end to end or to focus in on specific stages or planning factors. The sets of questions raised are meant to be a broad but not exhaustive set of triggers to help you develop clear strategic responses to the challenges and choices that confront you. The aim of this initial publication is to provide the initial stimulus; subsequent outputs from the *Association of the Future* program will provide a range of more detailed tools and resources for defining and implementing the future of your association.

We recognize that associations may have existing processes for strategic and operational planning and that these processes may be an ideal mechanism through which to address the questions raised here. We also recognize that other associations may choose to set up activities specifically to work through the framework and explore these questions. Hence, the framework is designed to support you whether it is done as a group, individually, with the board and volunteers, with staff, through consultants, through member consultation or any combination.

Section 5
Conclusions
Developing an Action Plan

5.1. Choosing a Course of Action

We hope this report has laid out a very clear sense of the fundamental changes that are shaping the environment, opportunities, and life choices being presented to our members and the resulting implications and opportunities for the associations and nonprofits. How you choose to react is a matter for you, the board, and your staff to decide. As we hope we've made clear, there isn't a single set of solutions that will work for every organization. We have tried to provide enough stimulus and resources to help you understand the trends and to drive debate in your association. We have also provided a strategic choice-making framework to help you work through the implications of these trends across every aspect of your organization. So what happens next?

There are a number of ways of using the resources, insights, and tools provided here. Outlined below are a number of different possible starting points (these could also be run together as part of a larger review or as one-off activities).

5.2. Choosing the Scale of Change to Pursue

In light of the sheer scale and implications of some of the trends and challenges, and the uncertainty over their long-term impact, one natural response would be to shun big-picture thinking and focus on the tactical. The temptation to pick the trends off one by one and deliver point solutions is understandable—and hugely tempting. However, changes will not arrive in a manner so neatly packaged that you can just deal with each one individually or during a single workshop session. They will combine and interact in often surprising ways, and it is essential to continually monitor these changes and revisit your strategic conversations about them. Therefore, we encourage you to think through all the questions in the entire framework, even if you then choose to focus on a vital few areas of change rather than on large-scale transformation.

The progression through these four stages is likely to be iterative; for example, your choice of technology will be highly dependent on whom you want to serve, what you want to provide to members, how you want to deliver it, and the kind of organization you want to be. So, if you are considering outsourcing IT activities, you will need to be clear on the services you want to offer. However, if you are doing it in-house, you will inevitably have to make tough decisions about the choice of technologies to adopt. One of the prime drivers for designing the framework in this way was to force a deliberate separation of what you want to do from the discussions of the delivery mechanisms and costs. All too often, we see good ideas being sidelined because of initial concerns about their likely cost or delivery capability, whereas a deeper understanding of the purpose and benefits of an activity could lead to a broader and more innovative search for delivery solutions.

It is also important to recognize that different people will perceive change at different rates—for example, although many are adapting to the changing nature of work brought about by globalization, some have yet to feel it in their daily lives or comprehend its significance. These differences could become more marked over time. The most common mistake when thinking about the future is to overestimate the impact of change in the short run and underestimate the implications of change in the long run. Historically, we know that most forms of change can happen in a relatively slow and predictable way (e.g., demographics). Others can be abrupt and disruptive such as the end of the Cold War and the events of 9/11. Others still can follow a more nonlinear pattern with periods of slow development followed by rapid and more disruptive impacts (e.g. the advent of the internet).

Fundamental changes take time to evolve into a critical component of our daily lives. The internet is a classic example; after the bursting of the dot-com bubble in 2000 and 2001, few would have anticipated just how deeply the web would be integrated into business and our personal lives. Many organizations are only just beginning to tap the power of web-based services and social interactions to transform their business, extend their offerings, and enhance customer service. One of the biggest changes the web is bringing about is the move to more collaborative enterprises and open approaches to innovation, in which outside ideas are positively encouraged. The rate of adoption could be rapid as firms see the economic payback. The implications for associations and their members could be immense.

5.3. Preparing for Change

Before addressing the strategic choice framework, it is worth spending some time thinking about how you can develop change-ready organizations. This means acknowledging that the only things you can be certain of are that fundamental shifts are happening and will continue to happen—and that you can have no certainty about how they will play out (especially when trends collide). It is also hard to predict what the second- and third-order effects will be as individuals, organizations, governments, and society as a whole respond and adapt to changes in the world around them—what unexpected and unintended outcomes could result?

If it's not clear how the U.S. economy will fare in the next five, ten, or twenty years; if experts are unsure about the impact of Baby Boomers retiring; if it is too early to tell how social networks will transform associations; if you cannot be certain how member needs and priorities will evolve—should you even bother worrying about the future? Should you just focus instead on becoming incredibly agile and learn to adapt fast in an ever more quickly changing world?

Although flexibility, adaptability and responsiveness will be vital, you do not have to sit back and wait for change to happen to you. There are things you can do to improve your capacity to handle uncertainty and prepare for the future. Depending on your current operating style, this may fit naturally with how you already work, or it may require changes in the way you think, plan, and act. Some of these critical challenges in developing a change-ready organization are explored below.

5.4. Developing a Tolerance for Uncertainty

The first stage in handling uncertainty is actually learning to live with it and making it a core part of your organization's strategic thinking. We are entering an era in which we do not know how all of the factors at play will influence the economy, business prospects, employment, lifestyles, and health. Under such circumstances, you cannot make a single set of assumptions about key

factors such as membership numbers, dues income, event attendance, the nature of the "competition," or the evolution of members' needs in line with your capabilities. Instead, you need to learn how to work with uncertainty and consider a range of possibilities for each of the key factors that drive your association.

Asking these "what-if" questions about all of your core assumptions will help ensure that you have a plan B and plan C should things not turn out as you had expected in planning.

Critical here is making sure that your board, volunteer leaders, staff, and members understand that good leadership in the 21st century demands that you have alternative plans and that you regularly test your assumptions about the changes ahead. This may even require specific training for key staff on issues such as planning under uncertainty and decision making with imperfect information.

5.5. Environmental Scanning

The best way of understanding what is changing in our world and what might be coming next is to devote some time to thinking about it. Many associations may not find it feasible or necessary to conduct full environmental scans. The scan presented here is designed to act as a baseline to which you might add key sector-specific trends, issues, and developments. With limited time and budget available, it may be more appropriate to devote internal resources to four key activities:

• Sharing the results of these scans with staff, boards, volunteer leaders, and members, asking them to identify and analyze additional trends, issues, and developments that should be on the radar screen.
• Analyzing the data collected to assess what these trends, issues, and developments could mean for members and their needs.
• Identifying the resulting implications for your association.
• Determining how you should respond.

5.6. Research

The purpose of this study is to raise critical questions. In many cases a natural response is to seek further insights into how these questions could be answered: for example, *"How are other organizations changing their HR policies and leadership styles to handle multiple generations in the workplace?"* or *"How are members using social networks?"* Although the temptation may be to commission new research or conduct member surveys, time and cost implications are associated with both courses of action, and members may develop survey fatigue. Given that you will need to develop a tolerance of uncertainty and learn to live with imperfect information, possible strategies would include

• Seeking out research that may already have been conducted elsewhere and accepting that although it may not be perfect, it may be sufficient,

• Collaborating with another interested party to reduce costs,

• Having a single "question of the week" on your website (although these will not provide full-blown analyses of membership attitudes, they do provide an instant pulse),

• Identifying research partners who may be willing to do pro bono research for the association as a training vehicle for their staff and as a means of gaining additional visibility, and

• Commercializing research outputs either by seeking sponsors or by reselling the reports to a wider audience.

5.7. Extending Your Networks and Perspectives

As an association professional, you are used to networking extensively within your sector and with the broader association community. However, many of the ideas, trends, and solutions that you need to know about could come from beyond these two communities. A critical part of the personal development of leaders, executives and staff going forward will be to network across sectors to gain new perspectives on the issues they are facing and new ideas on how to address them. Leaders need to seek out forums that bring people together from across multiple sectors—such as the online social networks, executive breakfast clubs and the Chambers of Commerce.

In the private sector, it is now common for organizations to bring in a range of outsiders such as artists, scientists, healthcare professionals, and students with no knowledge of the sector to provide an independent perspective on key issues for the organization. Key roles of these groups are challenging the organization's perspective, asking naive questions, and raising the big, undiscussable issues that all organizations have. Associations and nonprofits may find this an increasingly valuable mechanism for extending their radars and understanding the broader impact on society of new trends and developments.

5.8. Scenario Thinking as a Tool for Managing Uncertainty

Forecasts and trend projections typically use a set of assumptions about a single view of the future based on what has happened in the past. However, experience tells us that a number of factors, uncertainties, and sources of complexity can drive a forecast or trend line off course. Scenario planning is designed to help us work with uncertainty and capture complexity by exploring a range of plausible futures. Scenarios help us explore the possible development of and interaction between critical uncertainties such as economic growth, individual income, wealth, business trends, social trends, and key environmental issues. Scenarios can be developed at the levels of the global economy, a sector, or even an organization.

Scenario planning creates a range of storylines about different futures and explores the different ways in which key forces, trends, and issues may play out. These scenarios can help you *rehearse the future*, answer key questions about the external environment, and determine the different possible courses of action you might take. Analysis of the scenarios can help you determine actions you should take under any circumstances and the plan B and plan C actions you might pursue if events transpire to take you in a different direction from the future you were planning for.

Scenario planning can be a great tool for aligning multiple stakeholders and getting people to focus on solutions and where they are going rather than on problems and where they have come from. They can also help tease out a vision of where an association would fit, and what its role would be, under different possible futures. Such exercises can be powerful training tools for staff, executives, volunteers, and board members alike.

Scenario exercises can be done as both desk-based analytical exercises and participative consultations and engagement tools, with group sizes ranging from 2 to 2,000. The duration can run from a six- to twelve-month rigorous study to a one-hour workshop session to design a set of different newspapers from the future. In Appendix 5, we have included an example set of scenarios and the outline of an exercise to review the scenarios to determine possible implications for your members and your association. Practical guidance on how to develop scenarios and how to apply a range of other futures tools will be provided as part of future deliverables from the *Association of the Future* program. A range of web-based tools and resources, books, training courses, and consultants are available to help you undertake a full-scale scenario project.

5.9. Starting a Member Dialogue

Many associations have found it valuable to share the trends and patterns of change with members and ask them to identify additional trends affecting them. Members can be asked to explore the implications of those trends on their lives and the resulting requirements they have of your organization. You can then agree on a prioritized action list of those areas they most want help with. You could feed this into an overall strategic review or choose to deal with these priorities as individual initiatives. This exercise could be run through an email dialogue and/or through focus groups and workshops—possibly alongside or as part of existing events. It is important to get the board and volunteer leaders to be part of this process so that they can hear the voice of the customer and be part of the dialogue. The action list presented in Appendix 4 could provide a range of practical ways to drive forward the ideas and opportunities generated from such dialogue.

5.10. Engaging Your Staff

You should also consider running an exercise with your own staff similar to that outlined above. Staff could be asked to focus both on the trends affecting them as individuals and those impacting members. Task forces could be created to drive forward practical actions on a vital few initiatives that would make a significant difference for members and/or staff.

5.11.Set Up a Strategic Task Force

If you have already read enough to think that a fundamental review is required, you may want to establish a task force that could comprise staff, board members, volunteers, and members—and possibly some invited outsiders to challenge your thinking and ask the unaskable questions. This might start with a review of the trends, using the framework provided in Appendix 6. This could be followed by a scenario review exercise (Appendix 5) to examine the implications and opportunities created by different possible macroeconomic scenarios. Finally, the task force could use the insights, ideas, and priorities emerging from the trends and scenarios workshops to lead the organization through a strategic review using the Strategic Choice Framework presented in Section 4 and Appendix 3.

5.12. Mapping Your Personal Future

One of factors that can hold an organization back from embracing and pursuing a different future is a CEO's lack of comfort with the changing landscape that is unfolding. If the CEO struggles to see his or her own future in this emerging picture, the temptation can be to ignore the warning signs or to resist change. In contrast, it can be a powerful motivating factor for staff, executives, and boards if the leader has clearly thought about the future, has considered how it will affect him or her personally, and has a clear sense of what he or she wants to achieve. An example process for mapping your personal future is presented in Appendix 7.

5.13. A Call to Action

Associations and nonprofits will be faced with a powerful and evolving set of challenges over the foreseeable future. How you respond now will have a critical bearing on the outcome for your association. In turbulent times in which no single organization or nation has all the answers, the opportunity clearly exists for associations and nonprofits to make a valuable difference in the lives of their members and the communities they serve. The first decision you have to make is whether you want your future to be a set of responses to the things happening around you, or something that you help define and create. The choice is simple: Do you want to be a recipient of the future, or an active participant in designing it?

Designing Your Future
Key Trends, Challenges, and Choices Facing Association and Nonprofit Leaders

---

Appendices

Contents

Appendix 1
The 50 Key Trends

The Trend Description Framework

Presented on the following pages are the 50 trends that emerged from the process of environmental scanning, member review, and prioritization described earlier in this report. By means of these processes we identified a total of 50 key trends that our analysis suggests are already making an impact, or could over the next five years, both globally and in the United States. These trends could have a direct effect on the association community as well as on the economy and on government, governance, individuals, professions, businesses, and industry sectors in the United States—all of which have further implications for associations.

The trends were categorized by their origins by using the STEEP framework:

- Socio-demographic (starts on page 47)
- Technological (starts on page 77)
- Economic (starts on page 91)
- Environmental (starts on page 127)
- Political (starts on page 137)

For each key trend we have compiled a detailed profile that includes the following information:

- **Description:** an explanation of the trend, including supporting data where relevant; source references have been noted, where appropriate;
- **Timeframe:** the time during which we believe the trend could have an effect on at least half the population of the United States (note: *this, by its nature, is very subjective; some associations and individuals are already affected by these trends, but others may not see it on their "radar screens" for many years)*;
- **Potential Impact:** depicts the trend's impact on society as a whole;
- **Implications and Opportunities for Associations:** examples of possible implications for overall policy and strategy, as well as opportunities for associations to develop new activities;
- **Functional Implications and Opportunities:** examples of possible implications and opportunities related to what is delivered to members and the way in which associations organize to deliver;
- **Example Industry Implications:** highlighting possible impacts for specific/all sectors; and
- **Sources and References:** showing where the underlying data was derived.

Socio-demographic Trends

1. Generation Y (Millennials): digital, "civic," and connected

Key Question

How will the Millennial generation influence the nature of work, expectations for membership services and social-policy issues?

Description

The Millennial generation (born 1980-1999) is the most observed and studied generation in U.S. history. Often referred to as "Digital Natives," they are said to be "always on, always connected"—constantly exchanging messages, surfing the web, and participating in social networks via their computers, mobile phones, or game consoles.[1, 2]

Raised to be active team members in structured recreational and academic activities, Millennials are also expected to be a civically engaged generation focused on institution building and positive social change.[1, 3] High school and college volunteering rates are on the rise, as is the youth voter turnout—as evidenced by the 2008 Democratic Presidential nominations. The 2008 election was expected to be the third consecutive Presidential election to show an increase in youth voter turnout.[4] Most studies suggest that Millennials are more politically tolerant than their elders on issues related to immigration, race, sexuality, and gender and believe strongly in issues related to the environment.[4] A study released in 2008 by UCLA's Higher Education Research Institute found that of 260,000 college freshmen surveyed in the fall of 2007, more than 66.3 percent said it is "essential or very important" to help others—the highest percentage to say so in 25 years.[5]

Connectivity is a major lifestyle trait for the Millennials. Unlike members of previous generations, teenagers and young adults report strong ties with their parents, and there are few signs of widespread youth culture rebellion in American society on the scale experienced in the late 1960s and 1970s.[1] Millennials are often described as confident, having received a parenting style aimed at building self-esteem at an early age. They are comfortable living more transparent lives on the web with individual profile pages on social networking sites such as MySpace and Facebook and video testimonials on YouTube. Much of their web use revolves around connecting with friends.[5, 6]

Timeframe

Now–2010

Potential Impact

- Millennials are expected to be a major force for social change as they enter their young adult and family stage of life development.
- Growing political involvement—in Pew surveys in 2006, nearly half of young people (48 percent) identified most with the Democratic Party, whereas just 35 percent affiliated most with the GOP. This trend appeared to be growing during the 2008 U.S. Presidential nomination campaigns, possibly making the Millennial generation the least Republican generation.[2, 6]

Implications and Opportunities for Associations

- Associations need to revisit all operational activities, from communications to event design, to explore how they can be adapted to cater to the differing requirements of this emerging generation.
- Regular industry specific research is needed to understand the changing needs, attitudes, and expectations of the emerging workforce—particularly in relation to professional development, volunteerism, and association services.
- Pressure for transparency toward civic policy issues (and social causes) important to Millennial members may open room for associations with a clear social responsibility strategy seen to "do something good for mankind" to flourish with this generation.
- Leadership and boards of nonprofit organizations will need to consider how to incorporate this new generation into their volunteer leadership and governance structures, creating engagement mechanisms (formal structures, live forums, conference streams, web tools) that allow this younger generation to participate fully and self-organize around the issues and topics of greatest interest to them.

Functional Implications and Opportunities

• Requires a fresh look at association human resource policies and staff development strategies in addressing recruitment, development and retention, conflict resolution, attitudes toward work, mentoring, collaboration, and support for innovation.

• This generation is typically highly technoliterate and is growing up with high expectations of what technology can do for it. Associations may need to evaluate, adjust, and invest more frequently in information technologies flexible and capable enough to handle increasingly diverse member requirements for personalized services, new training programs, and communication strategies. The cost of supporting such requirements may drive collaboration between nonprofits in the development of such solutions, encouraging the use of third-party solutions on a "rental" basis (software as a service [SaaS]).

• Associations may want to develop systems to monitor and study the implications of emerging civic issues important to different generations as current and potential future members.

Example Industry Implications

• This generation is increasingly making employment decisions based on employers' Corporate Social Responsibility (CSR) and environmental policies.

• The desire for greater say and more responsibility could lead to a growth in freelance and independent workers and the creation of more new enterprises with younger leaders.

Sources and References

1. http://lifecourse.com/news/millennialssurvey.php

2. http://people-press.org/reports/pdf/300.pdf

3. www.civicyouth.org

4. www.usatoday.com/life/lifestyle/2006-06-28-generation-next_x.htm

5. www.civicyouth.org/quick/youth_voting.htm

6. www.millennialmakeover.com; http://millennialmakeover.blogspot.com

2. Millennials increasingly seeking overseas experience

Key Question

How might associations serve the needs of Millennials seeking to gain experience abroad or in the United States, developing programs and partnerships that create opportunities to work or volunteer overseas and leveraging the resulting experiences to the benefit of the wider membership?

Description

The number of U.S. Millennials (those born from 1980 to 1999) studying abroad has risen steadily in recent years, with an increase of 144 percent in the last decade, up from only 84,403 in 1994/1995.[1] According to a U.S. State Department annual report, in 2006 the number of students studying abroad reached 205,983—an increase of 8 percent over the previous year.[1] The range of opportunities for young Americans to work abroad within the private sector is also increasing as more companies expand their global operations.[2]

According to the Institute of International Education, "While 45 percent of all U.S. students abroad study in perennially popular destinations in Western Europe (#1 United Kingdom, #2 Italy, #3 Spain, and #4 France), there were major increases in the number of students going to other host countries, including a 35 percent increase to 6,389, up from 4,737 the previous year, in students going to China, now the eighth-leading host destination for American students and the only Asian country in the top 10."[1]

Timeframe

Now–2015

Potential Impact

- Younger Americans are recognizing and taking advantage of the tremendous opportunity of being present during the transformation of emerging economies in Asia and South America and free market hubs such as Dubai and are increasingly seeking such global experiences that will benefit their careers.
- Millennials' overseas experiences could strengthen global connections for U.S.-based industries.
- Millennials may be the first U.S. generation to have a significant proportion of its members leave the country to pursue large portions of their careers, if not their entire adult lives, overseas.

Implications and Opportunities for Associations

- Proactive associations may seek to create programs that generate overseas opportunities for their members and encourage overseas members to gain experience working in the United States.
- Younger members could provide the impetus for establishing association chapters in key overseas markets and for driving responses to global cultural and economic shifts in associations that have yet to act.
- As barriers to entry fall and business practices around the world become more visible via the internet, associations can increasingly serve domestic and international members across a range of jurisdictions.

Functional Implications and Opportunities

- Associations and especially professional societies will need a more globally oriented workforce to understand the needs of professionals working internationally. Associations may choose to make overseas experience a key criterion in future staff recruitment.
- Professional memberships and their leadership will need to be more open to global membership and chapter structures, recruitment for annual meetings, expanding accessibility of educational material, and revisiting sources of revenue for a global base.

Example Industry Implications

- The travel and tourism sector is increasingly recognizing the value of having U.S. staff train overseas and of recruiting staff from overseas to help provide a more personalized guest experience for visitors coming from increasingly diverse geographic backgrounds.
- Recent research from Thunderbird University has found that the top-performing managers in global businesses tend to have experience with working in multiple cultures and speak at least three languages.[3]

Sources and References

1. http://opendoors.iienetwork.org/?p=StudyAbroad

2. http://media.www.arbiteronline.com/media/storage/paper890/news/2007/09/04/Biztech/American.Expatriates.Take.Risk.On.Chinas.FastGrowing.Economy-2947998.shtml

3. http://media.www.theticker.org/media/storage/paper909/news/2003/11/03/News/Lecture.Offers.Insight.Into.Benefits.Of.Knowing.A.Second.Language-1779895.shtml

3. Rising life expectancy, aging global populations

Key Questions

How will associations respond as lifespans increase, changing lifestyles and patterns of economic development?

What services will be required by an older population and membership base?

Description

Alongside population growth, the world's aging population will be the demographic story of the 21st century. Since 1945 the life expectancy of citizens living in the wealthier countries around the world has increased by one year every five years. Expanded access to basic healthcare, nutrition, and safe water supplies has increased the global life expectancy.[1] The American Life Extension Institute believes that average life expectancy in the United States will reach 100 by 2029.[2] Some scientists, such as Cambridge geneticist Aubrey de Grey, argue that aging is a disease curable in our own lifetimes. As a result, they say that the life expectancy of even mature adults could extend to 500 or even 1,000 years.[3, 4]

Aging has wide-ranging implications related to wealth distribution, pensions and social services, healthcare, financial services, consumer spending, industry sector makeup, labor markets, and political policies. The UN report "World Population Aging" (2002–2007 update) indicates that by 2050, those aged 60 and over will comprise one third of the population in developed regions.[1] Those aged over 60 represented 8 percent of the global population in 1950, rising to 11 percent in 2007, and are forecast to reach 22 percent by 2050.[5]

The global ratio of workers aged between 15 and 64 to older persons could decrease from 12 to 1 in 1950 to 4 to 1 by 2050. Asia and Europe will age faster than other regions. By 2015 the EU will have 26 percent more people in the 50–74 age bracket and a third more aged over 65. This will be accompanied by a 16 percent decline in the 15–44 cohort. In the United States the proportion of the population aged over 65 years is projected to increase from 12.4 percent in 2000 to 19.6 percent by 2030.[1, 5] Over the same time period, life expectancy in China is expected to reach 75, in the Russian Federation 72, and in India 71.[3, 6]

Timeframe

Now–2015

Potential Impact

- Increasing financial strains placed on organizations, governments, and families to meet funding liabilities and expectations for services targeted at aging populations.
- Potential for conflict if resources or political policies are diverted to service older generations at the expense of younger ones.
- Employers will need to consider how they accommodate a workforce that could range in age from 16 to 85, and how to specifically cater to the needs of an older workforce.

Implications and Opportunities for Associations

- Major implications for the design of products, online tools, events and conferences, and membership categories (e.g., life membership models, benefits, and services for older populations).
- Potential growth in associations who service an aging population and support members past retirement age.
- Potential opportunity to provide services to help individuals prepare for longer lifespans and to assist organizations in catering to the differing needs of an increasingly diverse employee age range.

Functional Implications and Opportunities

- The challenge of shaping membership strategies (e.g., communication, retention, recruitment, programs, and services), leadership development, and workforce strategies to cater to a potentially increasingly wide variation in the age of the members and the association's own staff.
- The demand for new data and relationship management systems as the aging population adds to the diversity of the membership base and its values, behaviors, and cultures, as well as to the diversity of the potential volunteer pool.

• The challenge of financing retention after retirement—what is the current cost of servicing lifetime membership, and what are the potential financial liabilities of supporting the long-term profile of the membership base? What are the staffing implications (e.g., increased healthcare costs), and how appropriate are legacy business models?

• The increasing challenge for associations and organizations to capture the "know-what," "know-how," and "know-who" institutional knowledge base of an increasingly age-diverse workforce that could be stepping in and out of regular work, possibly creating new service opportunities.

Example Industry Implications

• Drives growth in healthcare, leisure, travel and tourism, assisted living, security services, continuing education, and financial services.

• Brings a rise in organizations staffed by active seniors working on a part-time or full-time basis after retirement.

Sources and References

1. www.un.org/esa/population/publications/WPA2007/wpp2007.htm

2. www.worldhealth.net/news/100-year_lifespans_the_norm_by_2029_pred

3. www.worldhealth.net/p/4236,6721.html

4. http://news.bbc.co.uk/2/hi/uk_news/4003063.stm

5. www.lifesite.net/ldn/2007/aug/07081605.html

6. www.mckinsey.com/mgi/publications/demographics/index.asp

4. Widening generational gap: values, attitudes, behaviors, technoliteracy

Key Question

How do we move beyond stereotypes to understand and value the attributes of all generational cohorts, encouraging respectful understanding and collaboration among them?

Description

America is at a crossroads as multiple generations with quite possibly very different outlooks on work, life, and technology meet in the workplace. Some workplace specialists, as well as a range of studies, are starting to identify gaps between senior manager Baby Boomers (born 1946–1964), rising managers from generation X (born 1964–1980), and newer, younger Millennial workers (born 1980–1999).[1]

More than 60 percent of U.S. employers say they are experiencing tension between employees from different generations. A Lee Hecht Harrison survey also found that more than 70 percent of older employees are dismissive of younger workers' abilities and that nearly half of employers also say that younger employees are dismissive of the abilities of their older coworkers.[2]

Research regarding values and beliefs shows increasingly marked differences emerging between generations in U.S. society.[2, 3, 4] Baby Boomers are those 77–80 million Americans born from 1946 to 1964 who are often described as idealistic, individualistic, personal values–oriented, and less trustful of government and authority. Baby Boomers were front-and-center during the significant changes of the twentieth century—the era of broadcast media, mass-market advertising, civil rights, the birth control pill, and the personal computer.

Generation X represents the 40 million Americans born from 1964 to 1979. They are often described as having spent their youth living under the shadow of the larger Baby Boomer generation. They are typically characterized as pragmatic, independent, and distrustful of traditional hierarchy. Generation X was at the forefront of the internet revolution and remains a major force of entrepreneurial activity in knowledge economy sectors.

Millennials are the 78–80 million Americans born from 1980 to 1999 who are often described as civic, confident, team-oriented, and optimistic. Their worldview has been shaped by American economic prosperity and the rise of the internet and personal technologies. Their hovering "helicopter" parents typically believed in a philosophy of "protect and nurture," raising their children to be team-oriented, supported by a sense of high self-esteem that sees "everyone gets a trophy." Unlike the Baby Boomers, who are said to be inwardly focused and distrustful of authority, Millennials are often described as civic and support wider institutional strategies for social change. They are more likely to work within the system and assume multiple roles within teams.[1, 4]

Technology is a critical source of intergenerational tension. Pew internet studies repeatedly show that adoption rates appear to be fragmented as younger generations more readily adopt and embrace technological developments than their older counterparts (colleagues, bosses and teachers) do.[6, 7] Millennials are more likely to embrace the collaboration and productivity tools that are changing the learning experience by allowing users to explore, share, and cocreate information in highly interactive ways.[7] Millennials are also more transparent and willing to reveal aspects of their multiple online and offline personalities, blending their personal and work lives with fewer boundaries. Despite efforts to design these tools using the most intuitive steps, research suggests that many older users still struggle to learn and adapt to them—and the gap appears to be growing.[6, 7]

Timeframe

Now–2015

Potential Impact

- Having four generations in one work environment presents opportunities to blend the experience, knowledge, and social relationships of older staff with the innovative energy of youth, evolving business policies, practices, and communication styles to work in a multigenerational environment.

- Potential exists for increased tension between generations created around differing perspectives on the purpose of work, benefit packages, personal happiness, work–life balance, learning styles, work styles, the role of technology, communication styles, performance feedback reviews, and preferred working hours.
- Generational views could vary widely regarding technology usage, digitally facilitated relationships, participation in social networks and personal connectivity (SMS, email, and online interaction versus phone and face-to-face), transparency, and accountability. This will also lead to greater pressure for organizations to support an increasingly wide range of preferred communication styles, engagement approaches, and technology tools.

Implications and Opportunities for Associations

- The need for research on best practices and the allocation of time and resources toward understanding the motivations of each generation regarding joining associations, as well as their perceptions of desired membership benefits, in order to blend different age groups and resolve intergenerational issues.
- The potential to provide programs and services to help organizations handle intergenerational differences through best-practices guidance, education, and training focused on mentoring, succession planning, communication styles, and media, negotiation, managing cross-generational employees and teams, conflict resolution, financial planning, and healthcare.
- The possible creation of opportunities to train members in emerging technologies.

Functional Implications and Opportunities

- Regularly updated research will be required to understand evolving generational values, needs, and expectations—particularly as economic conditions change and individual priorities alter with them.
- This may directly affect the design and delivery of all aspects of association operations, including strategy, governance, volunteer participation, products and services, delivery mechanisms, communications, and pricing structures.
- The cost of developing multiple technology-delivery platforms may be prohibitive for many associations, leading to collaboration or the rental of third-party offerings.
- Staffing/professional development will require regular reevaluation of roles and duties to maintain the ability to understand and serve different generations of members and staff while providing relevant training and technical support for a range of generations having different attitudes toward technology.
- This may lead associations to collaborate on research, sharing best practices in formulating and monitoring strategies in order to best resolve issues and gaps.

Example Industry Implications

- This will likely create issues for industries having a higher percentage of multigenerational workers.
- Many industries now find themselves in a constant and expensive cycle of train-deploy-replace to ensure that they are providing their staff with the latest personal productivity technologies that are required by a new generation of tech-savvy, demanding employees.

Sources and References

1. www.nasrecruitment.com/TalentTips/NASinsights/RecruitingManagingTheGenerations WhitePaper.pdf

2. www.lifecourse.com/pubs/books.php

3. http://pewresearch.org/pubs/526/marriage-parenthood

4. http://people-press.org/commentary/display.php3?AnalysisID=86

5. www.pewinternet.org/report_display.asp?r=162

6. www.marcprensky.com/writing/Prensky%20-%20Digital%20Natives,%20Digital%20Immigrants%20-%20Part1.pdf

7. www.nmc.org/pdf/2008-Horizon-Report.pdf

5. Baby Boomer retirement and unretirement; talent shortages

Key Question

How will associations address the needs of the individual and of employers, as well as the impact on their own organizations, caused by the Baby Boomer cohort's approach to retirement?

Description

The aging of the U.S. Baby Boomer (born 1946–1964) workforce could redefine our notions of retirement and workforce demographics as older people chose a wide range of post-retirement employment and leisure options to address personal needs and financial pressures. The Bureau of Labor Statistics predicts that in 2010 there will be 52 percent more people in the 55–64 age bracket than there were in 2000. Workers over the age of 55 are expected to grow from 14 percent of the labor force to 19 percent by 2012,[1, 2] when the Baby Boomer cohort will be 48–66 years old.

The U.S. population will continue to age, with the annual growth rate of the 55-and-older group projected at 4.1 percent, nearly four times the rate of growth of the overall population. It is anticipated that by 2012 youths (aged 16–24) will constitute just 15 percent of the population, whereas prime-age workers (aged 25–54) will make up about 66 percent. The share of the 55-and-older age group will increase from 14.3 percent of the population in 2002 to 19.1 percent by 2012.[3, 4]

It is assumed that many potential retirees may continue to work out of financial necessity or for reasons of professional and personal fulfillment. A recent study by the University of Michigan Retirement Research Center found that "nearly one-half of retirees followed a non-traditional retirement path that involved partial retirement and/or unretirement and that the unretirement rate among those observed at least five years after their first retirement is 24 percent. The unretirement rate was even higher among those retiring at younger ages (as high as 36 percent among those retiring at ages 51 to 52)."[5]

Although an overwhelming 76 percent of Baby Boomers intend to continue working past the traditional retirement age of 65, many are looking for second careers as entrepreneurs or temporary employees. A recent survey found that some 71.2 percent of Japanese men in their early 60s were still working, in comparison to 15 percent in France, 33 percent in Germany, and 57 percent in the United States. In the United States, 66 percent expect to work for pay after retiring. Of these, 27 percent plan to keep working to make ends meet, and 19 percent so that they can afford "extras."[3]

The Bureau of Labor Statistics forecasts that the civilian labor force (supply) will grow by 62.1 million, and that the jobs available (demand) will grow to 164.5 million, by 2014.[2, 4] A wide range of U.S. industries, from oil and gas to IT and nursing, are expected to face considerable talent shortages as the first wave of Baby Boomers begins to start retiring in 2010. McKinsey & Co. predicts that over the next three decades the demand for experienced IT professionals between the ages of 35 and 45 will increase by 25 percent, even as the supply decreases by 15 percent.[1]

Timeframe

2011–2015

Potential Impact

• The Baby Boomer population could redefine our notions of later life stages by challenging expectations regarding part-time work, leisure, volunteerism, family roles and structures, and continuing education and skills development. Employers could increasingly look to retain this generation to counter potential issues of leadership gaps, loss of expertise, and talent shortages.

• Many U.S. companies and nonprofits have not trained, prepared, or secured sufficient numbers of mid-level managers to fill the executive ranks nationally. A talent pool shortage among those with executive quality potential significantly affect the level of competitiveness of U.S. industries and the quality of service from the national public and nonprofit institutions.

• Immigration may be seen as one solution, assuming policy changes on visa restrictions. In 2007, American colleges and universities received 27 percent fewer graduate applications from international students than in 2003. The number of F-1 visas issued to international students fell 10 percent between 2000 and 2001.[2, 5]

• Organizations will need to rethink recruiting strategies to attract and retain retirees and adapt policies to accommodate aging workers who might delay full retirement for more flexible, part-time schedules.

Implications and Opportunities for Associations

• Associations will need to anticipate the diversity of retirement preferences among an aging workforce as well as the new class of workers that could emerge to work past retirement, requiring association services and programs tailored and priced to reflect their changing needs and circumstances.

• Associations may be able to benefit from the individual and organizational customer opportunities created by the needs of Baby Boomers going into unretirement. Traditional employment may be impractical, allowing associations to take on the role of retraining their older members to reenter or remain in the workforce (e.g., increased focus on lifetime learning, reward systems, compensation packages, volunteerism, performance reviews, securing knowledge transfer, and reaffirming personal relationships with partners and clients).

Functional Implications and Opportunities

• The organizational implications of filling leadership positions with retired Baby Boomers.

• The challenge of maintaining relevance of content, services, and membership categories to different generations.

• The human resources strategy of retaining and attracting experienced senior managers and executives who want to continue past retirement age but do not want to commit to long-term, full-time employment positions (e.g., flexi-time, part-time, tele-work, and retirement packages).

Example Industry Implications

• The aging workforce is especially critical in the healthcare sector and the oil and gas industry, where 66 percent and 65 percent of respondents, respectively, cite the issue as a significant challenge.[3] A shortage of more than 1 million nurses, amid a workforce of 3 million, is expected by 2012. Immigration may be a partial solution—the number of foreign-educated nurses coming into the country more than tripled, from 4,000 in 1998 to 15,000 in 2004. Foreign-educated nurses now represent as much as 10 percent of all practicing nurses in the States.[3, 4]

• The nonprofit and philanthropic sectors are expected to face significant losses in top executive leadership.[3]

• The U.S. Bureau of Labor Statistics' Top 10 occupations affected by Baby Boomer retirement (by end 2008) are[4]

- Management analysts
- Social workers
- Industrial engineers
- Lawyers
- Financial managers
- Registered nurses
- Public administration administrators and officials
- Personnel and labor relations managers
- Police supervisors and detectives
- Postal clerks

Sources and References

1. www.informationweek.com/story/showArticle.jhtml?articleID=205601557

www.apa.org/monitor/nov04/coverstory.html

2. www.bls.gov/opub/mlr/2004/02/art3abs.htm

3. www.management-issues.com/2006/8/24/research/greying-workforce-an-opportunity-to-be-grasped.asp

4. www.bls.gov/opub/mlr/2007/11/contents.htm

5. www.mrrc.isr.umich.edu/publications/papers/pdf/wp085.pdf

Additional Resources

1. www.buckconsultants.com/buckconsultants/Portals/0/Documents/PUBLICATIONS/Press_Releases/2007/pr_06_11_07.pdf

2. http://jasoncorsello.blogs.com/jason_corsellos_weblog/2006/05/are_you_worried.html

3. www.bls.gov/oco/reprints/ocor001.pdf

4. www.cio.com/article/31832/Knowledge_Management_in_

5. www.brookings.edu/interviews/2002/1017nonprofits.aspx

6. http://epochservices.net/kit/wp.pdf

6. Increasing political and economic impact of diversity— minorities one third of the U.S. population

Key Question

How will associations ensure that they are relevant, representative, and attractive for a changing demographic makeup?

Description

An increasingly diverse population will continue to affect every aspect of U.S. society and could have a significant influence on the United States' political and economic outlook. In 2007, the U.S. minority (non-white) population passed the 100 million mark and now makes up one third of the U.S. population.[1] Although minorities do not vote as one or have completely identical purchase patterns, they have become key target segments for political campaigners and commercial marketers.

Some states, such as Texas and California, are becoming "majority-minority" states, where no single group holds a majority population. The U.S. Census reports that "nearly one in every 10 of the nation's 3,141 counties has a population that is more than 50 percent minority." In 2006, eight counties that had not previously been majority-minority increased the total to 303.[2]

Some forecasts suggest that Hispanics could rise to one of every four members of the U.S. population by 2016.[3] According to U.S. Census Bureau figures published in May 2007, Hispanics remain the largest minority group, with 44.3 million in July 2006, representing one in seven (14.8 percent) of the total population. Blacks were the second largest minority group, totaling 40.2 million in 2006. They were followed by Asians (14.9 million), American Indians and Alaska Natives (4.5 million), and Native Hawaiians and other Pacific Islanders (1 million). The population of non-Hispanic whites who indicated no other race totaled 198.7 million in 2006. With a 3.4 percent increase between July 1, 2005, and July 1, 2006, Hispanics were the fastest growing minority group. Asians were the second fastest growing minority group, with a 3.2 percent population increase during the 2005–2006 period. The population of non-Hispanic whites who indicated no other race grew by 0.3 percent during this one year period.[1]

Hispanics represent nearly half the growth of immigrant populations coming into the United States.[4] The economic influence of Hispanics is growing even faster than their population. Nielsen Media Research estimates that the buying power of Hispanics will exceed $1 trillion in 2008—a 55 percent increase over levels in 2003. As the American population becomes more diverse, cultural traditions are increasingly "crossing over" ethnic boundaries, as in the case of the Quinceañera—the Latin American celebration of a girl's 15th birthday—which is joining the Sweet Sixteen party as a teen rite.[5]

Timeframe

Now–2010

Potential Impact

- The United States is moving closer to an era of majority-minority population in which no single ethnic or racial group will hold a majority percentage.
- Foreign-born minority populations are increasingly raising concerns over the impacts on their communities of immigration policies, counter-terrorism strategies, healthcare, social services, and trade agreements.
- Immigration will remain critical in providing a source of mass labor and higher-end knowledge workers, especially as studies continue to suggest that immigrants are key driver of innovation and economic growth.[6, 7]
- Rising diversity will continue to shape old and new traditions, testing the attitudes and tolerance of individuals and communities absorbing new populations into neighborhoods, schools, and work environments.

Implications and Opportunities for Associations

- How reflective is association membership of the broader population mix in U.S. society? What strategies are required to address any perceived gaps?

New association opportunities will evolve as more industries and professions develop around new ethnic and racial minority groups.

Associations will need to regularly revisit policies and training regarding immigration- and minority-relevant issues.

This issue creates opportunities to address diversity and social inclusion through research, program delivery (conferences, seminars, e-learning, and website access), volunteer leadership, governance, and communications.

Functional Implications and Opportunities

Are systems in place for measuring and monitoring changes by minority group, geographical shift, industry makeup, and association membership?

Social networks, mentor programs, and new organizational structures could provide a way of monitoring the needs of a diverse community through seeing the topics they discuss regularly and the specific issues they raise.

Example Industry Implications

New businesses will continue to develop around the needs of immigrant and minority communities

Key industries in certain regions (e.g., construction, healthcare, and food service) will remain heavily dependent on immigration and minority populations for a significant proportion of their labor force.

Sources and References

1. www.census.gov/Press-Release/www/releases/archives/population/010048.html

2. www.census.gov/Press-Release/www/releases/archives/population/010482.html

3. www.wfs.org

4. www.prb.org/Articles/2006/HispanicsAccountforAlmostOneHalfofUSPopulationGrowth.aspx

5. www.dmnews.com/The-US-Hispanic-Population—One-Market-or Many/article/92236/

6. www.businessweek.com/smallbiz/content/jun2007/sb20070608_805263.htm

7. http://goliath.ecnext.com/coms2/gi_0198-315468/Immigrants-drive-economic-growth.html

7. Redefining work–life balance

Key Question

How will associations serve the needs of members, employers, and their own staff for effective work–life balance programs, services, and solutions?

Description

As life expectancy rises and the length of the working day for many of us increases, individuals and organizations are constantly reevaluating what constitutes the right work–life balance or "work–life blend." The tradeoff between income, consumption, and working hours is becoming an increasing choice point for many adult workers. The productivity boom in the U.S. economy during the twentieth century created a strong consumer culture—people made more money, so they bought more goods and services. As concerns over working hours and sustainable consumption increase, nearly a third of U.S. workers recently polled said they would prefer more time off rather than more hours of paid employment.[1, 2]

A 2007 Monster.com work-life balance survey found that 89 percent of polled employees placed importance on work–life balance programs such as flex-time and telecommuting when evaluating new jobs. However, only about half the HR professionals polled considered their companies' work–life balance initiatives important. The survey also found that only 29 percent of workers rated their employer's work–life balance initiatives "good" or "excellent"; 58 percent felt their employer "encourages working too much."[3]

Timeframe

Now–2010

Potential Impact

- Workers' priorities are changing, and more people are trading long work hours and financial rewards for increased time for themselves, their families, and leisure activities.
- It is now commonplace among major employers to offer solutions through programs, services, and more flexibility in work schedules. Beyond workshops and training programs, some workers have found solutions around nontraditional work arrangements, including freelance work, telecommuting, flex-schedules, job-sharing, and balancing alternative work schedules between parent work schedules.
- Some specialists believe that because of "always on, always connected" technology, work–life balance has diminished as employees are continuously available, connected, and expected to work 24/7. Concerns exist that work–life balance may take be taking a back seat because of increasing pressures from global economic competition, the economic downturn, and organizations downsizing or freezing hiring.

Implications and Opportunities for Associations

- As terminology shifts from talking about "work–life balance" to "work–life blend," programs, services, coaching solutions, and other solutions may require a higher level of personalization and interactivity.
- Like other employers, associations have to be effective in recruiting the best talent and securing high-quality volunteer input. Key to this will be enabling balance in the lives of employees (regardless of generation) and constantly monitoring the pressures on staff and volunteer time commitments.
- Associations may be able to offer sector- and profession-specific advice, best practices, case studies, and program-impact testimonials.

Functional Implications and Opportunities

- Human resource policy adjustments may be required to reflect more flexible work scheduling options.
- Opportunity exists to create measurable goals and standards that realize work–life balance and test productivity gains among less stressed workers.

Example Industry Implications

- The issue of work–life balance and its effect on worker fatigue is becoming of increasing importance in sectors where public safety is a prime concern—(e.g., air-traffic control and medicine).
- The economic cost of stress-induced errors and high levels of worker burnout have led to a stronger focus on

stress management and work–life programs in the financial services sector.

Sources and References

1. www.aicpa.org/pubs/jofa/aug2006/lewison.htm

2. www.ispi.org/pdf/suggestedreading/11_lockwood_worklifebalance.pdf

3. http://phx.corporate-ir.net/phoenix.zhtml?c=131001&p=irol-newsArticle&ID=1074041&highlight

8. Funding and chronic diseases shaping healthcare challenges

Key Question

What role might associations play in the search for effective solutions to national-level challenges related to the rising burden of healthcare funding for individuals and employers?

Description

Healthcare is likely to remain front-and-center as a priority issue for government, employers, and the citizen during the next 10–20 years. Based on current levels of provision, the U.S. Congressional Budget Office's projections suggest that, in the absence of changes in federal law, total spending on healthcare will rise from 16 percent of gross domestic product (GDP) in 2007 to 25 percent in 2025, 37 percent in 2050, and 49 percent in 2082. Federal spending on Medicare (net of beneficiaries' premiums) and Medicaid will rise from 4 percent of GDP in 2007 to 7 percent in 2025, 12 percent in 2050, and 19 percent in 2082.[1, 2] At the same time, approximately 89.6 million Americans—more than one out of three people (34.7 percent) under 65 years of age—were uninsured at some point during 2006–2007.[3]

The United States must also deal with a wide range of age- and lifestyle-related diseases. The costs of servicing the overweight and obese are expected to continue rising. The cost of obesity to U.S. business is approximately $13 billion annually in direct health costs. Combined with the costs of disability, absenteeism, and lost productivity, U.S. companies today pay about 8 percent more in health claims costs alone because of overweight and obese employees. In 2006, between half and two-thirds of men and women in 63 countries across five continents—not including the United States—were overweight or obese. The World Health Organization forecasts that by 2015, approximately 2.3 billion adults globally will be overweight, and more than 700 million obese.[3]

Timeframe

Now–2020

Potential Impact

• Workers and their families will see more of their income spent on healthcare or may refuse treatment if they cannot afford it—resulting in potentially greater costs (and lost productivity) to the economy over the long term. Many older workers may choose to work past normal retirement age to maintain healthcare coverage.

• Ever-increasing pressure will be put on state and federal governments, as well as on hospitals and insurance companies, to come up with system-wide solutions to the healthcare crisis. Employers might also become leaders in experimenting with strategies to combat healthcare costs.

• City, county, and state healthcare providers will continue to find themselves stretched beyond capacity in providing services to the uninsured or underinsured (e.g., the emergency room crisis).

Implications and Opportunities for Associations

• Associations may be able to provide information, best practices, solutions to address budgetary pressures, and advice on healthcare services and the management of healthcare budgets.

• This may be a potential opportunity to provide accurate data to the government on the affects of healthcare funding liabilities.

• Associations in healthcare are being adversely impacted by reducing reimbursement rates, declining job satisfaction, and less financial ability to participate in associations on behalf of target members.

Functional Implications and Opportunities

• Associations may seek to test the viability of using their aggregated buying power to provide group membership plans for supplemental healthcare insurance or alternative coverage. For example, for the CEO Clubs—a nonprofit U.S.-based business association for CEOs—the healthcare package alone is seen as being worth more than the membership fee.[5]

• The association sector may be able to investigate new health insurance products collectively, helping to make such products available not only to the association market but also to society as a whole.

Example Industry Implications

- All major industry sectors are affected by healthcare funding challenges. Most immediately affected are healthcare providers, state and local governments, and large companies with excessive healthcare and pension liabilities because of an aging employee base. For example, in the automobile industry, the sheer scale of the $18 billion healthcare and pensions liability was a major impetus to Daimler selling an 80.1 percent stake in Chrysler for just $7.41 billion to private-equity firm Cerberus Capital Management. Daimler paid $36 billion for its stake in 1998 but only received $1.45 billion of the $7.41 billion; the rest went back into the business, and $600 million of that was reinvested in the company.[6, 7]

Sources and References

1. www.kiplinger.com/businessresource/summary/archive/2008/health-costs-cbo.html

2. www.ft.com/cms/s/0/f4312d0c-b49f-11dc-990a-0000779fd2ac.html

3. www.familiesusa.org/resources/newsroom/press-releases/2007-press-releases/new-report-finds-896-million.html

4. http://news.bbc.co.uk/1/hi/health/7057951.stm

5. www.ceoclubs.org/

6. http://articles.moneycentral.msn.com/Investing/Dispatch/Chryslersale.aspx

7. www.autoblog.com/2007/05/14/cerberus-buying-chrysler-for-7-4-billion/

9. Growing popularity of online education relative to that of classroom-based courses

Key Question

How might online learning change the nature of association services in the expanding field of professional development and distance learning?

Description

A growing cross section of the world's population is emerging that is at home with the web and that fully expects part of its education to be delivered online. The proportion of students taking some element of their courses online is rising in the United States and abroad, especially in Asia. U.S. on-campus student enrollment with mostly classroom-based education in degree-granting institutions stood at 17.9 million in 2005–2006.[1] Nearly 18 percent of students were receiving some of their education online. Nationwide, in autumn 2005, nearly 3.2 million students at degree-granting institutions were taking at least one course that had at least 80 percent of its content delivered online (e.g., web-enabled, "hybrid" [blended], or online-only). Today more than 96 percent of the very largest institutions (more than 15,000 total enrollments) have some online offerings—more than double the rate observed for the smallest institutions.[2]

Two-year associate's institutions have the highest e-learning growth rates and account for over half of all online enrollments from 2002 to 2007. Baccalaureate institutions began the period with the fewest online enrollments and have had the lowest rates of growth.[2]

Timeframe

Now–2015

Potential Impact

- The shift to online education is growing not only in the formal education system, but also in professional development and continuing education required for certification. Students and instructors are attracted by the ease of use and personalization inherent in asynchronous online instruction.
- Online education promises to expand access (by learner life stage, geography, and time commitment) and could eventually reduce the cost of delivering education around the nation and the world. A Sloan-C study expects most of the growth to occur within large institutions that already have existing online offerings and experience in the field. Despite quality concerns about student learning and "diploma mills," a 2003 Sloan survey found that "57 percent of academic leaders rated the learning outcomes in online education as the same or superior to those in face-to-face. That number is now 62 percent, a small but noteworthy increase."[2]
- Online education could provide a mechanism for rapid and supplemental training to meet talent or labor shortages in certain industries. It also refocuses educational development and delivery to incorporate interactive participation, self-directed learning, and outcomes measurement.

Implications and Opportunities for Associations

- This development may create opportunities for associations to expand their roles in delivering educational and training services to members and major industry sectors. It could supplement (or replace) physical classroom–based courses delivered in traditional settings.
- Associations could deliver "just in time," interactive, and on-going life-long learning education and training—responding quickly to emerging issues in workforce development and to changing member requirements.
- Associations could provide a platform enabling members to articulate and aggregate their demand for online solutions, making approved training providers able to then bid for and deliver those courses to interested members.

Functional Implications and Opportunities

- This development, however, challenges associations to become more innovative and responsive in delivering more competitive market-oriented education services keeping pace with technological developments, advances in member adoption rates, and increased acceptance of new delivery modes.

• Although it extends the reach of associations in servicing a wider audience, it might also challenge current service-delivery models.

• Associations may need to explore how to share the costs of developing technologies to support online learning interactions (e.g., video, virtual spaces, mobile, collaborative) that enrich such experiences and make them more effective, also exploring new pricing models (e.g., pay per module, bulk purchase by organizations).

Example Industry Implications

• Could change the training of college faculty in the education system.

• Could see the rise of private online education markets to support major industries.

• Could lead to new forms of virtual academic institutions and to increased global competition for continuing education (CE) offerings.

Sources and References

1. http://nces.ed.gov/programs/digest/2006menu_tables.asp

2. www.sloan-c.org/publications/survey/pdf/making_the_grade.pdf

10. Increasing economic power of women

Key Question

What role should associations play in closing any gender gaps and advancing economic empowerment of women?

Description

Despite substantial progress, significant earning gaps still remain between female workers and their male counterparts. The U.S. Bureau of Labor Statistics reports that "between 1979 and 2006, the earnings gap between women and men narrowed for most major age groups. The women's-to-men's earnings ratio among 35- to 44-year-olds, for example, rose from 58 percent in 1979 to 77 percent in 2006, and the ratio for 45- to 54-year-olds rose from 57 percent to 74 percent. At all levels of education, women have fared better than men with respect to earnings growth. Earnings for women with college degrees have increased by about 34 percent since 1979 on an inflation-adjusted basis, while those of male college graduates have risen by 18 percent."[1]

In line with rising incomes, female spending power is also increasing. "Women's decision-making authority has grown in part because more households are headed by women—27 percent (in 2005), a fourfold increase since 1950. Female buying power has grown, too. In the past three decades, men's median income has barely budged—up just 0.6 percent—while women's has soared 63 percent."[2] Consumer marketing firms often cite the estimated figure that women control 80 percent of family consumer spending.

Women's ownership of business is also rising steadily. The Center for Women's Business Research (CWBR) estimates that as of 2006, in the United States there were an estimated 10.4 million privately held firms in which 50 percent or more the equity was owned by women, accounting for two in five (40.2 percent) of all businesses in the country. These firms have $1.9 trillion in annual sales and have 12.8 million employees. CWBR also states that over the past two decades, majority women-owned firms have grown at about twice the rate of all firms (42 percent vs. 24 percent).[3]

Globally, women are accruing a greater share of wealth and exercising more economic power. In the UK, one study estimated that 53 percent of millionaires are likely to be female by 2020, and that by 2025 women will control 60 percent of the nation's private wealth.[4] In Canada, women's financial power is growing—there are around 821,000 female entrepreneurs, contributing in excess of C$18 billion to the economy.[5]

Timeframe

Now–2010; 2011–2015

Potential Impact

- The performance of females over males at every level of the education system globally is still not fully reflected in the hierarchies of organizations,[5] or in wage rates for similar jobs.
- The increasing proportion of women-led businesses should contribute to a shift in management styles and practices.

Implications and Opportunities for Associations

- It is imperative that associations ensure that they understand and adopt emerging best practices in terms of ensuring full and equal participation, opportunity, and reward for women in the workplace.
- Potential exists for associations to provide training, case studies, best-practice program designs, consulting, and mentoring services to help employers develop and implement transparent, effective, and sustainable solutions.

Functional Implications and Opportunities

- Continuous research is needed on the changing roles, needs, and expectations of female members—possibly shared across associations.
- The challenge of developing female-specific programming that takes into account other factors such as generation, culture, and ethnicity is increasingly complex.
- Potential exists for the provision of members having professional training and development that is specific to the changing needs and lives of women.

Example Industry Implications

- Industries such as the association and meetings sectors are in many respects acting as role models where women have the opportunity to lead and fulfill their potential in other ways.

Sources and References

1. www.bls.gov/cps/cpswom2006.pdf

2. www.businessweek.com/bwdaily/dnflash/feb2005/nf20050214_9413_db_082.htm

3. www.nfwbo.org/national/index.php

4. www.economist.com/world/britain/displaystory.cfm?story_id=9341098&CFID=5744580&CFTOKEN=92392792

5. www.guardian.co.uk/business/2007/oct/30/genderissues.banking

11. Growing role for "social entrepreneurship"

Key Question

What support could associations offer for the needs of social entrepreneurs within their profession or industry sector?

Description

"Social entrepreneurship" applies "practical, innovative and market-oriented approaches to benefit the marginalized and the poor." A social entrepreneur is one who seeks to create social change while balancing budgets and possibly even making a profit by using sustainable business practices. Social entrepreneurship efforts introduce new products, services, financial models, healthcare schemes, and processes to address key areas of social need and are often highly localized and culturally relevant to local communities.[1] Social entrepreneurship is a term often used to describe for-profit ventures in "conventional sectors" that also strongly focus on giving back both by donating profits and by committing staff time to particular causes.

The concept has been popularized by the widely told story of the micro-credit efforts of the Grameen Bank in Bangladesh and the recent book by David Bornstein—*How to Change the World: Social Entrepreneurs and the Power of New Ideas*.[2] Grameen's founder, Mohamed Yunus, made his first 15 loans with just $27 and went on to establish a bank that made micro-loans to small farmers to help them establish their own businesses, thereby transforming their economic prospects. A key feature of the Grameen model is the high repayment rates—reaching 98 percent in many areas—a factor often attributed to the fact that loans are made exclusively to women.[3]

More than 30 social entrepreneurship programs offering degrees or certificates are now offered by colleges and Universities across the United States.[4] Social entrepreneurship efforts are often funded by nonprofit and private-sector foundations seeking a more measurable and sustainable return on their investments.

Timeframe

Now–2020

Potential Impact

- Social ventures with different profit expectations can play a key role in addressing issues that prevent market growth and development and have the potential to help transform key sectors by acting both as partners and competitors to existing players.
- Social entrepreneurship efforts have captured the creative business imagination of young and old alike and could become a major growth opportunity in the years and decades ahead for individuals seeking work that offers the potential for strong personal and social fulfillment.
- Social entrepreneurship could fill a large void in efforts to address market failure, alleviate poverty, and confront some of the world's biggest social challenges. The long-term impact could be a reduction of financial stress placed on individuals and governments in emerging economies.

Implications and Opportunities for Associations

- Social entrepreneurs could establish "for-profit" alternatives to associations with the returns going back to address key causes of interest to their customers/members.
- Associations will need to explore how best to serve the needs of social entrepreneurs in their membership by looking at best practices, certifications, and evaluation standards.
- This situation creates the opportunity to positively promote social entrepreneurship and provide solutions that help members establish social ventures.

Functional Implications and Opportunities

- Social entrepreneur–backed ventures could be possible partners for the delivery of key association products and services.
- Associations may want to benchmark social ventures to see what can be learned about their commercial models, customer relationships, and operational structures and processes.

Example Industry Implications

- Social ventures such as microfinance institutions are seen as critical enablers in helping the poorest members of society access the finance required to help start their own microbusinesses and take themselves permanently out of poverty.

- Social ventures are becoming increasingly popular in sectors such as travel, tourism, and food service, in which founders seek to meet ecological and ethical goals while running a commercial enterprise.

Sources and References

1. www.ey.com/global/content.nsf/International/Strategic_Growth_Markets_-_Entrepreneur_Of_The_Year_-_Social_Entrepreneurship

2. www.howtochangetheworld.org/

3. http://en.wikipedia.org/wiki/Grameen_Bank

4. www.aacsb.edu/members/communities/interestgrps/socialpgms.asp

12. Evolving trust: declining trust in government and media

Key Question

How can associations establish themselves as "trust brands" and help ensure the highest standards of ethical behavior, transparency, and accountability in their professions or sectors?

Description

According to the eighth annual Edelman Trust Barometer, business is more trusted than either government or media in every region of the globe. Edelman's survey of 3,100 opinion leaders measures levels of trust in institutions, companies, and sources of information in 18 countries. Business is more credible than government or media in 13 of the 18 countries surveyed in 2007. The survey also found that more respondents in 16 of the 18 countries felt that companies have a more positive than negative effect on society.[1, 2]

In the United States, 53 percent of respondents say they trust business, an all-time high for the survey. This is a recovery from a low of 44 percent in 2002, which came in the wake of the Enron and WorldCom crises. In the three largest economies of Western Europe—France, Germany, and the UK—trust in business stands at 34 percent, which is higher than trust in media and government at 25 percent and 22 percent respectively.[3, 4]

In three of the four fast-growing developing nations known as the "BRIC" countries (Brazil, Russia, India, and China), business is trusted more than government, media, or non-governmental organizations (NGOs). In the fourth—China—business is trusted by 67 percent of respondents but trails government, which is trusted by 78 percent.[4]

A recent National Nonprofit Ethics Survey by the Ethics Resource Center shows that for the first time the nonprofit sector is rated no higher in ethical performance than government or business because of a range of factors that include board misconduct, executive management conflicts, and litigation.[5]

Timeframe

Now–2010

Potential Impact

• Declining trust in government can both erode elected officials' mandate to act on behalf of the people and restrict their willingness to consider innovative or risky solutions to contentious issues such as healthcare funding, pensions, social security costs, or educational standards.

• The media world continues to become more fragmented, putting the spotlight on their strategies, policies, and political stances. As the major media outlets search for sustainable business strategies and models for the digital era in the struggle to maintain their core audiences, many are becoming more overt in "adopting a position" to attract or win back particular audience groups.

• Audience expectations are changing in response to the growth of "advocacy journalism," which attempts to persuade audiences in one direction. People are finding new ways to receive and share information—either via alternative media sources (e.g., the blogosphere and news-feed aggregators) or self-generated media (e.g., citizen journalism).

Implications and Opportunities for Associations

• Associations will face a constant challenge in remaining trusted and relevant in a world of changing values and attitudes.

• Trust could be a major theme for associations to pursue in future programs and research activities.

• Associations may wish to assess how much they are trusted by key stakeholders relative to other groups in society, seeking to establish a leadership position on trust—delivered through all their activities.

Functional Implications and Opportunities

• Associations need to ensure all internal and external facing activities convey and build trust. Socially responsible associations could certify supply chain enterprises, exhibitors, and service providers as Responsible Partners™.

• Associations might also form entities such as "integrity committees" of volunteers and staff that expand participation, transparency, and accountability.

• Meetings will need to be more open; members will need to be more thoroughly tapped for input, and accountability will need to be fully embraced.

Example Industry Implications

▪ Firms will increasingly want to assess the trust and brand credentials of the media channels they use.

▪ Word of mouth could remain the strongest mechanism for building or destroying trust in a brand.

▪ Audited social responsibility reporting is a growth industry, following a Global Reporting Initiative (GRI) standard, and is increasingly a prerequisite to doing business with certain organizations and attracting investment from particular sources of funding.

Sources and References

1. www.edelman.com/image/insights/content/Full Supplement.pdf

2. www.edelman.com/news/ShowOne.asp?ID=146

3. www.slideshare.net/edelman.milan/edelman-trust-barometer-2007/

4. www.globescan.com/news_archives/bbcreut.html

5. www.ethics.org/research/

13. Increasing interest in philanthropy and volunteer work

Key Question

How will associations leverage the 21st-century dynamics of volunteerism and member engagement across Millennials and Baby Boomers?

Description

Research suggests that young children and teenagers across the nation are getting involved in volunteer work more than ever before.[1] Technology is a key driver as young people are increasingly exposed to and connected with the problems of the world via the internet and television. At the same time, technology is simplifying, popularizing, and, to some extent, democratizing philanthropy—meaning that causes have more access to potential supporters and making giving easier and more fashionable for people of all ages and means.

According to data collected over the past 30 years by the U.S. Census Bureau and the Bureau of Labor Statistics, Americans over the age of 16 are volunteering at historically high rates, with 61.2 million giving their time to help others in 2006.[1] This time is invested in activities such as mentoring students, beautifying neighborhoods, and restoring homes after disasters. Although the adult volunteer rate of 26.7 percent for 2006 was down slightly from the 28.8 percent recorded from 2003 to 2005, the percentage of American adults volunteering today is close to its highest rate in the past 30 years. These include late teens, Baby Boomers, and the over-65s. In addition, more and more young people are becoming involved in their communities through school-based service—learning and volunteering.[1]

Philanthropy is also changing. The Giving USA Foundation estimated philanthropic giving at $295.02 billion in 2006, setting a new record.[3] This represents 2.2 percent of gross domestic product, remaining above the 40-year average of 1.8 percent for another year.[3] Estimated giving by U.S. foundations for international purposes reached a record $3.8 billion in 2005.[2] This increase represents a 12 percent inflation-adjusted gain over 2002—far surpassing the 2 percent rise in overall giving in the same period and double the amount in 1998. In the United States, between 1994 and 2004, domestic giving of the foundations that are active internationally declined from 91 percent to 82 percent because of the increase of the proportion of international giving.[3, 4]

Timeframe

Now–2015

Potential Impact

- The rise in social volunteerism (and required community service) could change both the landscape of issues considered important on the national political scene and expectations for institutional support to assist this new level of civic engagement.
- Volunteerism is seen as having a clear impact on community building by solving social problems, reducing crime, and improving local economies, as well as supporting philanthropic giving to fill gaps left in publicly funded social services and community development.

Implications and Opportunities for Associations

- Associations could play a strategic role in raising awareness and focusing on social responsibility issues that encourage volunteerism and increase member engagement.
- The rise in youth volunteerism creates an opportunity to align with the interests of this cohort and encourage them to become members.
- Associations could promote their own volunteer leadership roles as an opportunity for individuals and employers looking for opportunities combining service with personal development.

Functional Implications and Opportunities

- Associations may want to review policies and practices for forming volunteer committees and taskforces to ensure they are open and attractive to those with the greatest propensity to volunteer.
- Volunteer strategies (e.g., recruitment, rewards, and recognition) will need constant review to ensure their relevance to younger, more digitally connected members, encouraging them to communicate what they are doing.

Example Industry Implications

• Increasing willingness to volunteer may help overcome certain types of staff shortages in the healthcare and service professions.

• Risks exist, however, of volunteers being used as "no-cost labor" and being built into the business models and pricing assumptions of some organizations.

Sources and References

1. www.nationalservice.gov

2. www.un.org/unfip/Docs/Foundations_DECCapital FlowsDec06.pdf

3. www.cafonline.org/pdf/International%20Comparisons %20of%20Charitable%20Giving.pdf

4. www.philanthropy.iupui.edu/Research/givingusa.aspx

14. Deepening personalization of products, services, communications, and experiences

Key Question

How should associations respond to growing trends toward personalization, and how can they compete with potentially better-funded private-sector competition for member attention?

Description

As the incremental cost of delivering services via the internet drops to almost zero, the potential to personalize products and services grows. Technology is enabling personalization of even physical products such as cars and their features, books, clothing, laptops, and sporting goods.[1, 2] In the mobile phone sector, users are already able to receive personalized advertising messages, and the potential to identify individuals through 3G technology allows for completely personalized advertisements to be shown on public display screens as you approach them.

In 2004, a Business Week cover proclaimed "The Vanishing Mass Market." Although mass brands have not disappeared, consumer markets are becoming more fragmented and niched.[3] Companies across a range of consumer product sectors are experimenting with enabling "mass customization" allowing consumers to choose personal preferences when related to product design, color, texture, and functionality.[3, 4] For example, Archetype Solutions is personalization company that works with Lands End, Target, and JC Penney to automate the process of creating custom clothing with unique patterns based on measurements submitted by customers; the clothes are then manufactured and shipped directly to the customer.[2]

Timeframe

Now–2020

Potential Impact

▪ The concept of personalization is likely to extend from the current round of largely web-based and high-end custom-built product and service offerings to encompass all the goods and services we consume online and in the physical world (e.g., custom-grown food, personal fabricators).

▪ Developing a genuinely personalized offering requires vendors to have deep understandings of customers and the different elements of product and service experiences that they may want personalized.

Implications and Opportunities for Associations

▪ Personalization places major pressures on an organization's business models, product cost, and pricing strategies and can be highly labor intensive—and it does not eliminate the need to provide quality service.

▪ Is the concept of personalization compatible with the current association model and the range of members' expectations for quality of services (e.g., pricing models, product features, on-demand services)?

▪ Faced with a range of alternative providers of content, meetings, and networking, members could increasingly demand that associations provide true personalization.

▪ Associations may see an opportunity in becoming a "one-stop shop" for a range of approved vendors who can provide personalized services to members. A new revenue stream could emerge from aggregating, interpreting, and reselling the data gathered on members' personalized choices.

Functional Implications and Opportunities

▪ Associations will need to consider how personalization would work in their contexts, what elements could be personalized, how would they be delivered, and how to structure the pricing model(s).

▪ A fundamental rethink may be required of internal structures, budgeting, funding sources, and delivery models in order to provide personalized products and services.

▪ Potential exists for providing a totally customizable member portal into which members could import other third-party web pages and content.

▪ Automation could be critical in helping components offer tailorable options to members at the local level.

Example Industry Implications

▪ Organizations that can take advantage of lower employment costs around the world can use outsourcing as a model for providing greater personalization—e.g., many personal tutoring and counseling services make use of staff in offshore locations to deliver personalized services to U.S. and European customers.

▪ In education, there is increasing discussion over the concept of personalized degrees. Students would literally tailor their entire course, selecting the lectures, units, personal tutorials, virtual world seminars, and online offerings that make up a degree. They could even opt to take physical and online classes from a range of different faculty in multiple institutions.

▪ There will be a growth in businesses providing customization and personalization tools for both the physical and online worlds.

Sources and References

1. http://iaacblog.com/erikthorson/?p=39

2. www.mckinseyquarterly.com/Eight_business_technology_trends_to_watch_2080_abstract

3. www.businessweek.com/magazine/content/04_28/b3891001_mz001.htm

4. www.businessweek.com/bwdaily/dnflash/nov2004/nf20041123_3634_db_081.htm

Technological

15. Internet continues transforming government, governance, and business

Key Question

How might the evolution of member needs, further technology development, changing economic circumstances, and cost pressures impact the way in which associations make use of the internet?

Description

The internet continues to change life as we know it—especially in the areas of governance and commerce. The "web" is changing our expectations of governance—with citizens expecting greater transparency, heightened accountability, and seamless delivery of services. The web is also changing commerce by reducing the complexities of business transactions and expanding our channels for media consumption, communication, and engagement. Over the last ten years, the means of engaging with the internet have also evolved from surfing static pages to far greater user interaction through social media such as blogs, wikis, social networks, and virtual worlds.

The web continues to expand globally. Internet World Stats reports close to 1.3 billion worldwide internet users as of December 2007. Global usage grew 265.6 percent from 2000 to 2007; however, there is still a long way to go; penetration of the global population is only around 20 percent. E-commerce and web-based advertising continue to grow exponentially. U.S. online retail reached $175 billion in 2007 and is projected by Forrester Research to grow to $335 billion by 2012.[1, 2]

The next decade will see tremendous changes in the user base on the web. It is estimated that nearly 1.5 billion of the world's citizens will have internet access by the end of 2008, and that a third of those will have access to a high-speed connection. For the last three years China has been the world's largest exporter of information and communications technology (ICT). In 2008, it will overtake the United States as the country with the largest number of internet users. For the first time, China will have more broadband subscribers than the United States. By 2010, 21 percent of China's households are expected to have broadband.[3]

According to a report by Cisco Systems, Inc., internet traffic will nearly double every two years through 2011, driven by high-definition video and high-speed broadband services. 40 percent of that traffic will be on the internet, and the rest will be generated by commercial video services. Internet video streaming and downloads are beginning to take a larger share of bandwidth and are forecast to grow from 9 percent of all traffic in 2006 to 30 percent in 2011, according to the report. Cisco believes internet video-to-TV could exceed internet video-to-PC as early as 2009.[4]

Timeframe

Now–2010

Potential Impact

- The web continues to evolve as a platform with global reach for organizing our lives, conducting business, influencing political processes, and delivering government services.
- As time and cost pressures on the citizen grow, there will be increasing expectations for those who serve them to provide content, education, testing, engagement, and events via the web.
- The growing popularity of web-based video could facilitate more "face-to-face" interactions over the web and greatly enhance organizational communication and customer service.

Implications and Opportunities for Associations

- A growing expectation exists that association services be delivered seamlessly via the web and evolve in more personalized manner. There will also be increasing demand for web services to be more open to member input, facilitating two-way engagement in the creation and distribution of content.
- This creates the opportunity to serve a global audience and to source content from global providers.
- In the face of growing concerns over revenues and budgets in a market turndown, electronic channels offer the potential to reduce costs for delivering

services, migrating members from paper to electronic delivery.

- Social media technologies can be leveraged to bring more members into the governance process of membership organizations, increasing the focus on niche communities.

Functional Implications and Opportunities

- The ease with which new content and applications can be made available on the web creates a strong imperative to ensure that material is easy to use and navigate—careful attention needs to be paid to ensure a simple and consistent user experience.
- Associations will need to ensure that they have adequate bench strength in key areas such IT, networking, and website development—this may mean sharing resources across associations or "renting" resource from third-party vendors.

Example Industry Implications

- More Americans will use the internet to research products before traveling to shops to make the actual purchase. Online shopping is expected to grow at an annual rate of 17 percent, resulting in forecast sales of $1 trillion by 2012.[2]
- In the healthcare industry, physicians are converting thousands of pages of patient records to digital files and reaching patients using social media tools.
- The traditional banking and investment community is facing stiff competition from online firms such as ING.

Sources and References

1. www.internetworldstats.com/blog.htm
2. www.internetworldstats.com/stats.htm
3. www.businessweek.com/globalbiz/content/feb2008/ gb20080213_175972.htm?campaign_id=rss_tech
4. www.xchangemag.com/hotnews/78h1610327.html

16. Social media explosion creating new approaches for engagement, communication, publishing, and marketing

Key Question

How can associations fully exploit online social media within the budgetary resources available to them?

Description

Social media technologies (i.e., blogs, wikis, and social networking sites) are increasingly seen as tools for encouraging political engagement and bringing members into the governance process. Organizations are increasingly turning to "crowd sourcing" sites that can bring large communities together for online dialogues with businesses and governments.[1] According to research from Strategy Analytics, social media services such as MySpace, Facebook, YouTube, LinkedIn, and Flickr are expected to attract over one billion broadband users within five years. Robust growth is anticipated in the number of social media users over the next five years: from 373 million broadband users this 2008, to over 1 billion in 2012, representing 75 percent of all broadband users.[2]

Blogging is also increasingly seen as a mainstream communications channel for companies: 52 percent of Fortune 500 companies have corporate blogs. 120,000 new blogs are created every day. Japanese is the number-one blogging language (37 percent), followed by English (33 percent) and Chinese (8 percent). Ohmynews is a popular South Korean online newspaper/blog written by 60,000 "citizen reporters."[3] An increasing number of businesses, associations, and even government agencies are also adopting "wiki"-style solutions to engage broader communities in the dissemination and updating of collective knowledge. For example, the American Library Association has a wiki-style website for adding or modifying information about threatened federal libraries.[4]

Social networks are becoming a prime source for information, contacts, learning, and research and are being increasingly used for business to consumer and business to business communications:

• The most popular site, MySpace, claims over 200 million registered users and accounts for approximately 5 percent of all internet visits. In South Korea, 18 million people—30 percent of the population—have accounts with the Cyworld service, including 90 percent of those aged 20–29.[2] In India over 40 million are signed up to the Hi5 network. eMarketer estimates that social network marketing will reach $1.3 billion by the end of 2008 and $2.5 billion in 2011.[5]

• During 2007, around 37 percent of the U.S. adult internet population used online social networking at least once a month. eMarketer expects that figure will rise to 49 percent by 2011.[5]

• Gartner Research estimates that up to 80 percent of U.S. internet users could become members of virtual worlds by 2011.[6] Retailers are setting up their own stores within virtual worlds, allowing users to view and purchase virtual goods.[7, 8] Other corporations are using virtual worlds for immersive employee training.[9]

Timeframe

Now–2015

Potential Impact

• Social media tools are becoming mainstream and are changing expectations as individuals want to be involved in the cocreation, dissemination, and endorsement of information and communication messages.

• Many organizational leaders are starting to look at social media and networks as essential tools for expanding their customer base by engaging them in more genuine and deeper dialogues, and creating a platform for customer-designed and developed products and services (e.g., "wisdom of crowds," such as Sermo as a free platform for discussion among MDs or—in the case of Creative Crowds from Holland—assembling national and global communities on behalf of commercial clients).[10]

• Social networks can extend and strengthen innovation and collaboration processes. P&G estimated that there were two million professionals outside the organization with the same capabilities as their 7,500 internal R&D staff. Their social network enabled Open Innovation process created a mechanism for "bringing them in" and now has over 3 million people actively engaged in its networks—sharing ideas and collaborating on the development of new products and process.[11]

• Social networks can also transform relationships within organizations by enabling individuals to share more extensive information about identities than just basic bio-data. These tools facilitate informal sharing and the development and testing of new ideas among colleagues. Social media are also proving to be powerful communication and project-management tools that avoid email overload and ensure that everyone knows where to find the latest thinking on an issue or the most recent version of any document.

Implications and Opportunities for Associations

• Offers mechanisms to build stronger relationships and have deeper information exchange among association staff and with members (e.g., collaborative production of content, management of user profiles).

• Social media–based platforms could "compete" with existing associations and possibly evolve as more trusted "member-led" alternatives (e.g., web-only memberships). Raises the issue of whether associations should compete with social networking platforms or leverage those that exist—signing up to all of the main networking sites and creating association member-only forums for networking within each site.

• Associations must overcome a wide range of user behavior challenges to accommodate varying levels of experience, fluidity, and interest in emerging social web tools and services.

• Offers the potential for associations to create new products and services born out of engagement with social media. Tools could be used to facilitate collaborative, team-oriented activities, projects, and experiential learning activities—particularly those involving a large body of knowledge, a broad web of facilitators, "expert" contributors and moderators, and highly decentralized participants.

Functional Implications and Opportunities

• Associations may need to replicate, replace, or even retire some existing means of facilitating community engagement as the nature of human communication changes and the resource challenge and costs of servicing multiple channels become bigger and bigger issues.

• To capture emerging generations, the ways associations communicate and engage with members may need to become far more distributed and organic, rather than

centralized and planned. This will affect not only marketing- and web-based products, but also governmental affairs, chapter relations, continuing education, and all member-facing services.

• This could challenge the capability of internal IT departments to balance demands of internal policies and investments with dynamics of changing web experiences in the marketplace. For example, many live services seem to exist in a perpetual "beta-test" stage of development—with the end-users living with and reporting bugs in return for early access to the software. Would association members be so willing to use unfinished software applications?

Example Industry Implications

• Most industry and government sectors are beginning to experiment with social media as it provides a powerful platform for expertise sharing among members of professional disciplines.

• Social media are already being embraced by sectors with products or services that require continued innovation and development based on real-world experience and user feedback. For example, IBM and Cisco have made extensive use of virtual worlds to host all staff conferences and to create innovation centers where third parties can collaborate with them on new product development.[12]

• In financial services, a number of banks now have personal advisors supporting their customers over the web via video.

• The InnoCentive website is widely used by corporate R&D units to list their most pressing technical issues and offer financial incentives to anyone who can solve them. Yet2.com is a web platform that enables companies to license or sell patents that they haven't as yet exploited.[13]

Sources and References

1. www.globalexpertbase.com/wp-8-276.html

2. www.strategyanalytics.net/default.aspx?mod=Report AbstractViewer&a0=3688

3. Survey: www.fringehog.com

4. http://wikis.ala.org/readwriteconnect/index.php/ Main_Page

5. www.dmillionews.com/Social-network-marketing-spend-to-reach-25B-in-11-eMarketer/article/95500/

6. http://metaversed.com/25-apr-2007/gartner-2011-80-internet-users-will-have-second-life

7. www.virtualworldsnews.com/2007/12/gartner-20-of-r.html

8. www.virtualeconomicforum.com/blog/2007/07/06/south-korea-to-tax-virtual-worlds-and-goods/

9. www.trainingzone.co.uk/cgi-bin/item.cgi?id=177109&d=680&h=0&f=0&date

10. www.creativecrowds.com/

11. www.fastcompany.com/resources/innovation/watson/011005.html

12. Reported in Cisco presentation to Apply Serious Games conference London June 28th 2007

13. www.innocentive.com/ ; www.yet2.com/

17. Rise in mobile and location-based web services as "smart" phones displace laptops

Key Question

As society becomes more reliant on handheld devices, how might associations evolve their offerings to accommodate more mobile "always on, always connected" audiences?

Description

With over 3.2 billion mobile phones in circulation globally at the start of 2008,[1] they have become the most widespread form of personal technology—outstripping the laptop, TV, and credit card. Global sales of the new generation of "smart" phones now outstrip sales of laptops. With a wide range of applications migrating to the palm of your hand, in the next five years, your mobile phone could become your credit card, banker, ticket broker, concierge, and shopping partner. The proliferation of personal digital devices, such as cell phones and portable games, is expected to replace laptops as the primary digital interface for most users.[2]

As a step up from WiFi, a new standard for broadband wireless metropolitan access networks (WiMAX) will enable far easier access to the internet from a range of devices, including mobile phones. The mobile WiMAX market is forecast to have a compound annual growth rate (CAGR) of 198 percent between 2008 and 2012.[3] This will enable the accelerated development of so-called "location-based services," which provide services and information (e.g., media and advertising) to individuals based on their geographic location—as determined through small portable computing devices or smart phones.

InStat™ predicts that the U.S. location-based services (LBS) business market could grow to from 582,000 to 1.1 million subscribed devices by the end of 2010.[4] LBS applications could range from safety and security to commercial logistics, location-based advertising, consumer transportation information services, and family location services with which parents can monitor their children.

Timeframe

2011–2015

Potential Impact

- The increasing power, capacity, functionality, and speed of handheld devices, and the commoditization of these products, means that our key "personal computing device" of tomorrow might fit in our pocket—making mobile payments, storing our data, providing us web access, and receiving location-based information, services, and targeted marketing messages.
- Location-based tracking and real-time updates could change the dynamics between attendees, exhibitors, and organizers at events, colleagues and work environments, consumers and brands, and parents and children, including teenage drivers.

Implications and Opportunities for Associations

- This could become a new delivery channel for associations—attracting younger members (e.g., member alerts via text messages).
- Likely to be huge divergence of demand and willingness to pay for mobile-enabled content and services.
- Could enable personalization of event attendance—participants could be flagged when key phrases or topics are raised in a seminar and enable higher levels of interactivity between presenters and delegates—whether or not they are in the room.

Functional Implications and Opportunities

- The cost of establishing mobile enabled applications and LBS may need to be shared across associations.
- Database security and delivery of personal information to handheld devices may raise policy issues related to privacy and security.

Example Industry Implications

- Could affect the transportation and logistics sector. The precise point-to-point tracking of objects and sealed freight containers could significantly improve security within cities, along borders, and at ports.
- New industries will be created around LBS (e.g., transportation information, personal security, targeted advertising, and digital maps). Some within mature industries

will benefit, and others could be disrupted—for example, LBS could enhance or replace existing directory-inquiry services.

Sources and References

1. www.inc.com/magazine/20080201/a-pocketful-of-marketing.html

2. www.wfs.org/fsrvmar07.htm

3. www.semiconductor-today.com/news_items/2008/FEB/RESMAR_040208.htm

4. www.in-stat.com/press.asp?ID=1630&sku=IN0602898MBM

18. Cybercrime, cyberwar, and cyberterrorism

Key Questions

How can associations best leverage their investments to protect themselves and members against a growing cyberthreat?
Is there potential for collaboration across associations?

Description

A range of cyberthreats are evolving, creating increased risk and extra workloads for individuals, organizations, and governments alike. Around 120 billion junk messages are sent worldwide every day, and the spam business is now estimated to be worth $200 billion a year.[1] Spyware, viruses, and phishing caused an estimated $7.1 billion of damage to U.S. computers alone in 2007. An estimated 60 million people had personal data exposed in 2007, resulting in an estimated $20 billion spent on clean-up costs and lost productivity worldwide. In addition, 48 percent of organizations do not have a policy for notifying customers when their private data may be at risk.[2, 3]

There is also growing concern about state-sponsored cyberattacks. McAfee believes approximately 120 countries have been developing ways to use the internet as a weapon and the targets are financial markets, government computer systems and utilities. McAfee says that China is at the forefront of the cyberwar. In response to rising levels of cyberthreat, the global internet security market is expected to grow at an annual rate of 16 percent from 2006 to 2010 to reach $58.1 billion annually.[4]

Timeframe

Now–2010

Potential Impact

- Many questions persist about the security of today's online networks as organizations spend more time and resources to protect valuable data.
- Concerns are rising over the possibility of a systemwide collapse (often cited as a "wildcard"—a low-probability, high-impact event) and the risk of a new management regime emerging to exercise far greater control and monitoring of internet usage in an attempt to prevent future cybercrime.

Implications and Opportunities for Associations

- Associations may increasingly have a role in sharing best-practice advice and guidance on cyberprotection across their membership base. They may also want to participate in conversations on industry standards.
- Associations may play a larger role in influencing national policy on cybercrime—balancing risk prevention with personal freedoms.
- A growing challenge exists of ensuring that mail from associations is not filtered out by spam- and identity-protection services.

Functional Implications and Opportunities

- Associations will need to plan for higher IT security costs as the range of cyberrisks grows.
- As the range of services offered online increases and potentially new forms of data are stored online (e.g., healthcare and financial information), this could require higher levels of security protection.
- Increasingly frequent reviews will be required to assess the completeness and robustness of association contingency plans for cyberthreats and system failures.
- What provisions are in place to address liability for lost or stolen identity data? Policies will be required that balance concerns over information security with the need for accessibility.

Example Industry Implications

- Cybercrime has spawned a whole new cyberprotection industry that is expected to experience continued growth for the foreseeable future.
- For industries such as financial services, the costs of cyberprotection and compensating customers for fraud are rising; even rumored security breaches can have a direct impact on share prices.

Sources and References

1. www.vnunet.com/vnunet/news/2204964/spam-focus-shifting-spreading-malware

2. www.consumerreports.org/cro/electronics-computers/computers/internet-and-other-services/net-threats-9-07/state-of-the-net/0709_state_net.htm

3. www.networkworld.com/community/node/21646

4. http://news.zdnet.com/2100-1009_22-6220619.html

19. Nanotechnology: the next trillion-dollar market?

Key Question

How can associations engage members and third-party experts in early conversations and development of road maps that explore the transformational impact of nanotechnology and other scientific advances?

Description

Nanotechnology is now entering sectors as diverse as healthcare, auto manufacturing, and food production. Lux Research estimated sales of nanoscale products and nanotechnology systems to be $300 million in 2005.[1] The National Science Foundation estimates that the global nanotechnology market could be worth $1 trillion by 2015.[2] Lux forecasts that sales of products incorporating nanotechnology could reach $2.9 trillion by 2014.[1]

A major driver of market growth is the adoption of nanotechnology by major industries. For example the worldwide automotive industries' turnover in products and components incorporating nanotechnologies was valued at $8.6 billion in 2007 and is forecast to top $54.2 billion by 2015. By 2020, the value of nanotechnology components in the automotive industry is forecast to hit $137.4 billion.[3]

The United States has the largest share of global investment in nanotechnology. The U.S. market had a share of 28 percent in 2005, followed by the Japanese market, with about a 24 percent share. Western Europe also had a quarter of the market, with major investment in core countries such as Germany, the UK, and France. Other countries, such as China, South Korea, Canada, and Australia held the rest of the share.[3, 4]

Timeframe

2011–2015

Potential Impact

- Nanoscale components have the potential to add tremendous value and expanded performance to everyday products, from concrete, plastics, and cotton to the sophisticated machinery used in building semiconductor chips.
- Nanotechnology and the businesses and markets it spawns are expected to be a fundamental driver of job creation in the years and decades ahead.

- Ethical debates about the safety of nanoscale science and nanoscale engineering are likely to continue for many years until a sufficiently strong evidence base of applications in the field exists on which to base long-term judgments.
- Concerns persist over unknown liabilities regarding the safety, health, and environmental impacts of nanotechnology processes.

Implications and Opportunities for Associations

- Nanotechnology is a multi-disciplinary science and technology area that has implications across almost every major profession and industry sector. The first challenge may be to raise awareness and educate the community on nanotechnology and its potential impact.
- May create the opportunity to provide products, services and a knowledge exchange between members with experience in the use of nanotechnology in their sector.
- Associations may seek to be central to—and even facilitate—the ethical, scientific, and commercial debates about nanotechnology in their sectors and professions. Associations may also seek to lobby for funding of research and development programs.

Functional Implications and Opportunities

- Associations may feel the need to give their staff regular updates on the impact of emerging science and technology developments on their members.
- Nanotechnology could be the catalyst for associations deciding that the impact of science and technology is such that they need to increase the attention paid to it and receive regular advice on new and emerging developments that could affect their community. They may decide to create a paid or voluntary post of chief scientific advisor or appoint a panel of scientific advisors. This would then lead to subsequent decisions on how best to incorporate and act on scientific advice.

Example Industry Implications

- Nanoscale science and engineering is likely to have an impact on every major industry from materials science, energy, and healthcare to transportation and electronics. Associations connected with workplace health and safety are already devoting a great deal of educational programming to the health-related impacts of nanotechnology.
- Possibly the two biggest industry challenges are recruiting and retaining scientists and engineers with the right skill sets and developing the necessary creativity and innovative mindset to envisage and capture the full potential of nanotechnology.
- According to Research and Markets' report [4] on The World Nanotechnology Market (2006):

  - The nanofood market could soar with a CAGR of 30.94 percent from 2006 to 2010 to attain a market value of $20.40 billion by 2010.

  - The market for textiles using nanotechnology is expected to reach $115 billion by 2012.
  - The U.S. market for nanotech tools is projected to increase to nearly $900 million in 2008 and then triple to $2.7 billion by 2013.

Sources and References

1. http://cohesion.rice.edu/CentersAndInst/ICON/emplibrary/Nanomaterial%20Volumes%20and%20Applications%20-%20Holman,%20Lux%20Research.pdf

2. www.nasa.gov/centers/ames/pdf/80090main_09_03Astrogram.pdf

3. www.asonano.com/news.asp?newsID=3448

4. www.researchandmarkets.com/reports/c40321

20. Energy: increasing demand and rising costs accelerate the search for alternative sources

Key Questions

What impact could rising energy costs have on the cost base of members and associations?

What strategies should associations be adopting to reduce energy demand?

Description

The U.S. Energy Information Agency (EIA) predicts that total world consumption of energy will increase by 57 percent between 2004 and 2030.[1] The largest projected increase in energy demand is for the non-OECD region, largely in countries such as China, India, and Brazil. It is likely that hydrocarbon fuels (oil, natural gas, coal) will account for as much as 80 percent of this demand, but the fastest growth sectors could be in alternative energy technologies.[1, 2]

The global market for "green energy" technologies such as biofuels, hydrogen fuel cells, and solar and wind energy rose to $40 billion in 2007. The "green tech" market is forecast to more than quadruple to $167 billion by 2015, and the market value for renewable energy consumption worldwide is projected to increase from $95.8 billion in 2007 to $124.4 billion in 2010 and $198.1 billion in 2015.[2, 3] Morgan Stanley estimates that yearly global sales from clean energy sources like wind, solar, geothermal power and biofuels could grow to as much as $1 trillion year by 2030.[4]

Timeframe

Now–2020; 2020+

Potential Impact

• Energy has become a priority issue for the 21st century, being closely tied to economic growth, global geopolitics, and environmental concerns around sustainability of resource consumption and climate change.

• International organizations are rallying to frame sustainable long-term energy policies to address serious concerns about meeting demand in the next twenty-five years without sacrificing the planet's ecosystems.

• The United States will have to address the challenge of energy independence as net imports are expected to continue to meet a major share of total U.S. energy demand to 2030.[1]

Implications and Opportunities for Associations

• This creates the opportunity for associations to provide platforms for expertise exchange and possibly additional products, services, and best-practice materials on energy efficiency and carbon reduction in their sectors.

• Associations will need to decide what role they should play in the setting of future industry best-practice standards and guidelines around energy management and the reduction of environmental footprints.

Functional Implications and Opportunities

• This issue encourages associations to ask whether they are adopting best practices in energy efficiency and advanced energy-management solutions across all association activities—such as group buying, green fuels, eliminating the use of paper, ecolighting, carpooling, and selection of green venues.

• Associations may want to assess the impact on their finances of an energy price rise of 10, 20, 50, 100, or 200 percent, defining what their strategies are to counter rising costs (such as emphasizing web-based delivery models).

Example Industry Implications

• Every industry and organization is influenced by rising costs of energy; the greatest impact could be felt within energy-intensive industries such as manufacturing and transportation.

• The energy industry is expected to expand considerably over the next fifty years, with much of this growth occurring around new energy technologies not currently at an advanced commercial stage. U.S.-based companies could play a significant role in the growth of this industry.

Sources and References

1. www.eia.doe.gov/oiaf/ieo/world.html

2. www.eia.doe.gov/oiaf/aeo/production.html

3. www.all-energy.net/Industry_Headlines.html?startat=481&max=40&HeadlinesSect=General

4. www.reuters.com/article/latestCrisis/idUSN18449059

21. Evolving personal technology "ecosystems": intuitive, visual, and smart

Key Question

Given the rate of technology evolution, what might be the most effective and engaging strategies for delivering future member services?

Description

Personal technologies will continue to evolve, changing the way in which we use them for communication, media consumption, work, leisure, and education. Web and communication technologies are becoming more intuitive and easier to use. The keyboard and mouse could soon lose popularity to new interfaces based on touch and voice controls that make technology use easier for wider audiences. The web is also becoming more visually oriented with the advent of web-based video and the emergence of 3D virtual worlds. Within a decade, hundreds of millions of users could connect "face-to-face" via video-based web experiences as "telepresence" technologies move out of the corporate video conferencing suite to become mainstream on our laptops and desktops.[1]

The power of the tools available to individual users is also changing. Today young web users in schools are already using near-professional quality software to create and edit their own video productions (e.g., Final Cut) and learning to use 3D modeling tools (e.g., Google SketchUp) that allow them to simulate real-world physics in a virtual landscape such as Second Life.

A major future advance to personal productivity will be the emergence of the "Semantic Web," a set of features, standards, and tools that will make it far easier for people and other machines to search for content. The aim is for the web to become "smarter" and more automated, with intelligent software applications handling simple tasks currently dependent on human involvement. The Semantic Web is an extension of the current web that will allow us to find, share, synchronize, and combine information more easily. Documents and information about documents will be stored in a machine-readable format that will enable far simpler search through and access to data stored across the web. Although some elements exist, most of the components of the Semantic Web are still in the R&D phase.[2, 3]

Interfaces are also changing around new display technologies. Flat-panel LCD displays are dropping in price and OLEDs (organic light-emitting diodes) are being developed as flexible and transparent plastic screens only a few millimeters thick. OLED displays could change the nature of computing within our homes—turning multiple surfaces into potential display panels. OLED also increase the likelihood that we will see ultra-thin mobile devices.[4]

Artificial intelligence (AI) applications use advanced software algorithms to automate tasks normally requiring human intervention and a level of decision making. AI applications are expanding around credit card fraud detection, data mining of conversations on social networks, and in laboratories for drug discovery and medical diagnosis.[5] They are also being incorporated into semi-autonomous vehicle systems (e.g., adjusted suspensions systems, adaptive cruise control systems) and are growing most rapidly in the financial sector. Studies estimate that a third of all stock trades in the United States were driven by automatic algorithms in 2007,[6] contributing to an explosion in stock market activity. Between 1995 and 2005, the average daily volume of shares traded on the New York Stock Exchange increased to from 346 million to 1.6 billion.[7] The next wave of AI applications will be used in energy system management and customer relationship management (CRM).

Timeframe

Now–2020

Potential Impact

- The web is still in its infancy; only 20 percent of the world had access in 2007. Similarly, consumer devices have not yet reached maturity in terms of global reach, design, and functionality. Today's most novel tools could become commonplace in tomorrow's work environment.

• In the years and decades ahead, hundreds of millions of new users will come online and connect with each other using personal technology experiences that look very different than the ones we know today. Software and consumer electronics hardware will continue to change how we live in the world.

• Artificial intelligence applications could soon disrupt many knowledge economy jobs by challenging humans in performing fundamental work tasks. They might also help to fill talent shortages of human capital and improve organizational decision making based on advanced tools for pattern detection and analysis.

Implications and Opportunities for Associations

• This raises the challenge of ensuring staff stay up to date with the technology being used by members and society at large, evaluating the resulting return on investment in hardware, software, and staff training.

• It also creates an opportunity to provide insights into new technologies, best-practice guidance, "technology catch-up," and advanced technology training and guidance.

Functional Implications and Opportunities

• Potential for automating workflows, monitoring membership relationships, and monitoring dialogues across social networks and discussion forums to spot emerging themes and potential issues.

• Association's web interactions could migrate more heavily from voice and text to video-based interfaces.

Visualization systems based on video and 3D could offer a more engaging way of conveying analysis and insights on complex issues and help improve online learning and group decision making.

Example Industry Implications

• Major potential impact on industry sectors that could be influenced by hundreds of millions of new web users who use vastly different tools, as well as on industry sectors that require "high-touch" customer interfaces.

• AI applications are already used to perform advanced calculations and synthesis of massive data sets used in business analytics (e.g., business prospecting, quality assurance, auditing). They will increasingly be used across a range of industries from real estate to bio–life sciences.

• Augmenting the healthcare workforce—Japanese robots are currently employed in both receptionist and elderly caregiving roles.

Sources and References

1. www.telepresenceoptions.com/2008/01/study_why_europeans_will_aggre/

2. www.infoworld.com/article/08/01/15/sparql-semantic-web_1.html

3. http://en.wikipedia.org/wiki/Semantic_Web

4. www.physorg.com/news1098.html

5. www.nytimes.com/2006/11/24/business/24trading.html

6. www.iht.com/articles/2006/11/23/business/trading.php

Economic Trends

22. Uneven economic growth

Key Questions

How robust are associations' strategic plans in the face of a range of possible future economic scenarios?

What would be the response to a "worst-case scenario"?

Description

Economic growth, often measured as a percentage of aggregated GDP, is the increased value of goods and services produced by an economy. Since the end of the Cold War, global economic growth has been driven largely by an expansion of free-trade agreements, investments to enhance productivity, worker training, and more market-friendly policies in places such as Asia, Europe, and the Americas. The expectation now is that growth patterns will vary across the world with the developing economies of Asia, Africa, the Middle East, and Latin America expected to show the greatest growth—partly through rising domestic economic activity and partly through increased international trade—especially between developing nations.

In its first-quarter 2008 World Economic Outlook, the International Monetary Fund (IMF) forecast that global economic growth would fall to 3.7 percent in 2008 and 2009—1.25 percent lower than in 2007. It estimated a one in four chance of a global recession as a result of global growth falling below 3 percent. It estimated that the U.S. economy would grow by just 0.5 percent in 2008 and 0.6 percent in 2009—contracting in the first half of 2008. The big concern for the global economy is the impact of a prolonged U.S. slowdown—whereas the United States contributes 28 percent to world GDP, China accounts for only 5 percent. In fact, the whole of Asia, from Turkey to China, contributes 24 percent, less than the United States alone.[2]

The IMF forecast that real GDP growth among the major industrialized economies would fall from 2.2 percent in 2007 to just 0.9 percent in 2008 and 2009. At the same time, growth in the "newly industrialized Asian economies" was expected to fall from 5.6 percent in 2007 to 4.0 percent in 2008 and 4.4 percent in 2009. Although the United States accounts for the largest share of total GDP, global economic growth is dominated by China—which has seen more than a decade of annual growth in double digits—and India (which has experienced growth of 6–8 percent for several years).[3] The IMF highlights that nearly half of global growth during 2007 came from three countries—China, India, and Russia (7 percent). It estimated that China could expand by 10 percent in 2008, with India following close by at 8.4 percent.[4]

Timeframe

Now–2010

Potential Impact

- Growth in the developing world has seen a massive improvement of living standards in many countries. Since 1977, China and India have taken over 400 million and 150 million people, respectively, out of poverty and into a self-sustaining existence.[3]
- Although domestic consumption and trade between developing regions will drive growth, the developing world's economy has not decoupled from the United States and Europe, and any prolonged slowdown could have significant impact across a number of still-fragile emerging economies.
- Sustaining economic growth will require continued efforts to raise education levels and improve training. It also requires social and political stability, which can be threatened by energy supply and prices, commodity prices, widening income gaps, civil wars, conflicts, restricted access to clean water, costs of pollution, and ecosystem collapse.

Implications and Opportunities for Associations

- How closely should associations be monitoring global growth forecasts and the possible impact on their current and future membership base?
- How prominent is the "international dimension" in the services, annual events, and resources available to members?

Functional Implications and Opportunities

- This issue creates the opportunity for associations to develop guides and "roadmaps" for global markets to identify opportunities around rising income groups—both for their members and for their own marketing efforts.
- What would be the impact on budgets and operations if overseas or domestic demand for membership and related services rose or fell by 5, 10, 20, or 50 percent?
- What plans are in place to handle rising overseas membership?

Example Industry Implications

- Despite the rise of emerging markets, the U.S. domestic market will remain the world's largest for many years to come, and hence opportunities will continue to exist—although the competition may increase.

- Shifting patterns of global growth will lead to a number of firms reviewing their strategies around growth, markets, and from where they source their talent.

Some member industries and associations grow during downturns (e.g., foreclosure services, bankruptcy practitioners, discount retailers), but the majority finds its prospects more closely tied to the health of the economy.

Sources and References

1. www.imf.org/external/pubs/ft/survey/so/2008/RES018A.htm

2. www.finfacts.com/irishfinancenews/article_1012923.shtml

3. Fast Future estimates based on multiple national statistical reports and independent research studies

4. www.worldbank.org/depweb/beyond/beyond.htm

23. Growing financial market risks and uncertainty

Key Questions

What would be the impact of a slowdown over a period of one, three, or five years?

What mitigation strategies could be put in place now?

Description

The U.S. sub-prime meltdown has induced a crisis of confidence in credit markets across the globe. The result has been a loss of nerve across the lending sector, higher interest rates, a tightening of lending criteria, and the collapse of institutions that lost market confidence—such as Bear Stearns in the United States and Northern Rock in the UK.

The IMF estimated the "mark-to-market" U.S. subprime-based losses at U.S. $945 billion.[1] At the start of 2008, Goldman Sachs projected that if U.S. house prices fell a further 10 percent in 2008, up to 15 million people with prime, near-prime, and sub-prime mortgages could be in negative equity. Analysts suggest that if large numbers of those in negative equity defaulted on their mortgages, losses to lenders and investors could be between U.S. $1–2 trillion.[2] U.S. house prices actually declined at an annual rate of 25 percent in the three months to January 2008.[3] An April 2008 Credit Suisse research report suggested that up to 6.5 million U.S. home loans (nearly 12.7 percent of all U.S. residential borrowers) could be foreclosed by the end of 2012 because of falling house prices and a lack of available credit.[4] In addition, total outstanding U.S. credit card debt is estimated at U.S. $1 trillion, and the *New York Times* reported that the unregulated credit default swap market is twice the size of the U.S. stock market.[5]

Timeframe

Now–2010

Potential Impact

• The biggest concern is our inability to reliably estimate banks' true exposure to at-risk credit products.

• Alongside financial losses and layoffs in the financial sector, concerns exist that prolonged credit crisis will lead to firms across other sectors holding back investment plans and attempting to limit their costs.

Implications and Opportunities for Associations

• Associations may see a role in helping their members understand the changing landscape of global financial markets, the risks arising from the liberalization and deregulation of markets, and the impact on their sectors.

• Faced with domestic uncertainty, associations may choose to innovate, explore new geographic and service markets, and experiment with new revenue and business models; but others may become more risk-averse and less entrepreneurial.

• Associations need to anticipate the potential for a fall-off in discretionary spending by individual and corporate members that could impact membership renewals; the sale of products, services, training, and sponsorship; and event attendance. A range of strategic responses will need to be considered, including greater sponsorship, developing lower-priced products and services, new bulk discounting models to encourage corporate purchases, and greater focus on emerging market.

• To address short-term revenue problems, a range of temporary measures may need to be explored, such as discounting longer-term membership, encouraging prompt renewal by offering dues reductions or additional discounts on other products and services, and reducing the prices of online products, which have virtually zero cost of delivery.

Functional impact

• May create a role for monitoring industry exposure to risky financial investments.

• Increases the need to develop contingency business plans to address slowdowns of different severity.

Example Industry Implications

• Major private-sector capital investment projects are at increasing risk because of the rising cost of debt and the growing reluctance of banks to lend.

• The level of losses and layoffs in the financial sector is likely to continue into 2009 and possibly beyond.

▪ Could lead to a dramatic reregulation and restructuring of the banking sector.

Sources and References

1. www.imf.org/external/pubs/ft/weo/2008/01/index.htm cited in http://news.bbc.co.uk/2/hi/business/7338326.stm

2. www.rgemonitor.com/blog/roubini/244767

3. www.economist.com/world/na/displaystory.cfm?story_id=11016296

4. www.reuters.com/article/bondsNews/idUSN2233380820080422

5. www.nytimes.com/2008/02/17/business/17swap.html

24. Rising economic strength of China and India represents an increasing share of global GDP

Key Questions

How can U.S. associations benefit from the rising strength of China and India?

How can U.S. associations leverage the experience of those associations that are already in these economies?

Description

Almost 40 percent of the increase in global GDP in the next 15 years is forecast to come from China (27 percent) and India (12 percent). The United States is expected to account for 16 percent and the other BRIC economies (Brazil and Russia) just 2 percent each.[1] The Organization for Economic Cooperation and Development's (OECD) latest forecast suggests that China could overtake the United States as the world's largest economy before 2015 and account for about a quarter of world GDP by 2030.[2] Goldman Sachs now forecasts that India can maintain a growth rate of 8 percent through to 2020 and that its GDP will overtake the United States in dollar terms by 2050 to make it the second largest economy even as India's GDP per capita is expected to quadruple over the period from 2007 to 2020.[3]

The UN forecasts that in the period to 2050, of the major economies, only India's population will see a gain in its share of the 15–59 age group—a gain greater than the rest of the top seven economies combined. China could see a 15 percent reduction, and Australia, the United States, and the UK are expected to lose 5– 10 percent of this age group; a decline of around 5 percent is projected for Turkey, Indonesia, Mexico, and Brazil.[4]

China's middle class is estimated to reach over 500 million by 2012[5] and leads India in developing vibrant consumer classes with business models to match. India's launch of the U.S. $2,500 Tata Nano[6] as the world's cheapest car has raised consumer expectations about what they can afford. In both countries, global travel is now seen as a natural next purchase for the growing middle classes—and estimates from MasterCard have suggested that between 400 million and 1 billion Chinese and Indian consumers could be earning enough to travel internationally by the period from 2015 to 2020.[7]

Timeframe

2016–2020

Potential Impact

• The rise of China and India is opening up tremendous commercial opportunities for businesses, individuals, and associations who are willing to invest the time and effort in understanding them and what it takes to be effective and successful serving customers in these markets.

• Chinese and Indian businesses are seeking an increasing foothold in global markets—acquiring businesses, setting up operations, and forming partnerships and distributor relationships.

• The opportunity presented by China and India is also increasing competition for global investment resources—and more importantly—management time and attention in Western businesses. Their rise is also impacting the availability and price of raw materials and commodities.

Implications and Opportunities for Associations

• There is a large emerging market opportunity for associations to support their members—and the broader market—with training, advice, and guidance on how to do business and succeed in China and India, and for businesses from those markets looking to expand into the United States and Europe.

• Associations serving businesses that operate in global markets could come under increasing pressure to support their members in those markets.

Functional Implications and Opportunities

• Associations need to differentiate between the needs of existing U.S. members going into China and India and members from those markets.

• Associations serving global markets may have to start looking at the mix of language skills and cultural awareness among their own staff and at all of their internal processes and structures to see how well they support the service requirements of those markets.

Example Industry Implications

▪ The software sector has already engaged with India and other emerging markets and is increasingly establishing a presence in China.

▪ Those who can help with the development of civil society infrastructure, professional development, and knowledge transfer for key sectors will continue to be in high demand in both China and India for at least the next decade.

Sources and References

1. www2.goldmansachs.com/ideas/brics/index.html

2. www.oecd.org/document/11/0,3343,en_2649_201185_40277515_1_1_1_1,00.html cited in www.finfacts.ie/irishfinancenews/article_1012947.shtml

3. www2.goldmansachs.com/ideas/brics/BRICs-and-Beyond.html

4. http://scid.stanford.edu/pdf/SCID286.pdf

5. www2.goldmansachs.com/ideas/brics/index.html

6. http://news.bbc.co.uk/2/hi/business/7180396.stm

7. www.mastercard.com/us/company/en/insights/

25. Rise of the "Next 11" nations on the global stage

Key Question

What criteria are associations using to determine the target markets for their international expansion?

Description

The Next 11 (N-11) list was a term coined by Goldman Sachs to cover the next wave of emerging economies that have promising outlooks for global investors and could become top-20 economies by 2025—namely—Bangladesh, Egypt, Indonesia, Iran, South Korea, Mexico, Nigeria, Pakistan, the Philippines, Turkey, and Vietnam.[1]

The list was popularized in 2005, nearly two years after Goldman Sachs coined the phrase "BRICs" to describe the rise of Brazil, Russia, India, and China as the next great consumer economies of the 21st century. Goldman Sachs investment analysts selected the Next 11 based on performance against the key criteria of macroeconomic stability, political maturity, openness of trade and investment policies, and quality of education.[1, 2]

These economies have contributed around 9 percent of global growth over the last few years and could reach two-thirds the size of the seven current largest economies (the G7) by 2050. All have the potential to grow at around 4 percent annually over the next 20 years. Mexico and Indonesia have the potential to rival all but the largest of the G7, and Nigeria, South Korea, Turkey and Vietnam might all overtake some of the current G7.[3]

Timeframe

2020+

Potential Impact

- The "Next 11" countries could soon become significant centers for global investment as their national economies expand alongside rising domestic incomes. Expansion of imports and exports could lead to the same type of high growth currently experienced in China, India, and Russia.
- Foreign entrants need to understand that the character of the N-11 economies varies dramatically—ranging from relatively mature and stable economies with high per capita income, such as South Korea, to some of the poorest nations, such as Bangladesh, and those experiencing domestic or geo-political strife, such as Pakistan and Iran.

Implications and Opportunities for Associations

- This creates an opportunity to provide guides and specific materials covering key economic, political, social, and cultural factors for members thinking of entering these markets.
- Many of these nations will see the growth of the association community as part of building the fabric of civil society; this could create tremendous partnership and growth opportunities for existing associations.
- How geared up are associations to respond to unsolicited support requests from emerging nations?
- Growth of membership and participation in leadership from "Next 11" nations could change the composition and "social fabric" of associations.

Functional Implications and Opportunities

- This creates a need for developing a pool of advisors who have direct experience with these future growth centers.
- A challenge may come in trying to differentiate associations' own N-11 offerings from all the services and data already available.
- How frequently should associations review their internal service structure and processes in light of an increasingly diverse global membership?

Example Industry Implications

- Although much of the growth of these economies is rising from natural resources such as oil and increasing domestic consumption, the economies of some, such as South Korea, are already competing in many global sectors; all have ambitions to build a critical mass of globally competitive firms in key sectors.

Sources and References

1. http://en.wikipedia.org/wiki/Next_Eleven

2. www2.goldmansachs.com/hkchina/insight/research/pdf/BRICs_3_12-1-05.pdf

3. www2.goldmansachs.com/ideas/brics/BRICs-and-Beyond.html

26. Future U.S. growth fueled by rising immigration

Key Question

How well does the current portfolio of programs, services, and policy positions address the needs of immigrants in the target market for members?

Description

The UN estimates that a total of 2.2 million migrants will emigrate from poorer to richer countries every year until 2050. This includes up to 1.2 million Asians and 377,000 Africans migrating to developed economies annually.[1]

In 2006, foreign-born workers accounted for 15 percent of the U.S. labor force. If current trends continue, nearly one in five Americans (19 percent) could be an immigrant by 2050, compared with one in eight (12 percent) in 2005. By 2025, the immigrant, or foreign-born, share of the population is expected to surpass the peak during the last great wave of immigration a century ago.[2, 3]

The most recent U.S. census found that "immigrants accounted for over half the growth in the nation's labor force in the past decade, filling openings in factories and textile mills, restaurants and other blue-collar industries, according to a private analysis of government data."[4] The study of Census Bureau figures between 1990 and 2001 also found that recent immigrants helped fill openings that required more education, such as those in engineering firms and high-tech industries.[5] Immigration also plays a key role in the overall population growth within the United States. A recent report from the Pew Research Center projects that immigration could push the U.S. population beyond 438 million by 2050 (up from 303 million in 2008).[4] The immigrant influx has been felt throughout the country but was especially vital in the Northeast, where the new U.S. residents comprised nearly all of the net increase in the labor force.[3]

Timeframe

Now–2015

Potential Impact

- Most in-depth studies suggest that immigration is an important driver of economic growth. A recent White House study found that, "[o]n average, U.S. natives benefit from immigration. Immigrants tend to complement (not substitute for) natives, raising natives' productivity and income. Careful studies of the long-term fiscal effects of immigration also conclude that it is likely to have a modest, positive influence."[1]
- Immigration is not without controversy as issues remain regarding job losses, national security, taxes, and social services, as well as language and cultural barriers.
- Immigration is also being studied for its connection to entrepreneurial activities. The Kauffman Foundation's index of entrepreneurial activity is nearly 40 percent higher for immigrants than for natives.[4]

Implications and Opportunities for Associations

- Associations may want to collaborate on researching the tendency for immigrants to join associations, as well as what their prime needs are and their interest in volunteering and leadership.
- This creates opportunities to assist members in developing plans that anticipate significant shifts in U.S. policy toward immigration laws or enforcement.

Functional Implications and Opportunities

- A need exists to assess the policy implications and alternative scenarios for key industry sectors.
- Associations may want to look at their own programs, governance, content, communications, and staff recruitment policies to assess how effective they are with immigrant communities.

Example Industry Implications

- Over 22 percent of immigrants who arrived since 1990 worked in service occupations, compared with 19 percent of the total foreign-born population and 13 percent of native-born workers.[3]
- 13 percent of recent immigrants worked on assembly lines or as machine operators.[3]

Sources and References

1. www.un.org/esa/population/unpop.htm cited in www.brusselsjournal.com/node/1982

2. www.whitehouse.gov/cea/cea_immigration_062007.html

3. www.cbsnews.com/stories/2002/12/02/national/main531433.shtml

4. www.prb.org/Articles/2008/pewprojections.aspx

5. www.dallasfed.org/research/swe/2003/swe0306a.html

27. Rising U.S. personal and federal indebtedness

Key Questions

What impact could rising levels of debt have on association membership and income?

Could it create opportunities to provide debt management advice?

Description

U.S. personal savings rates (defined as a percentage of disposable personal income) have been in steady decline for two decades. This rate has been falling for 20 years, from 10.8 percent in 1984 to 4.8 percent by 1994. By 2004 it reached 1.8 percent, and it hit 0.4 percent in May 2005.[1] For 2005 as a whole, the personal savings rate in America was negative as consumers spent more than they earned during the year. In 2007 the U.S. personal savings rate averaged less than 1 percent.[2]

At the start of 2008, the U.S. national debt was approximately $9.1 trillion and equated to almost $30,000 for every American. It is forecast to rise to $10 trillion in 2009. U.S. debt is expanding by about $1.4 billion per day—or nearly $1 million a minute. Standard and Poor's estimates that the U.S. national debt will hit 350 percent of GDP by 2050 if current fiscal policies are maintained.[3, 4]

Timeframe

Now–2015

Potential Impact

- The level of personal savings has an impact on all aspects of the U.S. and global economy. It is a leading indicator for retail spending, housing markets, and major industry and service sectors.
- A low personal savings rate also places Americans in a vulnerable position that makes them less likely to absorb smaller shocks or price fluctuations such as higher gasoline or energy prices, food costs, or housing payments.
- As Americans save less, many find themselves in a tighter credit position, making it difficult to borrow or to pay down existing debts.
- The U.S. national debt continues to grow per capita and has already had a major impact on the U.S. dollar as the world's preferred currency—with many now switching to a basket of currencies, including the Yen and the Euro. The decline of U.S. interest rates and the resulting fall in the value of the U.S. dollar have wide-reaching consequences—for example, reducing foreign demand for U.S. treasury debt and increasing the inflow of investment funding to purchase U.S. assets such as businesses while driving up import prices but making exports cheaper.

Implications and Opportunities for Associations

- Members may question the return on their investment in membership dues with increasing vigor.
- This financial situation creates opportunities for associations to help members develop better "environmental scanning" and anticipatory skills to spot, assess, and plan for changing trends, possible future "shocks," and "inevitable surprises" to the system—such as declining global competitiveness, rising or spiking energy prices, further mortgage crises, inflation, recession, depression, corporate failures, war, or terrorist attacks.
- A falling dollar may make membership rates more attractive to overseas candidates and lead to an increase in international attendees at U.S. meetings.

Functional Implications and Opportunities

- This situation may encourage associations to revisit their business models and assess the robustness of their assumptions and strategies.
- Associations may want to develop alternative plans and budgets based on different possible economic scenarios.
- In the face of member scrutiny, associations will need to be more creative about articulating and demonstrating their value-added proposition and the risks/opportunity costs of not belonging.

Example Industry Implications

- This situation represents a growth opportunity for those targeting international markets and pricing in dollars.
- It also poses the risk of continued financial losses and layoffs in the financial services sector.

- The future may see the emergence of more "vulture funds" established to acquire distressed assets from individuals and corporations who cannot service their debts.

Sources and References

1. www.sfgate.com/cgi-bin/article.cgi?f=/c/a/2005/08/07/BUG5JE423K1.DTL

2. www.bea.gov/briefrm/saving.htm

3. http://edition.cnn.com/2007/US/12/03/us.debt.ap/

4. www.msnbc.msn.com/id/22081728

28. Growing challenge of maintaining physical infrastructure

Key Questions

What role can associations play in highlighting the costs of and potential solutions to current infrastructure challenges?

How might this problem influence the delivery of association services?

Description

The OECD estimates that every year through to 2030, roughly 2.5 percent of world GDP will be required to finance worldwide investments in telecommunications, road, rail, electricity, and water. The figure rises to 3.5 percent of global GDP when electricity generation and other energy-related infrastructure investments in oil and gas are included. The figure would be higher still if assets such as ports, airports, and storage facilities were factored in. Annual global infrastructure spending is estimated to average U.S. $2 trillion until at least 2015—with over 50 percent expected to come from emerging economies.[1]

The American Society of Civil Engineers estimates that $1.6 trillion is needed over a five-year period to bring the nation's infrastructure up to a "good condition." The U.S. National Highway System is composed of 163,000 miles of rural and urban roads. The Department of Transportation estimates that a third of the country's major roadways are in substandard condition—a significant factor in a third of the more than 43,000 traffic fatalities each year, according to the Federal Highway Administration.[2, 3]

More than one in four of America's nearly 600,000 bridges need significant repairs or carry more traffic than they were designed for, according to the U.S. Department of Transportation. There is also growing demand for adding new road capacity. The Texas Transportation Institute estimates that traffic jams waste 4 billion hours of commuters' time and nearly 3 billion gallons of gasoline a year.[4, 5] In 2005, congestion (based on wasted time and fuel) cost about $78.2 billion in the 437 urban areas, compared to $73.1 billion in 2004. The average cost per traveler in the 437 urban areas was $707 in 2005, up from $680 in 2004 (using constant dollars).[6]

In addition to transportation infrastructure challenges, the underground, aging, and inadequate sewer systems spill an estimated 1.26 trillion gallons of untreated sewage every year, resulting in an estimated $50.6 billion in cleanup costs, according to the U.S. Environmental Protection Agency.[4]

Timeframe

Now–2015

Potential Impact

- Inadequate infrastructure could limit economic growth and hinder U.S. competitiveness if it causes problems in the movement of people and freight and leads to inefficiency in energy, electricity, and water utilities.
- This may lead to increased use of alternative work models—e.g., flexible scheduling, telecommuting, teleconferencing, and online education—and the use of alternative product delivery channels such as the internet and mobile phones.

Implications and Opportunities for Associations

- Associations may be able to coordinate industry and individual member lobbying on national-level infrastructure issues.
- This problem impacts member travel, networking, conferences, time available for volunteering (e.g., pains of congestion), and overall quality of life.
- Associations may want to commission research into innovative infrastructure funding models, delivery options, and technologies to help facilitate a broader debate on addressing infrastructure challenges.

Functional Implications and Opportunities

- Associations may fill a role in calculating potential future liabilities for infrastructure-related costs that could have a bottom-line impact on operations for members.
- Associations may wish to facilitate the development of industry-level contingency plans related to potential infrastructure-related wildcards (e.g., infrastructure collapse).

• What-if analysis could be undertaken on critical association activities such as conferences, exhibitions and delivery of printed publications to assess the potential impact of worsening infrastructure issues or potential crises and to explore alternative response strategies and solutions.

Example Industry Implications

• Large potential growth around engineering services.
• Challenges for industries that are totally dependent on physical infrastructure (e.g., trade, logistics, transportation).

Sources and Reference

1. www.oecd.org/dataoecd/24/1/39996026.pdf
2. www.asce.org/reportcard/2005/index.cfm
3. www.msnbc.msn.com/id/7137552/
4. http://pewresearch.org/pubs/699/look-out-below
5. www.fhwa.dot.gov/tea21/suminfra.htm
6. http://mobility.tamu.edu/ums/report/congestion_cost.pdf

29. Nations competing on science investment to drive economic performance

Key Questions

What role can associations play in setting the agenda for science and technology investment at a national- and industry sector–level?

Can they create forums to facilitate strategic debate and connect innovators and producers?

Description

An underpinning assumption in most national strategies is that scientific advances and innovation will be key drivers of future economic performance. Global R&D investments in basic science and applied engineering continue to expand. Battle Research estimates that $1 trillion was invested globally in R&D efforts during 2006.[1] At the same time, the investment strategies and landscape of global R&D players are changing constantly in response to the role of innovation for global economic competitiveness.

Booz Allen Hamilton's Annual Innovation Study found that R&D spending caught up to sales growth in 2006. R&D spending by the "Global Innovation 1000" (the leading global spenders on R&D) rose in 2006 by $40 billion to $447 billion, a 10 percent increase. Companies headquartered in North America increased their absolute R&D spending by 13 percent, representing the largest source of dollar growth among the Global Innovation 1000. North American headquartered firms sustained their lead in innovation spending, having increased their absolute R&D spending by $21 billion in 2006, as compared with firms from China and India, which increased spending by only $400 million during the same period.[2]

Companies headquartered in China, India, and the rest of the developing world represented just 5 percent of overall corporate spending on R&D in 2006, but their five-year average growth rate suggests a desire to catch up quickly. China and India increased their 2006 spending by 25.7 percent over 2005, in keeping with a five-year average rate of growth of 25 percent.[3] Both China and India have ambitious plans to reduce their dependency on foreign R&D and to become technologically self-sufficient by the middle of the century if not sooner.

Academic R&D Funding in Decline

Within the U.S. private sector, investments in R&D projects based in university environments have been in steady decline and are at their lowest levels since the mid-1980s.[4] The National Science Foundation reports that "[t]he share of academic R&D support provided by industry peaked at 7.4 percent in 1999 and declined every year thereafter, reaching 4.9 percent in 2004."[4] Policy leaders are now talking about the continued outsourcing of basic science and applied engineering as a threat to U.S. competitiveness in the 21st century.

Globalization of R&D

Increasingly, transnational companies are investing more heavily in R&D centers abroad in places such as China and India, which graduate nearly twice as many scientists and engineers as American schools. The number of Asians earning science and engineering degrees has increased more than 50 percent in the past two decades, but the number of Americans receiving similar degrees has been stagnant.[5, 6] In recent years, China and India have captured a bigger proportion of the R&D budgets from transnational investors in the areas of bio and life sciences, materials engineering, and information technology systems.[7]

Timeframe

Now–2020+

Potential Impact

- Innovation from basic investments in science in the United States is expected to continue to create new industries and businesses, generate job growth, and shape the next 25 years in key U.S. sectors such as energy, information technology, life sciences, and biotechnology.

• For several decades, the United States had no serious competitors in the world of basic R&D investments across a wide range of industries. Looking forward, the landscape could be very different as emerging economies attempt to cultivate high value–added industries within their own borders. Foreign investors are responding by investing of time and resources as science becomes more globally competitive and cooperative.

• Scientific research is becoming more politicized as concerns rise over the value of intellectual property and the potential use of R&D for national security applications.

Implications and Opportunities for Associations

• Associations may seek to play an active role in tracking science and technology investment as R&D continues to drive long-term value creation and industry competitiveness.

• This may provide the opportunity to pool industry-wide resources for precompetitive research.

• It may also create the potential for coordinating lobbying at the professional- or sector-level to increase both the allocation of government funding to R&D and the number of places on science and engineering courses.

Functional Implications and Opportunities

• This creates the opportunity to provide services that outline and share "culture of innovation" factors, best practices, and case studies.

• Is there a role for chief science and innovation advisors and industry- or profession-focused innovation advisory panels?

Example Industry Implications

• Sectors such as pharmaceuticals are already aware of how much importance is placed on their R&D pipeline by investors.

• Increasingly, those in innovation-driven sectors will find themselves being ranked by investment analysts on measures such as their global R&D and innovation capability, spending, and competitiveness.

Sources and References

1. www.rdmag.com/ShowPR.aspx?PUBCODE=014&ACCT=1400000100&ISSUE=0509&RELTYPE=GR&PRODCODE=0000000&PRODLETT=BZ&CommonCount=0

2. www.industryweek.com/ReadArticle.aspx?ArticleID=15214

3. www.rdmag.com/pdf/R&D%209_05%20Global2.pdf

4. www.cra.org/wp/index.php?cat=24

5. http://electronicdesign.com/Articles/Index.cfm?AD=1&ArticleID=7457

6. www.ieeeusa.org/policy/issues/innovation/index.html

7. www.global-innovation.net/projects/grd/india/index.html

30. Growing economic importance of global knowledge economy—50 percent of U.S. GDP by 2010

Key Question

Are associations constantly assessing how to measure and increase the contribution of their profession or sector to the knowledge economy?

Description

Microsoft estimates that the knowledge economy, which includes financial services, information technology, business services, and the creative sector, accounts for 40 percent of U.S. GDP and is expected to rise to 50 percent by 2010.[1] Today, intangible assets, such as knowledge and skills, account for around 70 percent of the total value of companies in the S&P 500.[2]

In 2005 just over 40 percent of the European workforce was employed in knowledge-based industries. Between 1995 and 2005 employment across the EU knowledge-based industries went up 24 percent. In contrast, employment in the rest of the EU15 economy went up by just under 6 percent.[2]

Timeframe

Now–2010

Potential Impact

▪ Risk of U.S. knowledge-economy professions becoming less competitive than foreign competitors if the education system at every level doesn't deliver the skills, attitudes, and retraining required to serve the needs of knowledge-intensive businesses.

▪ Challenge of preparing people for changing working patterns and emerging models of knowledge-based organizations—e.g., more freelance workers, more mobile work styles, working on global teams, greater external collaboration, greater workforce participation, increasing foreign ownership, and portfolio careers.

▪ Increasingly, it is no longer seen as sufficient to hold a certain credential or job title or to be a member of a particular profession or association. Employers and society as whole are placing more emphasis on the individual's ability to demonstrate mastery of a compelling body of knowledge in real-life situations. Job interviews increasingly probe for evidence of the candidate's ability to use knowledge to respond to new problems and opportunities.

▪ For many professions, even technical know-how and practical application skills will no longer be sufficient, and what is considered "core knowledge" will include a greater "social" education. This could include a foundation in human organizational behavior, communications, information-seeking/research strategies and techniques, and more fluid leadership and organizational structures to accomplish missions.

Implications and Opportunities for Associations

▪ The capacity to create and deliver proven advancements in practical know-how could become an increasingly important part of an association's brand promise.

▪ Growing opportunity for associations to "back-fill" gaps in labor force capability through continuing education, retraining, and certification.

▪ Challenge of ensuring that association services and content are current and updated at the pace with which industry knowledge and best practices are advancing, as well as changing societal expectations of what it means to be a professional. The expanding definition and expectations of a "professional" could create new training and development opportunities for associations.

▪ How will the growth in telecommuting, freelancing, and collaborative ventures impact the vision and missions of associations?

▪ The increasingly cross-disciplinary nature of the knowledge required in many professions may lead to greater collaboration between associations on knowledge creation, training, and credentialing.

Functional Implications and Opportunities

▪ Challenges associations to look at internal structures—are they geared up to respond with speed and flexibility to evolving member needs and expectations in the knowledge economy?

▪ Needs assessments and marketing studies must be done to ascertain where to focus product development.

- Raises questions about the core knowledge required to be an effective association professional in the knowledge economy.

Example Industry Implications

- Knowledge-based businesses will increasingly source talent from a global pool—more companies are establishing R&D facilities in China, India, and the Middle East. For example, Microsoft's travel technology R&D center will be based in Dubai.[3]

- Knowledge-intensive industries such as IT are already experiencing skill shortages.

Sources and References

1. www.microsoft.com/uk/developingthefuture/default.mspx
2. www.theworkfoundation.com/Assets/PDFs/KE_Europe2.pdf
3. www.gulfnews.com/business/Technology/10185766.html

31. Global talent shortages increasing with economic growth

Key Question

Given the potential worldwide talent shortage, to what extent can associations step up to become part of the solution on a global basis?

Description

The pace of development across the globe is placing immense stress on the global talent pool. For some years, economies such as China and India have provided a near endless supply of well-educated high school and college graduates who filled key roles in Western businesses in areas such as R&D and software development. Increasingly these individuals are being lured back to their home countries by attractive salary levels and wide-ranging opportunities. In developing countries, the rapid development of their industrial base and national infrastructure is driving up demand—and hence salaries for professionals in these sectors, attracting candidates from the global market.

A 2007 ManPower survey reveals that 41 percent of U.S. companies had trouble filling positions in 2007. The figures are higher, at 62 and 61 percent, respectively, in New Zealand and Australia. France, at 40 percent; the UK, at 34; and Germany, at 27; had high but variable figures. By comparison, India and China had figures of 9 and 19 percent respectively.[1, 2]

Timeframe

Now–2015

Potential Impact

- Global talent and markets create incentives for U.S. corporations to become even more transnational.
- A shortage of suitably qualified talent domestically could hold back progress and reduce competitiveness—creating openings both domestically and abroad for foreign competitors. This will also create increased competition for a limited pool of talented managerial staff.

Implications and Opportunities for Associations

- Possible role for associations to develop industry-level foresight to model key talent supply trends, developing and evaluating alternative future scenarios and helping members prepare for an uncertain range of possible futures.
- The scale of the challenge creates an opportunity to develop and test a range of imaginative new solutions—such as accelerated learning, improving knowledge worker productivity, and facilitating improved knowledge management and exchange within and across industries and professions.
- A need exists for identifying core areas requiring special attention—e.g., science and math curricula in K–16.

Functional Implications and Opportunities

- HR function in associations may need to become much more global in terms of knowledge, experience, and competencies.
- May increase the expectation for associations to facilitate solutions and lobby at the national level for investments in education, training, and retraining and for more tolerant immigration policies toward skilled professionals and foreign students.
- As they compete with the private sector for a limited supply of high-quality, high-performing talent, associations may find it harder to attract the talent they need to drive their services and operations.

Example Industry Implications

- May encourage more firms to outsource and move to where the talent is located.
- May encourage more collaboration among industry competitors and result in more mergers, acquisitions, and industry consolidation.

Sources and References

1. www.manpower.com/investors/releasedetail.cfm?ReleaseID=235798
2. http://wistechnology.com/articles/4433/

32. Attractiveness of U.S. business environment weakens relative to that of other countries

Key Questions

How do associations see themselves playing in helping to ensure the future competitiveness of U.S. business?

If an association becomes truly international, can it still pursue national-level agendas?

Description

In 2007, America fell to ninth position in the *Economist*'s business environment rankings despite the attractiveness of strong fundamental features such as deregulated labor markets and technology leadership. The overall comparative attractiveness of America's business environment is predicted to decline further in the period to 2012 because of mounting financial and macroeconomic risks, increased protectionism at home and abroad, security concerns, and strained international relations. As a result, America could be overtaken in the rankings by Canada, Switzerland, Hong Kong, the Netherlands, and Australia.[1]

Recent high-profile cases in which the United States has rejected attempted takeovers (and mergers) of firms by Chinese- and Dubai-based business are cited as failures to allow the globalization model to function effectively and have been poorly received internationally. This has led some analysts to question whether the United States will remain a prime investment destination.

Timeframe

Now–2015

Potential Impact

- A "perfect storm" could be brewing within the United States around weakening financial foundations, a geographic shift in where corporations spend their R&D innovation dollars, and a labor force that is lagging behind other emerging knowledge economy centers on basic educational performance (e.g., Asia, Europe).
- Transnational corporations might accelerate their investment strategies outside of the United States in an effort to maximize their returns.

Implications and Opportunities for Associations

- A decline in U.S. competitiveness and the rise of other emerging economies could change the potential makeup of membership over a 10-year timeframe, for future revenues may increasingly come from members, content purchasers, sponsors, and exhibitors outside the United States.
- Associations with largely domestic audiences may find their value proposition and business models endangered if those sectors fail to improve their relative performance.
- Associations may consider it an imperative to scan the business environment for forthcoming drivers of change and use the insights to facilitate industry-level debate.
- Creates a potential new service stream around research- and case study–driven content, best-practice guidance, events, and knowledge exchange to help drive up competitiveness in key professions and sectors.

Functional Implications and Opportunities

- Will raise expectations for associations to lead strategic conversations and develop industry- and profession-level "roadmaps to the future" that ensure competitiveness.
- Associations may increasingly need to look at the skills they require to facilitate the kind of performance transformations they want to bring about.

Example Industry Implications

- Global opportunity and competition mean that firms will need to think about going global much earlier in their existence—declining U.S. competitiveness may make it harder to achieve these goals.

Sources and References

1. www.economist.com/markets/rankings/displaystory.cfm?story_id=10050677

33. Education falling behind employers' expectations

Key Question

What role can associations play in ensuring that employers have employees with the key skills required needed to be effective, innovative, and competitive in the 21st century?

Description

There is a rising of level of commentary coming from various sectors about the perceived gaps between the capabilities and aptitude of high school and college graduates and the needs of industry, especially in terms of written and verbal communication skills. There is also concern that the initiatives adopted have not closed the gap. For example, despite significant federal support for initiatives such as No Child Left Behind, six years later fourth-graders in the United States were doing no better in reading than they were in 2001. Moreover, according to the results of an international reading comparison, fourth-grade students from 10 countries and jurisdictions—including Russia, Hong Kong, Singapore, Italy, Sweden, and Canada all outperformed those in the United States. In 2001 only three countries had done better than the United States on primary-school reading.[1]

A 2005 survey for the National Association of Manufacturers found that 84 percent of employers felt that U.S. K–12 schools were not doing a good job of preparing students for the workplace. Fifty-five percent said schools were deficient in preparing students with basic employability skills such as attendance, timeliness, and work ethic, 51 percent cited math and science deficiencies, and 38 percent were concerned about reading and comprehension.[2, 3]

Timeframe

Now–2015

Potential Impact

▪ This will become an increasingly important focus in political debates if it slows down commercial organizations' ability to meet their strategic goals and remain globally competitive.

▪ It may also drive interest in accelerated (or supplemental) learning programs to address issues for high school and college students and adults with poor basic skills and behavioral issues.

Implications and Opportunities for Associations

▪ Could open up opportunities to help close the gap between the capabilities of high school and college graduates and employers' expectations, over time driving up membership numbers in key industry sectors.

▪ How do we identify critical needs?

▪ What is the appropriate level of association involvement in post-secondary education?

Functional Implications and Opportunities

▪ The education function in associations could become more important in a changing world in which life-long-learning is seen as critical and associations have the potential to be one of the main providers of adult professional education.

▪ This may drive new content or service opportunities for basic-level skills guides and materials aimed at those with poorer reading and mathematical skills.

▪ How well is the education system serving the needs of associations as employers? Over time, it could be even more difficult for associations to find competent professional staff who are able to communicate accurately and effectively.

Example Industry Implications

▪ Impacts a wide range of industries, from construction to service and healthcare.

▪ Educational institutions and systems are facing pressure to change to better prepare students for the world of work.

Sources and References

1. www.newsweek.com/id/73110

2. www.21stcenturyskills.org/index.php?option=com_content&task=view&id=203&Itemid=64

3. www.indiana-etc.org/pdfs%5CUrgency-Model-for-HS-Reform-by-P21.pdf

34. Pay-as-you-go and "freemium" services becoming more prevalent business models

Key Questions

What would be the impact of moving to a free membership/pay for service model on your association?

Which elements could be removed from the core membership offering to reduce the price and then as separate products and services—what impact could this have on membership numbers and overall revenues?

Description

A key area of innovation in recent years has been the creation of new business models, many of which revolve around pay-as-you-go "micro-payments" for individual transactions. In many cases these purchases might previously have been procured through an annual fee or subscription. The pay-as-you-go model has become increasingly popular for many web-based transactions and is now moving to the offline world (e.g., cell phone minutes, car share programs). For example, a start-up auto insurance operation in Dallas aims to make Texas the first state to offer drivers pay-as-you-go insurance policies.[1] A range of personal and business insurance transactions could be transformed by such pay-as-you-go policies. The challenge will be ensuring that federal and state legislatures and regulatory systems can keep pace.

The internet has also opened up new opportunities for online businesses adopting the "freemium" business model to provide their core product for free while generating revenues through additional paid services, advertising, and sponsorship.[2, 3] Exemplifying this is the medical website Sermo/Alpha MD, which provides access for over 50,000 physicians to share their expertise and opinions anonymously. The site is funded by commercial partners such as pharmaceutical companies and investors who pay between $100,000 and $500,000 annually to see the doctors' anonymized opinions on conditions and treatments and pose direct questions to the community.[4]

The freemium model is also moving offline. In 2007, Prince distributed his latest album for free in Britain's *Daily Mail* newspaper.[5] The band Radiohead lets fans choose their price—free if they want—when they download its latest album.[6]

Timeframe

Now–2015

Potential Impact

• Creates new openings for startup businesses with mindsets different from those prevailing in the sector—creating more competition and possibly lower prices in many areas.

• Providers of products and services sold by annual subscription or packaged price may be motivated or forced to look at how they can unbundle their offerings.

• The increasing application of "freemium" models could become a standard and enable more competition in the online and offline delivery of products and services across a range of industries.

Implications and Opportunities for Associations

• Associations could become more market-driven and explore the potential for pay-as-you-go and freemium approaches to expand the reach and sales of core services and third-party offerings.

• Many associations could see "freemium" services as a threat to their core business model as most association services are bundled into a base membership package that provides high value to members. If services are unbundled, some core activities that associations currently fund through cross-subsidy from the profits of other projects may not be viable if members are not willing to pay the true cost of delivery.

• A pay-as-you-go approach would provide clear insight into which services members valued sufficiently to pay for individually.

• Associations would need to define what constitutes core services as part of membership dues and which current standard services could be unbundled.

Functional Implications and Opportunities

• Challenges associations to think hard about how to market and maximize the value of individual offerings rather than relying on packaging them into subscription pricing.

- Pricing for pay-as-you-go would need to include full overhead allocation.
- Would introduce far greater volatility into budgeting and forecasting.

Example Industry Implications

- Pay-as-you-go could result in an expansion in access to services in many sectors (e.g., insurance, healthcare, software, technology, entertainment).
- May spawn a whole new set of online "software as a service" (SaaS) applications enabling organizations to "rent" technology and adopt different payment models without building the underlying systems.
- Could lead to a dramatic shift in cost structures.

Sources and References

1. www.bizjournals.com/dallas/stories/2007/12/31/story7.html?ana=from_rss

2. www.microsoft.com/presspass/press/2006/may06/05-21EmergingMarketConsumersPR.mspx

3. www.economist.com/theworldin/business/displayStory.cfm?story_id=10094757&d=2008

4. www.medscape.com/viewarticle/557924

5. www.guardian.co.uk/media/2007/jun/29/business.pop

6. www.nytimes.com/2007/10/02/arts/music/02radi.html

35. Global outsourcing market could hit $1.43 trillion: U.S. outsourcing deepens

Key Question

How might associations leverage the integration of global workforces into new membership opportunities and international expansion opportunities for key professions and major industry sectors?

Description

The global market for shared services and outsourcing is expected to grow to $1.43 trillion by the end of 2009, from $930 billion in 2006.[1] Gartner forecasts that by 2010 about 30 percent of Fortune 500 enterprises will outsource to three or more countries, from less than 10 percent today. Estonia, Uruguay, Azerbaijan, and Sri Lanka are just some of the emerging countries attempting to carve niches for themselves in this market.[2]

U.S. professional service companies are being compelled by their clients to consider offshoring and outsourcing as viable strategic solutions. For example, revenues from the offshoring of legal services are forecast to reach $640 million by 2010.[3]

Timeframe

Now–2010

Potential Impact

- The landscape of the global knowledge economy workforce in particular is evolving quickly as increasingly transnational companies seek to find the greatest talent and value around the world.
- The type of roles being outsourced and offshored are moving up the value chain—for example, investment banks are increasingly locating at least part of their investment research functions in locations such as India.

Implications and Opportunities for Associations

- Creates an opportunity to provide products, services, best-practice guidance, advice, and facilitation of knowledge exchange around outsourcing and offshoring core services in a sector.
- May drive down U.S. membership numbers if firms thin out their U.S. operations through offshoring and outsourcing, but could create opportunities to support their operations overseas.

- Global integration requires changes in the paradigms and thinking of associations, for many U.S.-based industries and companies are entering an era in which sector leadership is not guaranteed and best practices, innovation, and winning business models could come from a range of geographic markets.

Functional Implications and Opportunities

- Creates the challenge of how to service industries and firms that are effectively now a network of global relationships and alliances.
- May create the incentive for associations to look at the potential for extending offshore and domestic outsourcing of their activities beyond membership administration, event management, and content creation to cover other aspects of business operations—e.g., back office, publishing, IT, and web development.

Example Industry Implications

- Most major industry sectors now tap globally distributed teams and workforces in everything from R&D, product design, and marketing to customer service and billing.
- The outsourcing industry is now a major sector with its own dynamics, challenges, and development support requirements.
- In healthcare, "nighthawks" read medical images overnight (X-rays, MRIs, PET scans, and CT scans), but this gives rise to concerns about the credentials and quality control of overseas laboratories.

Sources and References

1. www.itbusinessedge.com/blogs/sts/?p=189

2. www.businessweek.com/technology/content/jul2007/tc20070730_998591.htm?chan=search

3. www.ilw.com/articles/2008,0125-ross.shtm

36. Global rise in entrepreneurship

Key Question

In light of the rising global economic importance of entrepreneurship, what role could associations play in the creation and growth of entrepreneurial businesses in their profession or sector, both nationally and internationally?

Description

Entrepreneurship is acknowledged as a critical driver of economic activity for countries at both ends of the economic spectrum. The ninth annual Global Entrepreneurship Monitor (GEM) Global Report (2007) found that early-stage entrepreneurial activity tends to be high in countries with lower per-capita GDP but declines in middle-income countries and then rises again in higher-income countries.[1, 2]

As per-capita incomes rises in high-income countries, so does the percentage of adults (18–64 years old) involved in early-stage entrepreneurship—defined as starting a new business activity. Cultural, demographic, and institutional factors are also at play. Many EU countries consistently have relatively low rates of early-stage entrepreneurship. Globally, Iceland (12.5 percent), Hong Kong (10.0 percent), and the United States (9.6 percent) show the highest levels. The lowest rates were found in Austria (2.4 percent), Puerto Rico (3.1 percent), and Belgium (3.2 percent).[1]

Among high-income countries, the United States (5.1 percent), Israel, Iceland, and Canada show the highest rates of "high-growth expectation entrepreneurship" (expecting to employ at least 20 employees five years from now). Among middle and low-income countries, China has the highest rate, followed by Argentina. Entrepreneurs are also looking at global markets—in some GEM countries, 40 percent of early-stage entrepreneurs expected 24 percent or more of their customers to come from outside the country.[1, 3]

Timeframe

Now–2015

Potential Impact

• Recent global growth in entrepreneurial activity suggests confidence in the economic outlook. It also implies that favorable support systems are in place in at least some economies—e.g., education systems producing innovative talent, a willingness of some banks and investors to support early-stage businesses, and customers in need of new products and services.

• In the developing world, there is a greater reliance on entrepreneurs to address the shortcomings of public bodies in delivering radical change. The private sector has been encouraged to provide the necessary impetus and execution skills to deliver progress, growth, and job creation. Regulation has been driven through to allow private ventures in areas as diverse as infrastructure, healthcare, telecommunications, consumer markets, and financial services.

Implications and Opportunities for Associations

• New opportunities may open up around the creation of associations serving different entrepreneurial sectors and entrepreneurs from groups not currently served or considering joining an association.

• Entrepreneurs are increasingly looking at communities and networks as potential for-profit opportunities— competing with nonprofits on value and service.

• Creates a potential opportunity to develop services aimed specifically at would-be and current entrepreneurs in a particular profession or sector.

Functional Implications and Opportunities

• What are the best-practice examples of entrepreneurial behavior in associations? How transferable are they?

• What lessons can the association community learn from the entrepreneurial sector both about customer relationships and about internal operations?

Example Industry Implications

• The creative, new technology, food service, personal, and household service sectors have in recent years seen a dramatic rise in entrepreneurial activity in the United States.

- In emerging markets, entrepreneurs are increasingly driving major infrastructure initiatives.

Sources and References

1. www3.babson.edu/ESHIP/research-publications/upload/GEM_2008_Executive_Report.pdf

2. www.gemconsortium.org/

3. www.economist.com/markets/indicators/displaystory.cfm?story_id=10180767

37. Rise in U.S. corporate and individual social responsibility

Key Questions

How can the social responsibility agenda be interpreted in an association context?

What role should associations play in driving responsibility discussions in the profession or sector?

Description

Social, environmental and corporate governance factors are seen as increasingly relevant to financial performance. Half of all Fortune 100 companies issue Corporate Social Responsibility (CSR) reports. In 2007, of the top 100 companies in America, 59 issued Corporate Social Responsibility reports—compared to nearly 90 percent within Europe and 61 percent in the rest of the world.[1, 2]

According to the 2007 edition of the "Report on Socially Responsible Investing (SRI) Trends in the United States" from the nonprofit Social Investment Forum (SIF), in the period from 2005 to 2007, SRI assets increased more than 18 percent, although all investment assets under management edged up by less than 3 percent. The Trends report identifies $2.71 trillion in total assets under management using one or more of the three core SRI strategies—screening, shareholder advocacy, and community investing. In the past two years, social investing has enjoyed healthy growth from the $2.29 trillion documented in the 2005 Trends report.[1]

At the start of 2008, nearly one out of every nine dollars under professional management in the United States was invested using socially responsible criteria— 11 percent of the $25.1 trillion in total assets under management at that time—as tracked in Nelson Information's "Directory of Investment Managers."[3]

Timeframe

Now–2015

Potential Impact

- Companies and organizations are operating in a world with higher expectations for CSR, transparency, and accountability related to the broader consequences of their actions beyond just their core operations.

- The pressure toward "social responsibility" is expected to increase from multiple directions—greater stakeholder involvement and citizen and nonprofit advocacy groups, as well as governmental and intergovernmental agencies tasked to address social justice and environmental issues.
- Some business and organization leaders are embracing the expectations toward "social responsibility" as a way of building premium brand value and addressing issues important to their core consumer base. Other leaders see greater transparency and accountability as a way to improve the bottom line.
- For-profit companies are starting to actively engage in their communities and take over activities that have traditionally been in the domain of nonprofit organizations.

Implications and Opportunities for Associations

- Associations can be the conduit to satisfy corporate and individual members' desire to "do good" and respond to expectations to respond effectively to changing societal demands for corporate responsibility.
- This creates the potential to monitor and share best practices, emerging issues, compliance strategies, and reporting, assurance, and peer indexes, as well as facilitating debate and expertise sharing among members.
- To be credible, associations may increasingly have to demonstrate their own dedication to responsible and sustainable business practices while taking care of their own triple bottom line—member value (profit), staff and community (people), and the environment (the planet).

Functional Implications and Opportunities

- This raises the potential for associations to report on their performance against the "triple bottom line" accounting principles.
- It also creates an education challenge: ensuring that all staff understand the association's CSR ambitions and measurement practices.

Example Industry Implications

- Corporate responsibility best practices can now be found in every major industry sector and business size.
- Some companies find that their Corporate Social Responsibility performance becomes a key marketing tool and an area where they can transfer knowledge and process to the local community—this is seen as particularly important when entering emerging markets and the national governments are keen to ensure best practice on Corporate Social Responsibility from new entrants.

Sources and References

1. www.csrweb.org

2. www.econtext.co.uk/cover_scans/InContext2006.pdf

3. www.socialinvest.org/news/releases/pressrelease.cfm?id=108

38. Evolution of tomorrow's company

Key Question

What are key aspects of today's association most ripe for transformational change?

Description

In the face of the continued transformation of economies, increased competition, and technological advances, the nature, strategies, and structure of companies will continue to evolve.

- Companies are more decentralized and networked, with increasingly distributed teams based around the nation and globe, involved in every aspect of product development and service delivery;
- Employees in some major industry sectors are increasingly more freelance and project-based;
- Most companies are adapting to higher standards for transparency and accountability in their practices (both internally and externally);
- Social networks and other social media are transforming the way companies communicate and share with staff, partners, customers, and other stakeholders;
- Leadership and human resource dynamics are changing. Most industry sectors will experience a major generational transfer of knowledge. Women are playing more leading executive-level roles;
- Companies based in developing nations are increasingly focused on higher-value tasks (e.g., India's call centers are transforming into accounting and consulting centers); and
- Companies will look at an increasingly wide range of approaches such as complexity theory and chaordic science[1] to find the right models with which to manage the 21st-century organization.

Timeframe

Now–2016

Potential Impact

- The expectation should be for continued evolution in structure, scope, business models, and the use of technology.
- A new model will need to emerge that allows firms to compete in a turbulent global marketplace without necessarily increasing the workload and stress levels of individual workers.

Implications and Opportunities for Associations

- How well do associations understand the changing needs of domestic and foreign businesses that operate in their sectors or that use the professionals they serve? Who pays the dues when companies are loose networks of distributed intelligence and productivity? Will individuals pay their own way for "continuous education"?
- This creates an imperative for collaborative research to ensure that associations understand the forces and factors shaping the future, the impact on members, and the implications on members' needs of the associations that serve them.
- It also creates a potential leadership role for associations: facilitating strategic conversations about the future of their sectors or professions that address the opportunities and challenges associated with a changing environment and workforce dynamics.
- Traditional "territories" for associations may have to be rethought—alliances, partnerships, and other arrangements with sister organizations in other countries may increasingly be the norm.

Functional Implications and Opportunities

- This situation will drive the need for continual investment in alternative, flexible technologies that are mobile, social, and compatible with alternative work arrangements, as well as IT and consulting staff to support regular transitions.
- A possible role for associations may emerge in identifying trends, monitoring drivers of change, and communicating alternative future landscapes relevant to major professional and industry sectors.

Example Industry Implications

- The rate of transformation within a sector will be determined by multiple factors. For example, a combination of cost pressures, the emergence of large new target markets, and the search for talent could drive many to establish their corporate headquarters in locations such as China, India, Dubai, and Singapore.

Sources and References

1. www.chaordic.org/

39. Continued shift in global wealth and spending power

Key Question

Are associations "following the money"—monitoring shifts in patterns of income and wealth in the United States and beyond and assessing the potential impact on membership numbers and revenues?

Description

The U.S. share of global spending is forecast to decline from 32.5 percent to 30.9 percent from 2005 to 2020. The spending of the EU 25 is also expected to drop by 4.9 percent to 22.3 percent. In contrast, Russian spending could increase by more than 100 percent to 2.7 percent of the global total, and China is projected to nearly triple its share to 8.4 percent, up from 3.3 percent in 2005.[1]

The McKinsey Quarterly estimates that "almost a billion new consumers will enter the global marketplace in the next decade as economic growth in emerging markets pushes them beyond the threshold level of $5,000 in annual household income—a point when people generally begin to spend on discretionary goods."[2, 3] By 2015, consumer spending power in emerging economies could nearly match the spending power of Western Europe. It is estimated that 100 million Chinese households will achieve European income levels by 2020. Furthermore, the Hispanic population in the United States will have spending power equal to that of 60 percent of all Chinese consumers.[3]

The Brookings Institute estimates that "the middle class in poor countries is the fastest-growing segment of the world's population. While the total population of the planet will increase by about a billion people in the next 12 years, the ranks of the middle class will swell by as many as 1.8 billion—600 million just in China." It forecasts that by 2020, the world's middle class will grow to include 52 percent of the total population, up from 30 percent now. "The middle class will almost double in the poor countries where sustained economic growth is fast lifting people above the poverty line."[3, 4] It is estimated that half of India's population could be "middle class" within a few decades, and that India's individual purchasing power will climb from $2,149 in 1999 to $5,653 per person by 2020—and $16,500 by 2040.[5]

Timeframe

Now–2020; 2020+

Potential Impact

• The growth of the world's global middle class will be a major driver for political and social changes in the coming decades as individuals and families in emerging markets embrace new lifestyles and values. This shift in global spending power could bring greater parity among the world's nations.

• Some economists point to the rising "anxious middle" working class in developed economies, where workers feel threatened by globalization and free trade.

• The economic shift will also surface controversial elements of socioeconomic justice and degradation of the environment for the sake of economic growth.

Implications and Opportunities for Associations

• A rising global middle class will expand the market opportunity for most U.S. industrial sectors and service companies—and, potentially, the associations that serve them.

• This creates an opportunity for U.S. associations to explore previously unconsidered markets, developing new partnerships, expanding membership and operations, and providing and acquiring content and services from peer global organizations.

• Associations may want to conduct research to model the relationship between income and wealth levels and association membership, projecting the potential impact on membership levels and demand in the United States and key markets internationally.

Functional Implications and Opportunities

• Associations may need new strategies and tactics for attracting the emerging middle class in target markets, expanding their capabilities to deliver services—company members could reside in an increasing number of locations around the globe.

• Staff in all external service areas will need to be prepared to deal with multiple cultures, languages, and expectations.

Example Industry Implications

- Sectors that develop the deepest insight into the emerging middle class will be best positioned to tap those markets—for example, UK food retailer Tesco sent teams to live with Chinese families to learn about their lives, their needs, and how best to sell to them.[6]

- In cases in which automation is eliminating traditional middle-class jobs such as bank staff and airline reservation clerks, sectors are being forced to rethink pricing models, product and service offerings, and target markets.

Sources and References

1. www.eiu.com

2. www.worldbusinesslive.com/article/609473/world-bank-predicts-rise-global-middle-class/

3. www.investopedia.com/articles/07/global_trends.asp

4. www.foreignpolicy.com/story/cms.php?story_id=4166

5. www.theglobalist.com/DBWeb/StoryId.aspx?StoryId=2195

6. http://business.timesonline.co.uk/tol/business/industry_sectors/retailing/article626406.ece

40. Shifting patterns of global inequality and unmet needs

Key Questions

To what extent should associations be looking to attract funding from wealthy philanthropists?

Do associations have any duty to serve the needs of the poorest in society?

Description

The United Nations estimates that close to 3 billion people still live on less than $2 per day, and 1 billion in "extreme poverty"—on less than $1 a day. This number has fallen by 130 million worldwide since 1990, despite the addition of 800 million people to the world population during the same period.[1, 2, 3] Research from the OECD and Deutsche Bank suggest that although the average German spends 14 years in education, and Americans 13, the figure falls to 8 for South Africa, 6 for China and only 5 for India.[4, 5]

At the same time, wealth creation continues among the world's top asset holders. Forbes' 2008 billionaire research found the number of global billionaires crossing the four-figure mark to reach 1,125 with a net worth of $4.4 trillion, up $900 billion from 2007. America has a total of 469 billionaires, accounting for 42 percent of the world's billionaires and 37 percent of their total wealth—down 2 percent and 3 percent, respectively, from 2007. Russia is in second place, with 87 billionaires; Germany third, with 59; and India fourth, with 53. Although half of the world's 20 richest were from the United States two years ago, only 20 percent are today. India has the largest grouping among the top 10—Lakshmi Mittal, Mukesh Ambani, Anil Ambani, and KP Singh. In Asia, India is followed in its number of billionaires by China (42), Hong Kong (26), Japan (24), and Australia (14). The list includes 226 newcomers—including 77 from the United States, 35 from Russia, 28 from China, and 19 from India. The highest growth rate came from India, rising at over 50 percent. At this rate, India will have almost 3000 billionaires by 2020. Even if these growth rates were to fall to between 10–25 percent, India would be on course for between 160 and 770 billionaires by 2020.[6]

The 2007 World Wealth Report (Merrill Lynch and Cap Gemini) showed a rise in the number of millionaires globally to 9.5 million people who control $37.2 trillion in wealth assets. Many believe that these figures underestimate the true figures by at least 100 percent. The millionaire population increased 8.3 percent between 2005 and 2006. By 2011, that wealth is expected to grow to $51.6 trillion. In North America, the number of financial millionaires grew 9.2 percent to 3.2 million. Their total wealth grew by 10 percent to $11.3 trillion. The number of "super-wealthy," with financial assets of $30 million or more, grew 11.3 percent worldwide to 94,970, and their total wealth grew by an even more astounding 16.8 percent to $13.1 trillion.[7, 8, 9]

Despite the rise of the super-wealthy, there are concerns that global total wealth could actually decline. A recent McKinsey study suggests that "over the next two decades, absent dramatic changes in saving behavior or returns earned on financial assets, growth in household financial wealth will slow by more than two-thirds, from 4.5 percent historically to 1.3 percent going forward. This slowdown, coupled with rising expenditure and inflation will cause the level of household financial wealth to fall some 36 percent, or approximately $31 trillion. The U.S. portion of this shortfall could reach $19 trillion."[10]

Timeframe

Now–2020+

Potential Impact

- Continued high rates of poverty, unmet social needs, and widening income gaps can limit the growth and expansion of global markets, leading to greater social and political instability. Poverty prevents poor countries from devoting sufficient resources to detect and contain deadly disease, educate younger populations, train workers, and build critical infrastructure.
- The scale of wealth assets held by the super-rich segment suggests the emergence of a global class of multi-millionaires and billionaires who will exert greater influence on business and society around the world.

Implications and Opportunities for Associations

▪ Associations may want to research the wealth profile of target economies to understand where members might come from and what proportion of their income they might be willing to invest in membership associations that could help advance their prospects.

▪ Associations may increasing be called upon to consider their social responsibility and provide tangible solutions and support for global goals to address unmet need—possibly through initiatives such as the UN Global Compact.

▪ If associations can demonstrate that they are adding critical value to society, they may be able to attract attention and long-term funding from philanthropists.

Functional Implications and Opportunities

▪ Associations could conduct assessment of gaps and unmet needs related to industry sector markets (as suppliers, producers, or consumers) based around the world, or provide tools and practices for monitoring progress.

▪ Research foundations may need to become increasingly sophisticated in seeking out wealthy philanthropists who see the value of the association's research agenda.

Example Industry Implications

▪ A growing for-profit industry is emerging to advise the wealthy on how best to target their philanthropic investments.

▪ The "ultra-luxury" goods market is expected to remain relatively robust in the face any economic turndown.

Sources and References

1. http://news.bbc.co.uk/1/hi/world/americas/4185458.stm

2. http://sedac.ciesin.columbia.edu/povmap/

3. http://unstats.un.org/unsd/demographic/products/vitstats/

4. www.oecd.org/topic/0,3373,en_2649_39263294_1_1_1_1_37455,00.html

5. www.dbresearch.com

6. www.finfacts.com/irelandbusinessnews/publish/article_10002168.shtml

7. http://stonesoupstation.blogspot.com/2008/03/for-first-time-ever-number-of.html

8. www.ml.com/media/79882.pdf

9. http://blogs.wsj.com/wealth/2007/06/27/more-millionaires-than-ever/

10. www.mckinsey.com/mgi/publications/demographics/index.asp

41. Changing patterns of U.S. income, wealth, and savings

Key Question

Should associations be offering services that address the long-term financial planning needs of individual members?

Description

The latest data on U.S. citizens shows a massive divergence in wealth, income, and savings across age groups and within cohorts such as the baby boom generation (born 1946–1964). Accounting for nearly 30 percent of the U.S. population, the Baby Boomer generation is important not only because of its size, but also because it represents the wealthiest generation in the United States, with an estimated annual spending power of over $2 trillion. As boomers age, they are likely to diverge into three distinct tiers: about 20 percent will be very well off in retirement (including a segment who will be extremely well off: the top 1 percent of boomers hold more wealth than the bottom 80 percent); about 50 percent of boomers will scrape by on savings, retirement accounts, and home equity; and a vulnerable 25 percent or so will face senior citizen status with few assets.[1]

There is also growing concern over income gaps and stagnant wages. A recent historical review of tax returns by the Center for Budget and Policy Priorities looked at long-term patterns around income gaps. In 2000, the richest 2.8 million Americans had $950 billion after taxes, or 15.5 percent of the $6.2 trillion economic pie. The poorest 110 million Americans had less, sharing 14.4 percent of all "after-tax money." But the higher incomes of the last decade did not lift all people equally; the gap between rich and poor more than doubled from 1979 to 2000.[2]

From 1973 to 2005, although U.S. family incomes virtually stagnated for the lowest quintile, they grew more than three times as rapidly for the top 5 percent than for those in the middle-income group. The personal savings rate in the United States has fallen from an average of 9.1 percent in the 1980s to an average of 1.7 percent so far this decade.[3] The U.S. Department of Commerce reports that as of summer 2007, the American personal savings rate was just 0.5 percent.[4, 5]

Timeframe

Now–2010

Potential Impact

- Opportunities for upward mobility among the poorest in society may become rarer because of a combination of declining average wages, expanding income gaps, rising costs of living, falling housing valuations, spiraling costs of energy, food, and healthcare, and increasing costs of secondary education. In some cases, these cost rises are outpacing even dual-income working-class families. The result could be a less competitive labor force, creating shortages of domestic workers for knowledge-economy jobs.
- A growing wealth gap, and failure to lift people out of poverty, could lead to increased social tensions.

Implications and Opportunities for Associations

- Opportunities to provide advice on confronting a wide range of emerging financial situations for U.S. workers (e.g., facing retirement with no savings vs. expected asset transfer from wealthiest Baby Boomers).
- It may be necessary to assess the membership implications of widening income gaps and stagnant wages among certain labor force segments.

Functional Implications and Opportunities

- Associations will need to assess the implications of the changing personal financial landscape.
- It may be necessary to review strategies for attracting the wealthiest segments.

Example Industry Implications

- Sectors may increasingly skew their offerings to focus on wealthier segments. For example, the UK credit card company Egg recently cancelled the accounts of 161,000 card holders (7 percent of its customers) because their personal situation posed an "unacceptably high risk" and no longer met Egg's target customer profile.[6]

Sources and References

1. www.marketresearch.com/product/display.asp?productid=1466503&g=1

2. http://query.nytimes.com/gst/fullpage.html?res=9C03E6D8143DF936A1575AC0A9659C8B63

3. www3.brookings.edu/es/commentary/journals/bpea_macro/forum/200709goldin_katz.pdf

4. www.bea.gov/briefrm/saving.htm

5. http://finance.sympatico.msn.ca/savingsdebt/insight/article.aspx?cp-documentid=5951550

6. http://news.bbc.co.uk/2/hi/business/7222336.stm

Environmental Trends

42. U.S. organizations and investors focusing on green issues

Key Question

What role should associations play in driving the environmental agenda and advancing policies and best practices with members and industry sectors?

Description

Although progress has been made on many fronts in certain sectors, U.S. organizations may have lagged behind their European counterparts in addressing the reduction of their overall "environmental footprint." Although the adoption of greener practices is rising up the management agenda, the picture is not consistent. For example, the energy efficiency of office buildings, measured as energy use per square foot, has leveled off in recent years, following a dramatic growth in efficiency during the 1990s. Although employee telecommuting from home or remote locations for eight or more hours per week rose by 16 percent between 2000 and 2006, the percentage of employees carpooling or taking public transit to work dropped almost 10 percent over the same period.[1]

Performance on other key indicators has also been encouraging but inconsistent. For example, paper use, measured against gross domestic product, has declined by more than 20 percent over the past decade, and the recycling rate increased by 20 percent in the decade to 2006. However, although the amount of used computers and other e-waste more than doubled from 2000 to 2006, the amount of e-waste recycling grew by only about 20 percent.[1]

The investment community has recognized the scale of the market for technologies to help corporations and individuals improve their environmental performance. Venture capital investment in green-tech companies topped $5 billion in North America and Europe in 2007 and shows no signs of slowing down. The Cleantech Group's analysis shows that investment leapt from $3.6 billion in 2006 to $5.18 billion in 2007. Energy generation was the most active sector, with 172 deals, totaling $2.75 billion. Behind that was energy storage, at $471 million; transportation, at $445 million; energy efficiency, at $356 million; and recycling and waste, at $291 million. Cleantech Group said that the number of deals over $100 million increased, which it saw as "an indication of growing investor confidence."[2]

Timeframe

Now–2015

Potential Impact

- The global community will continue to look toward the United States to take a more active role in reducing carbon emissions and encouraging the development of environmentally sustainable technologies and industries. Meanwhile, emerging economies such as China and India will continue to argue that (1) they have to balance environmental protection with the need for economic growth to help take their populations out of poverty, and (2) carbon emissions and resource consumption should be measured on a per-capita basis rather than at the national level.
- Increasingly, major industries will be measured and compared on factors such as emissions, waste, and natural resource consumption. This will help drive adoption of greener policies and standards that are measurable and accountable to third-party verification. A priority will be integrating "cradle-to-cradle" product design and development with appropriate disposal solutions.

Implications and Opportunities for Associations

- This creates a possible opportunity for associations to provide environment-related products, services, and discussion forums for members, acting as clearing houses for the latest research and best practices.
- It also creates an opportunity for establishing industry-sector certifications, standards, and measurement strategies that can be tested by third parties who compare claims against actual environmental footprints.

Functional Implications and Opportunities

- Should associations lead by example and actively measure and drive down their own environmental footprints?
- How might environmental concerns change expectations for conferences and gatherings (for example, by

leveraging relationships with hotels and conventions centers to accelerate their greening efforts)?

Example Industry Implications

• This will increasingly put the spotlight in all sectors on those perceived to have poor green credentials (e.g., energy companies, heavy manufacturing, transport, construction, consumer electronics/appliances, computing, personal care, food, and home cleaning products).

• The emerging "green sector," or "clean tech," has the potential to become a major employer and new driver of innovation and growth in the economy.

Sources and References

1. www.csrwire.com/News/10886.html

2. www.news.com/8301-11128_3-9852833-54.html

3. http://blogs.wsj.com/environmentalcapital/category/alternative-energy/clean-tech/venture-capital/

43. Global consumption patterns challenge Earth's resource capacity

Key Question

Should associations "think the thinkable" and initiate conversations that challenge basic assumptions of a "business as usual" future, exploring alternative scenarios of economic growth severely challenged by the costs of limited resources?

Description

The UN projects a global population of 8 billion by 2025 and of 9.2 billion by 2050, up from 6.6 billion today.[1] Meanwhile, hundreds of millions of people in emerging economies are experiencing rising incomes and longer lifespans—driving up food consumption, increasing demand for clean water and energy, and placing increased pressure on all natural resources. The Worldwide Fund for Nature's (WWF) Living Planet Report says that human populations are using up Earth's natural resources at a rapid rate. The WWF estimates that if current consumption levels continue, we will require two planets' worth of raw resource supplies in the next 40 years. If global consumption levels rise to match those in Europe, three planets will be required, and if consumption rose to U.S. levels, five.[2]

Clyde Harrison of 321 Gold points out, "Today, 1 billion people consume two thirds of the world's raw materials. 5.6 billion people consume the other third and they are becoming more successful. The industrial revolution involved 300 million people. The emerging nation revolution involves 3 billion." China, with roughly 20 percent of global population, has 47 percent of the world's demand for iron ore, 32 percent of its aluminum demand, and 20 percent of its copper demand and consumes 6–8 million barrels of oil per day. The United States represents 4–5 percent of global population and consumes 25 million barrels per day.[3]

Timeframe

2011–2020

Potential Impact

- Rising prices of basic commodities could lead to increasing domestic strife—the first half of 2008 witnessed food riots in more than 30 countries because of rising food and energy prices.

- Many environmental analysts believe the world economy could be reaching a "limits to growth" threshold in which raw resource supplies cannot meet growing demand—leading to a sharp increase in the cost of living. The potential for geopolitical and domestic conflicts over access to and control of key resources such as oil, water, and agricultural land will increase commensurately.
- Economists have serious concerns about inflation and the rising cost of raw materials used for making everything from steel and concrete to food products.
- The "limits to growth" scenario is feeding new public policy debates as entrepreneurial business leaders move toward extracting raw resources in new places (e.g., the ocean floor, the Arctic) and is causing environmental groups to exert pressure to prevent unregulated mining of ecosystems, such as rainforests, that sit on top of valuable deposits.

Implications and Opportunities for Associations

- This creates the opportunity for associations to elevate the debate on issues related to resource management, materials science innovation, and organizational best practices in reducing resource demands and securing resources for future generations.
- It is also an opportunity for associations to help their industries or sectors find and research solutions not already identified by the government or within the industry.
- A "limits to growth" scenario of rising resource costs could slow the growth of major industry sectors[4] and could have an impact on member makeup and demand for services.

Functional Implications and Opportunities

- Associations could come under increasing pressure to develop organizational policies to ensure that their sustainability practices match member needs and expectations in an era of rising costs of natural resources.

• It could also create a stronger focus to consider the environmental impact of all decisions, from selecting event suppliers to travel planning.

Example Industry Implications

• The food service industry from diners to high-end restaurants could experience a softening of demand if it has to raise prices to cover rising input costs even as customers are becoming more nervous about economic conditions and rising costs of living.

• Investors will increasingly start to analyze businesses on their resource efficiency and their ability to drive down their consumption of increasingly expensive basic commodities.

Sources and References

1. www.un.org/popin/data.html

2. www.naturalnews.com/020873.html

3. www.321gold.com/editorials/harrison/harrison 032408.html

4. http://online.wsj.com/article/SB120613138379155707. html?mod=googlenews_wsj

44. Climate change a growing political and economic priority globally

Key Question

Who will lead and sustain industry-level conversations about the potential risks associated with climate change and the rapidly changing regulatory and political landscape of today's carbon-intensive economies?

Description

There is vigorous debate among scientists, politicians, and economists about the causes of and solutions to climate change. However, there is also growing consensus that human-induced climate change is a moral, environmental, political, and economic priority for governments, organizations, and citizens. Current levels of carbon dioxide and methane in the atmosphere are higher than at any time during the past 650,000 years. A 5–10 percent increase in hurricane wind speed, linked to rising sea temperatures, is predicted to approximately double annual damage costs in the United States to $150 billion by 2017.[1]

The 2007 UK Stern report on the economic impact of climate change suggests that 1 percent of global GDP (gross domestic product) must be spent on tackling climate change immediately. It warns that if no action is taken, floods from rising sea levels could displace up to 100 million people. Concurrently, drought could create tens or even hundreds of millions of climate refugees, and melting glaciers could cause water shortages for one in six of the world's population. Global warming has the potential to cut worldwide food production by 20 percent and worldwide income from agriculture by 16 percent by 2020.[2]

Stern suggests the economic impacts of unabated climate change could cost the world 5 percent of its GDP yearly. However, the report argues that shifting the world onto a low-carbon path could eventually benefit the global economy by $2.5 trillion each year. By 2050, markets for low-carbon technologies could be worth at least $500 billion.[2]

Timeframe

Now–2010

Potential Impact

• The world's total economic loss from weather-related catastrophes has risen 25 percent in the last decade. According to the insurance firm Swiss Re, the U.S. insurance industry's share of the overall $150 billion economic cost of U.S. catastrophes related to climate change could reach $30–$40 billion annually by 2017.[3, 4]

• Air pollution is estimated to cost China 3.8 percent of its GDP, and water pollution another 2 percent, according to the World Bank. China is far from alone—in the MENA (Middle East and North Africa) countries, environmental degradation is estimated to cost Egypt 4.8 percent of GDP, Syria 3.49 percent, and Tunisia 2.1 percent.[5]

• Coastal infrastructure could be affected by rising sea levels and flooding. For example, to protect the San Francisco Bay Area and the stretch of coast south of Santa Barbara from a 3.28-foot (1-meter) rise in sea level will require an initial investment of $1.52 billion, plus $152 million in annual maintenance costs. The probability of a major flood event there in the next 50 years is predicted to increase to a 40 percent chance over time.[6]

Implications and Opportunities for Associations

• Associations could play a role in coordinating research and action for members or industry sectors, identifying options, undertaking cost–benefit and risk analyses, formulating new climate change policy, and seeking to influence public sentiment to support political or economic responses.

• Associations could become prime sources of information, research case studies, and best practice materials, as well as platforms for expertise exchange in their sectors. Associations expect to come under increasing pressure to dramatically reduce their own carbon footprint and to identify strategies to limit the impacts of climate change.

Functional Implications and Opportunities

• This may accelerate the transition from carbon- or energy-intensive operational policies (e.g., paper-based to electronic communication; more virtual meetings rather than face-to-face events).

- Associations may need to expand policy analysis related to climate change.
- This could cause higher costs for associations (insurance, real estate acquisitions, and regional costs of living).

Example Industry Implications

- Industries with historically high emission levels are coming under increasing scrutiny and pressure to reduce those emissions to best-practice levels, complying with emerging carbon markets (e.g., energy, manufacturing, aviation, hospitality/travel tourism).
- Within each sector, responses will vary. For example, although many in aviation are mounting extensive PR and lobbying campaigns to defend their emissions performance, others are experimenting with a range of measures that includes testing alternative fuels (Virgin Atlantic) and offering customers the opportunity to "offset" their emissions by paying extra for their airfare (Silverjet).

Sources and References

1. www.dailymail.co.uk/pages/live/articles/news/news.html?in_article_id=413451&in_page_id=1770
2. http://news.bbc.co.uk/1/hi/business/6096084.stm
3. www.fundee.org/news/policy/outlook2007.htm
4. www.un.org/esa/sustdev/sdissues/consumption/Marrakech/sherif.pdf
5. www.chinaeconomicreview.com/dailybriefing/2007_11_20/World_Bank:_Chinas_air_pollution_costs_38_of_GDP.html
6. www.cier.umd.edu/climateadaptation

45. Rises in ecoliteracy, "green" practices, and ethical consumption

Key Question

What role should associations play in helping members understand and monitor the wide spectrum of attitudes, beliefs, and values related to ethics, sustainability, and environmental issues?

Description

The marketplace is responding to societal value shifts driven by diverse factors such as the environment, religion, political beliefs, and ethical concerns. Consumers are increasingly looking beyond price, quality, and convenience and applying a range of other filters in making purchasing decisions.[1] Environmental issues are at the forefront of these behavioral changes, and more sustainable "green" products are appearing on the major retailers' shelves.

Citizens are also becoming more active in their monitoring of environmental change and their pursuit of more ecofriendly practices. A host of new scientific and social tools, including sensor networks, pollution monitoring, and citizen alert groups (such as those using mobile phones to report pollution violations), are creating a rapidly growing awareness of the environment and increasing citizen activism.[2] Ecobehavior is also changing. Today, the United States recycles 32.5 percent of its waste, almost double what it recycled 15 years ago. Estimates put the recycling business in the United States alone at $250 billion annually.[3]

Timeframe

Now–2010

Potential Impact

- Businesses and public institutions are responding to an operational environment in which their actions are more transparent and they are increasingly held accountable for the broader consequences of their actions.
- Citizens, as consumers and voters, are taking a more active role in addressing issues important to their personal beliefs. Increasingly, they expect their preferred brands and communities to reflect respect for these beliefs in their organizational behaviors.
- Organizations are having to respond by making clear what their "brand promise" is on a range of issues of concern to society. Today we see environmental claims made as part of many marketing and branding efforts. The next step will be an increasing focus on assessing and validating those claims.

Implications and Opportunities for Associations

- Associations may seek to understand changing member priorities through regular polling to identify trends in values, expectations, and emerging issues. Associations might also anticipate potential conflicts between associations representing industries that are considered "polluters" and associations supporting green practices and policies.
- Associations could share the results of polling and broader scanning of new trends and developments to help the membership base anticipate societal shifts related to environmental and ethical issues.
- Associations may want to lead from the front in developing and implementing ethical and environmental best practices across all activities, from communications to events.

Functional Implications and Opportunities

- Associations will come under pressure to ensure that they are building and communicating clear and consistent messages about their environmental and ethical positions and practices and may need to support their claims with third-party verifications.
- Any sense of waste or poor environmental or ethical performance on the part of an association could become open to rapid debate through online member discussion forums and consumer-level social web forums.
- This creates the opportunity to establish ethical and environmental stewardship and certification programs and to help frame and monitor industry-level standards and protocols.

Example Industry Implications

- An industry of sustainable service solution providers is emerging to provide best-practice guidance on how to behave in a more environmentally sound, ethically aware, and sustainable manner.

▪ Every sector now has a body of case study material emerging regarding how the more responsive players are reacting to customers' environmental and ethical concerns.

▪ Industries that are directly involved in green practices will be strengthened, but other energy-intensive industries may need to refocus their efforts on meeting the expectations of members, partners, and regulating bodies.

Sources and References

1. www.iconoculture.com

2. http://fringehog.com/2007/05/10/theme-of-the-week-eco-literacy/

3. www.epa.gov/msw/recycle.htm

Political Trends

46. Diminishing U.S. political influence internationally

Key Question

In an era of multiple global political and economic powers, how can U.S. associations develop, maintain, or extend a leadership position as a trusted source for information, services, education, and professional training?

Description

The CIA/NIC "Mapping the Global Future: Report of the National Intelligence Council's 2020 Project" suggests that the era of American global dominance could end by 2020.[1, 2] The rise of China and India as political influences in the developing world, and the emergence and strengthening of alliances in Asia, Africa, and Latin America, are reducing U.S. influence on governments globally. At the same time, the weakening of the dollar, the increasing turbulence in the U.S. financial services sector, and concerns about a domestic recession are threatening to reduce the influence of the United States in global financial markets.

There has also been a rise in adverse global reaction to U.S. foreign policy. A 2007 BBC World Service poll of 26,000 people in 25 countries (mostly non-Arab) found that only 29 percent now feel the United States exerts a mainly positive influence on the world. That compares with 36 percent who felt that way a year before, and 40 percent two years earlier. When asked about the U.S. military presence in the Middle East, an average of 68 percent of respondents across the 25 countries answered that it provokes more conflict than it prevents.[3]

Timeframe

Now–2010

Potential Impact

- The shift to a "multi-polar" world is increasingly seeing countries such as China, India, Brazil, and a resurgent Russia, as well as groupings such as the EU and economic powers in the Middle East all seek greater political and economic influence.
- This could shift the allocation of foreign direct investment away from the United States, diminishing the role of the U.S. dollar as a preferred currency reserve and gradually changing the balance and location of global wealth assets held by corporations, governments, individuals, and non-state actors.
- An adverse political climate for the United States could impact the economy, leading to job losses and a decline of key industries. Conversely, a sustained period of a cheaper dollar could lead to more competitive U.S. exports and more firms seeking to manufacture in the United States.

Implications and Opportunities for Associations

- Associations that are not already truly global may have to accelerate their globalization plans if they are to meet members' needs and achieve their ambitions for international service delivery, reach, and influence.
- The realignment of global power and wealth opens up significant opportunities for associations to expand their global reach and membership.
- U.S. domestic industries could struggle—putting pressure on costs, discretionary spending, and employment levels and creating demand for services that help them expand outside U.S. markets.
- New association "competitors" could emerge from lower-wage economies able to offer similar or better content and services via the internet at lower prices.
- New skill sets and knowledge will be required by association members to help them perform effectively in diverse geographic markets.

Functional Implications and Opportunities

- Associations could be under increasing pressure from their non-U.S. members and companies with globally based teams to ensure that their content, communications, service offerings, organizational structures, and chapter relations models reflect the different languages and cultural norms, reference points, backgrounds, expectations, and experiences of non-U.S. audiences.
- There could be increasing opportunity to provide association members with political, economic, and cultural guidance and risk and opportunity assessments for the diverse geographic markets they are entering.

Example Industry Implications

• U.S. sectors that have traditionally been seen as global leaders (e.g., infrastructure, technology, healthcare) will face increasing competition trying to establish their presence in expanding emerging economies. For example, no U.S. or European firm has been successful in winning contracts to run mobile phone services in the developing world—the winners have typically come from China, the Middle East, and India.[4]

Sources and References

1. www.dni.gov/nic/NIC_2020_project.html

2. http://blog.washingtonpost.com/postglobal/drg/

3. www.voanews.com/english/archive/2007-02/2007-02-07voa58.cfm?CFID=34152627&CFTOKEN=49611671

4. Fast Future analysis (Unpublished)

Reference Resources

1. Fareed Zakaria, Newsweek, May 12, 2008: "The Rise of the Rest: It's true China is booming, Russia is growing more assertive, terrorism is a threat. But if America is losing the ability to dictate to this new world, it has not lost the ability to lead." www.newsweek.com/id/135380

47. India and China becoming "spokesnations" of the developing world

Key Question

How can U.S. associations respond to the possible emergence of large global associations growing rapidly from highly populous nations seeking rapid development of the professional and industrial sectors?

Description

As China and India's economic strength increases, they are also establishing a new role in global affairs as "spokesnations" for much of the developing world. Developing nation groupings such as the "G77," ASEAN, and the Shanghai Cooperation Organization are increasingly looking to China and India to lead their interests in global negotiations on issues such as climate change and at forums such as the UN, World Bank, IMF, and WTO. For many emerging economies, China and India offer an alternative development model closer to their own experience.

China and India are now major recipients of foreign direct investment. They are also starting to expand their own investments and diplomatic relationships abroad in Africa, Latin America, and the Middle East. As the world's leading manufacturer, China has started to push its own standards in industries such as electronics, consumer products, logistics, and supply-chain management. India is rapidly becoming a central hub for knowledge-economy service industries and is also expected to exert more influence internationally.

Timeframe

Now–2015

Potential Impact

- India and China see themselves as emerging global powers and are keen to build economic and political ties with nations around the world. Both have now become donor nations, providing aid and technical assistance to other rapidly developing nations, and are increasingly finding common ground on issues related to the environment and energy security, reducing their dependence on Western technology and patents.
- Both are pushing for full representation at the top levels of global bodies such as the UN, IMF, WTO, and World Bank, as well as regional ones, such as ASEAN.

Both are increasingly assertive in negotiations to ensure that global political, economic, and legal agreements do not have an adverse impact on themselves or other developing nations.[3]
- China and India are both wrestling with the environmental impact of economic growth—with the challenge of taking populations of over a billion out of poverty on a permanent basis, environmental performance has lagged on the priority list. Both are now focusing on driving a greener growth agenda and looking to leapfrog into an age of "clean-technology" industries.

Implications and Opportunities for Associations

- Both nations see the value of associations in building up civil society infrastructure, cocoordinating the voice of industries and professional groups, and driving up professional standards.
- Both could increasingly demand that the products and services offered by global associations are tailored to reflect local circumstances, laws, culture, and languages.

Functional Implications and Opportunities

- How do we best meet the needs of non-U.S. constituencies through service offerings, membership categories, chapter structures, policy positions, and communication strategies? For example, should membership be a single price globally, or priced in local currencies to represent a certain proportion of member income wherever they are in the world?
- Associations seeking to serve emerging economies will need to source partners capable of tailoring and creating materials appropriate to the needs of local markets.
- Could non-U.S.-based chapters become a platform for reaching members in other emerging economies?

Example Industry Implications

- Every commercial and industrial sector in both countries has experienced growth in recent years, and China and India are now driving growth of industries in other regions of the world (e.g., China's infrastructure investments in Africa).

• The burgeoning middle classes of over 400 million in China and over 150 million in India are driving a boom in consumer markets.

• Salaries and wages are rising in both countries, which may erode some cost advantages of outsourcing deals over time.

Sources and References

1. http://news.bbc.co.uk/1/hi/uk_politics/7199483.stm

48. Increasing political and economic transparency

Key Question

How can associations leverage and communicate to members the geographic and market opportunities that could arise from greater transparency?

Description

Long-term global studies of political and economic transparency suggest that an increasing number of nations are becoming more transparent on the back of rising national GDPs and continued economic integration. The annual *Corruption Perceptions Index (CPI)* (first released in 1995) ranks 180 countries by their perceived levels of corruption, as determined by expert assessments and opinion surveys. The least corrupt in 2007 was found to be Sweden, followed by Singapore, Finland, Denmark, and New Zealand. The lowest ranking went to Myanmar (# 180), followed by Somalia, Iraq, and Haiti. The United Kingdom ranked 12th and the United States 20th.[1]

The survey found scores to be significantly better in nations with higher levels of economic growth and integration into larger regional or global markets—including southern and eastern Europe and several African nations (Namibia, Seychelles, South Africa, and Swaziland). The transparency index found higher levels of corruption and less transparency in nations with stagnant or falling GDPs or that were consumed with war and conflict (e.g., Afghanistan, Iraq, Somalia, and Sudan).[1, 2]

Although there is always the risk of regimes becoming less transparent, there are also signs of hope. For example, despite irregularities in the process, Nigeria's presidential election in 2007 was only the second consecutive democratic election in its history. The new President Umaru Musa Yar'Adua has tried to lead by example, strengthening the corruption commission, sacking ministers suspected of corruption, and making a very early declaration of his personal assets.[3]

Timeframe

Now–2015

Potential Impact

• Political and economic transparency is a critical precursor to sustaining global economic growth and successful regional integration and will continue to rise in importance as an issue on the international policy agenda.
• Organizations will be increasingly sensitive to the importance of political and economic transparency and risk assessments as their strategies take them overseas.

Implications and Opportunities for Associations

• Associations could make themselves aware of the different indices (e.g., Ibrahim African Index, Bribe Payers Index) and share this information with their membership.
• Associations could evaluate best practices (e.g., reporting standards) and model guidelines for operating inside nations with high corruption and poor transparency ratings. Transparency in how governments operate, set standards, enact laws, and so on, can only benefit American organizations seeking to expand into new markets.
• This creates the opportunity to provide country guides and risk assessments and facilitate knowledge exchange for international economies.

Functional Implications and Opportunities

• Expectations for transparency and accountability are likely to spread beyond governments to private-sector businesses and nongovernmental organizations.
• Associations may want to evaluate their own transparency policies and practices against the best policies in the public and private sectors.
• Associations will need to invest more in research and analysis activities to identify the domains where transparency is important to members and the broader community, and whether standards are being met.

Example Industry Implications

• Transparency will become increasingly important for industries that require national or international regulatory oversight (e.g., food, agriculture, pharmaceuticals, finance).

- For those industries involved in major public sector works programs, such as rail, roads, and waterways, a very clear statement of operating principles is required to guide staff on how to handle situations that fall outside normal operating and ethical practice boundaries (e.g., requests for bribes).
- The healthcare industry is addressing issues of transparency related to physician practice, patient care, records management, and clinical trials.

Sources and References

1. www.transparency.org/news_room/latest_news/press_releases/2007/2007_09_26_cpi_2007_en

2. www.transparency.org/policy_research/surveys_indices/bpi

3. Presidential presentation to Nigeria's 13th National Economic Summit, Abuja September 5–7, 2007

49. Increasing global role for single-party states

Key Questions

What will the impact be on association policies and practices if associations choose to pursue opportunities in single-party states?

Description

Single-party states are governments formed by a single political party, in which no other parties are permitted to run election candidates. In most cases, parties other than the one in power are banned. Increasingly, those ruled by different forms of royalty and emirs are also referred to as single-party states in terms of their operating practices. Some nations, such as China, hold tremendous influence over global economic activities; others, such as Cuba have only held a fluctuating level of influence within their regions.

Single-party states, rich in natural resources or having strong economic growth, are actively using sovereign wealth funds as global investment tools outside their own countries and markets. China's wealth fund is estimated at $200 billion, Abu Dhabi's at over $800 billion, and the Singapore's government's at $300 billion.[1] These funds are increasingly active on the global stage and have been particularly prominent in their investments to prop up the balance sheets of Western investment banks during 2007 and 2008. The concern is that these funds are not always transparent and could be pursuing national political goals in their investment strategies—although there is little evidence of this in the way they have conducted their investments to date.

Sovereign funds have existed since at least the 1950s, but their total size worldwide has not increased dramatically until the past 10–15 years. In 1990, sovereign funds were estimated to hold $500 billion at most. The current total is an estimated $2–3 trillion and, based on the likely trajectory of current accounts, oil prices, and country growth forecasts, this could reach $10 trillion by 2012. Sovereign wealth funds are expected to be the primary investment vehicles for nations seeking to expand global assets (e.g., corporate equity, real estate). Including capital appreciation, the amount could swell to $12 trillion by 2015.[1, 2]

Timeframe

Now–2015

Potential Impact

- Single-party states hold control over financial policies and are able, in many cases, to make very rapid decisions in response to changing economic conditions (e.g., changing banking policies, increasing or decreasing foreign access to domestic markets, funding worker training programs). Some economists believe that single-party democracies such as Singapore can often make an easier transition into a market-based economy.
- Single-party states' sovereign wealth funds are creating dilemmas for policy makers. On one hand, they are providing much-needed investment and liquidity in key markets—such as the recent bail-out of global investment banks. On the other hand, there is growing concern—often even fear—about their intentions and lack of transparency.

Implications and Opportunities for Associations

- Operating or investing in a single-party state requires sophisticated analysis and good internal connections. The association community may want to undertake a community-wide evaluation on behalf of it is members.
- Will associations operating inside single-party states be forced to alter policies or organizational structures to accommodate local laws and customs? Can there be less democratic versions of chapters for the international arms of associations?
- An opportunity exists to establish an association for sovereign wealth funds.

Functional Implications and Opportunities

- How might single-party state strategies affect association strategies for growth and membership services?
- Single-party states may have simpler or more complex decision making processes but may also offer the best long-term route to establishing national standards in key sectors.
- To do business in single-party states, firms are learning to live with different legal and social frameworks.

Example Industry Implications

- Many industries trade with single-party states. In recent years, the hydrocarbon energy industry has seen significant challenges operating within single-party states eager to expand domestic influence and power.

Sources and References

1. www.economist.com/finance/displaystory.cfm?story_id=9230598

2. www.imf.org/external/pubs/ft/fandd/2007/09/straight.htm

50. Changing patterns of global governance—growing influence of non-state actors

Key Question

How well do associations and their members understand the global landscape of non-state actors that shape policy and dynamics in their sectors?

Description

The increasingly global nature of many of the challenges faced by society—such as climate change, rising food and energy prices, terrorism, and infectious diseases—is increasing the need for more global responses and coordinating mechanisms. Governance and responses to these issues is increasingly being led by pan-national organizations such as the UN and the EU. Global governance and international affairs are also increasingly being influenced by the role of non-state actors who use sophisticated communication methods and organizational structures to advance their issues and agendas for good and bad. Non-state actors include

• Those who operate within established laws, such as globally focused nongovernmental organizations (NGOs)—such as the Open Society Institute—to encourage free markets and political reforms.[1]

• Private, membership-only groups, such as the Bilderberg Group, that include influential individuals from a wide range of political and business interests who hold private annual meetings to discuss global issues.[2]

• Individuals with extreme wealth able to establish foundations (e.g., the Bill and Melinda Gates Foundation) with tremendous global reach and influence over the direction of scientific research and implementation strategies of the projects they invest in.

• Those acting outside domestic and international laws, including terrorist organizations such as Al Qaeda and criminal organizations who oversee the global drug trade, human trafficking, black marketeering, and other illicit activities.

There are blurring lines around new non-state actors such as private security and military contractors (PMCs). PMCs such as Blackwater receive multimillion-dollar contracts for overseeing operations in war-torn areas or for combating illicit drug trafficking. The PMC industry is estimated to be worth over $100 billion a year.[3, 4]

Illegal non-state actors control world illicit trade, which Havocscope.com estimates to be about $1 trillion per year. Counterfeiting and piracy are estimated at $521.6 billion, the global drug trade at $321.6 billion, trade in environmental goods at $55.7 billion, human trafficking at $43.8 billion, consumer products at $37.5 billion, and the illegal weapons trade at $10.1 billion. The World Bank estimates that up to an additional $1 trillion was paid in bribes last year as part of the estimated $0.5–$1.5 trillion laundered globally. Hence total criminal income could be over $2 trillion.[5]

Timeframe

Now–2015

Potential Impact

• As the range of global issues increases, so does the potential for international institutions to step in to establish governance and coordinate responses. Some nations may fear the loss of national sovereignty to these often unelected bodies.

• Non-state actors will continue to influence the evolution of globalization and international affairs.

• International governing bodies will continue to address the "blurring line" of rights and protection for non-state actors assuming more state-like roles (e.g., private military contractors).

• Terrorist and criminal organizations are expected to consume an increasing proportion of law enforcement and security budgets and drive regulation of everything from travel to internet usage.

Implications and Opportunities for Associations

• Greater demand from members seeking to understand and monitor the influence of non-state actors in key industry sectors and global markets.

• How might non-state actors change the landscape for businesses and nongovernmental associations operating on the global stage (e.g., strain on resources, monitoring the complexities of relationships and influence)?

Functional Implications and Opportunities

• Could legal non-state actors open up channels for associations to expand into new markets? Or might they prevent expansion into certain industry sectors or nations?
• Could illegal non-state actors initiate events that shut down global opportunities or complicate economic or geopolitical affairs?

Example Industry Implications

• Well-funded charitable organizations such as the Gates Foundation are expected to proliferate and influence both unmet needs and the political agenda, as well as the direction of funding strategies.
• Quasi-non-state actors such as PMCs are becoming an increasingly significant sector and could lead to challenging ethical and political debates about roles and responsibilities.

Sources and References

1. http://en.wikipedia.org/wiki/Non-state_actor

2. http://en.wikipedia.org/wiki/Bilderberg_Group

3. www.unitedpmc.com/companies.htm
www.sourcewatch.org/index.php?title=Private_Military_Corporations

4. www.millennium-project.org/millennium/Global_Challenges/chall-12.html

5. www1.worldbank.org/finance/html/amlcft/docs/Ref_Guide_EN/v2/01-Ch01_EN_v2.pdf

100 Emerging Trends
Political Trends

Title	Description
1. Declining power of the nation-state	The influence of nation-states is declining, and the divide between foreign and domestic affairs is breaking down in the face of increasingly global issues such as economic interdependency, the environment, natural resource supply challenges, and the rise of global terrorist networks. Individuals, nongovernmental organizations, pressure groups, and transnational groupings are wielding more influence than ever before, often bypassing state controls and working outside the reach of international institutions. www.bbc.co.uk/worldservice/worldagenda/pdf/gordon_corera.pdf
2. Increases in the number and kind of actors in international governance, with resulting challenges to policy-making	Increased potential for challenges to international regulatory and policy environments arising from increases in number and kinds of actors in international governance. Increasingly "multilevel governance" is likely—with more international, national, and subregional or local policy-makers, regulatory bodies, and private organizations challenging injustices, inequities, and cultural differences in regulations and standards. www.defra.gov.uk/science/ForwardLook/default.asp
3. Rising political and economic influence of a resurgent Russia	Russia's influence on the international stage is increasing caused by its large oil and gas holdings, which have helped lift its foreign currency reserves to $464 billion at the end of 2007, giving it the third largest holdings in the world, behind China and Japan. Russia is expected to be a top-ten economy, in GDP terms, for the foreseeable future. Personal wealth in Russia is also on the rise—it had 87 billionaires at the start of 2008, up from 7 in 2002 and the second largest number after the United States. The number of millionaires also grew—from 80,000 in 2002 to 119,000 in 2006. www.economist.com/theworldin/europe/displayStory.cfm?story_id=10092027&d=2008
4. Rising confusion over the path of development in Middle East	U.S. public perception over the path of development in the Middle East region remains fragmented. There are widespread fears related to continual support of terrorist organizations and foreign policy positions of unfriendly nations. Other concerns center on the increased reliance on petroleum and natural gas supplies and the increasingly powerful financial influence of Middle East–based sovereign funds, which are investing in more Western businesses. Yet, despite concerns, massive social and economic changes abound in places such as Dubai, Saudi Arabia, and throughout the Middle East, which are positively changing their physical landscape, demographics, cultural makeup, economic outlook, and global economic integration. www.fastfuture.com
5. Further European integration	The European Union is expected to keep growing from 27 member states at the start of 2008—potentially rising to 40 states. Croatia, the former Yugoslav Republic of Macedonia, and Turkey are the next candidates for entry. There is strong debate on what impact further enlargement will have on Europe's economic prospects and political unity and its influence on the global stage, which the EU is expected to continue to try to expand. www.fastfuture.com

Title	Description
6. Rise in global terrorism	Security will remain an important issue for most nations. A terrorism incident database is maintained by the RAND Corporation for the National Memorial Institute for the Prevention of Terrorism, which is funded by the U.S. Department of Homeland Security. Surveying incidents for the period January 1998 through August 2006 shows that the rates of terrorism fatalities and incidents have increased since events on 9/11. A fair portion of the increased activity is related to the war in Iraq—but not all. Removing Iraq from the picture shows an increase in the average monthly rate of terrorism fatalities of more than 10 percent for the post-9/11 period. The increase in the rate of incidents, counting Iraq, is 75 percent. www.comw.org/pda/0609bm38.html
7. Increasing demand for "tailored" governance	Citizens are likely to demand more immediate and personalized responses to their requirements, though they may not necessarily expect a direct interface with the government. In fact, the government is likely to become more "virtual" to its citizens, a trend accelerated by "e-government" initiatives. The expectation is of a greater dispersal of power from government to citizens. www.foresight.org.uk/user_media/Britain_in_2020.pdf
8. Micropolitans	The U.S. federal government has designated "Micropolitan statistical areas" to recognize changes outside cities and suburbs that have been brought on by development, migration, and the economic shift from farming and manufacturing to service industries. Once lost in the vast rural expanse beyond the nation's metropolitan areas, these "mini-metros" with rural sensibilities are emerging as political power centers and bases for companies seeking talented workforces and lower business costs. http://en.wikipedia.org/wiki/United_States_micropolitan_area
9. Increased litigation of international controversies in the United States	In the last five years, there has been an increase in attempts by parties operating in international commerce to gain access to U.S. courts to resolve disputes. The trend is forecast to continue, particularly in relation to forum-related issues such as personal and subject-matter jurisdiction, venue, and choice of law. www.forbes.com/businesswire/feeds/businesswire/2008/01/07/ businesswire20080107006406r1.html
10. Declining global water supply a source of interstate tension	Lack of clean water is responsible for more deaths in the world than war is. About one out of every six people living today do not have adequate access to water, and more than double that number lack basic sanitation. Agricultural irrigation consumes enormous quantities of water. In developing countries, irrigation often exceeds 80 percent of total water use. Meanwhile, access in rapidly expanding urban areas remains an enormous problem for emerging economies. By 2025, almost two-thirds of the global population will live in countries where water will be a scarce commodity. Deloitte & Touche estimates that more than 1 billion people will lack access to clean water in 2008. www.engineeringchallenges.org/cms/8996/9142.aspx www.guardian.co.uk/business/2007/dec/09/water.climatechange
11. Risk of global pandemics	Outbreaks of global pandemics such as SARS and avian flu are expected to increase significantly in the next decade as international travel—of both people and goods—increases. The number of global tourists is expected to rise from 565 million in 1995 to 1.6 billion by 2020. www.curevents.com/vb/showthread.php?t=88470

Title	Description
12. Rise in "antiglobalization" sentiments	Business and government leaders from around the world are reporting a rise in working-class anxiety and resistance to globalization. The rise of antiglobalization sentiment could lead to increased protectionism and a potential limitation to the expansion of global trade. www.stwr.net/content/view/1930/37/

Economic Trends

Title	Description
13. U.S. to remain the number-one foreign direct investment recipient	The United States will likely continue to be the beneficiary of global direct investment strategies. Between 2007 and 2011 the United States is forecast to remain the number-one recipient of foreign direct investment (FDI) at 16.75 percent of world total. Britain is ranked second for this period at 7.54 percent and China third at 5.79 percent. www.economist.com/markets/rankings/displaystory.cfm?story_id=9723875
14. BRIC economies of Brazil, Russia, India and China continue to exceed growth expectations	Goldman Sach's 2007 baseline projections for India's potential output growth show that the economy can sustain growth rates of about 8 percent until 2020, significantly higher than the 5.7 percent that Goldman projected in its original BRICs paper in 2003. Assuming the government continues to implement growth-supportive policies, India's GDP (in U.S. dollars) is expected to surpass that of the U.S. before 2050, making it the world's second-largest economy, after China.
	By the time China becomes an aged society in 2027, under all of the scenarios considered by Goldman Sachs, its per-capita GDP should have surpassed the "developed-economy" status of $10,000 (in 2005 terms). Russia is projected to have a real chance of catching up with living standards of the current G7 and increasing its per-capita GDP elevenfold in constant U.S. dollar terms between 2006 and 2050. Brazil is expected to use a surge of oil revenues to increase capital investments above today's 19 percent of GDP. Forecasts estimate that Brazil's investments reach 25 percent by 2015, when it should be able to sustain growth at 5 percent. www2.goldmansachs.com/ideas/brics/index.html
15. Increasing economic strength of Middle East states	Across the Middle East, the IMF expects a rise in GDP growth from 5.8 percent in 2007 to 6.1 percent in both 2008 and 2009. The IMF argues that the region is fairly well insulated from the chaos in global financial markets. However, major concerns are the impact of dollar devaluation and inflation—with recent figures of 20 percent in Iran, almost 14 percent in Qatar, 9 percent in the UAE, and 6.5 percent in Saudi Arabia. An estimated $1.8 trillion of investment in new construction and development projects is being undertaken across the Gulf Cooperation Council countries (Bahrain, Kuwait, Oman, Qatar, Saudi Arabia, and the UAE). www.imf.org/external/pubs/ft/weo/2008/01/index.htm www.meed.com
16. Airlines under pressure	The global airline industry continues to struggle to achieve profitability. After years of losses, the industry posted a profit of around $5.7 billion on a turnover of around $500 billion in 2007. However, rising energy prices have put pressure on

Title	Description
	margins and—according to the International Air Transport Association (IATA)—the sector is on course for a net loss of between $5 to 10 billion for 2008. The industry is currently carrying net debt of around $200 billion. www.iata.org
17. Rapidly increasing energy demands	The IEA (International Energy Agency) predicts that world energy demand will be 57 percent higher in 2030 than it is today. Hydrocarbons will remain the dominant source of primary energy, accounting for 84 percent of the overall increase in demand between 2005 and 2030. Chinese and Indian petroleum imports are expected to quadruple by 2030, further complicating today's global supply "crunch." Coal consumption is expected to jump by 73 percent between 2005 and 2030, with increased demand in China and India. Analysts such as the OECD expect that $22 trillion in investment in energy supply infrastructure is needed to meet projected global demand. www.finfacts.com/irelandbusinessnews/publish/article_1011728.shtml
18. Rising energy costs driving search for alternative sources	With crude oil prices rising to unprecedented levels, both business and government are aggressively seeking new forms of alternative energy, including biofuels, hydrogen, and renewables. With some analysts forecasting that oil prices could rise from up to $130 to $200 per barrel, the expectation is that investment in alternative energy sources could accelerate. www.altfutures.com/news/Nov07.htm
19. New generation hydroelectricity/ocean power	A new generation of free-standing turbines could liberate U.S. hydroelectricity from its dependence on dams. According to New Energy Finance, investments in companies proposing to make or deploy free-standing turbines rose from $13 million in 2004 to $156 million in 2007. Projects already underway include American Verdant Power's installation of a tidal turbine in New York's East River, as well as pilot projects in Nova Scotia with UEK, OpenHydro, and Canadian Clean Current. www.economist.com/science/tq/displaystory.cfm?story_id=10715508
20. The end of cheap food	Global demand for food is rising faster than the means of production. Approximately 1 billion people live on $1 a day. If food prices rise by 20 percent, 100 million more people could drop to this level, the common measure for absolute poverty. In real terms, food prices globally have jumped by 75 percent since 2005. A key driver is raising consumption in the developing world—the Chinese consumer, who ate 20 kg (44 lb) of meat in 1985, ate over 50 kg in 2007. The rising costs of food could lead to stagnant economic growth and is already a cause of civil unrest, with riots over food prices taking place in 30 countries at the start of 2008. www.economist.com/opinion/displaystory.cfm?story_id=11050146 www.globalpolitician.com/24162-economics www.economist.com/opinion/PrinterFriendly.cfm?story_id=10252015
21. Continued growth in spending on homeland security	Governments and businesses worldwide spent $59 billion in 2006 on homeland security. The market for security goods and services is expected to increase to $178 billion by 2015. Another major attack such as 9/11 has the potential to increase total spending to $730 billion. Major industries and aspects of everyday life could see a decrease in the availability of funding to support private- and public-sector programs and services. www.usatoday.com/money/industries/2006-09-10-security-industry_x.htm
22. The rise of Asian tourism	The World Tourism Organization estimated that nearly 37.5 million Chinese tourists travelled abroad in 2007, a 17 percent increase over 2006. They

Title	Description
	forecast that this could rise to 100 million per year by 2020. MasterCard estimate that 400 million Chinese and Indian citizens will have sufficiently high incomes to travel overseas by 2015. Online travel planning is poised to take off in Asia. By 2010, India alone will account for more than $2 billion in internet bookings, according to Euromonitor. www.traveldailynews.com/pages/show_page/23672 www.economist.com/theworldin/forecasts/industry.cfm?d=2008
23. Growth in the global travel and tourism industry	Global tourism hit 565 million visitors in 1995 and reached 898 million in 2007. World Travel and Tourism Council estimates growth to triple to 1.6 billion in 2020. East Asia and the Pacific, Asia, the Middle East, and Africa are forecast to record growth at rates of over 5 percent yearly, compared to the world average of 4.1 percent. The more mature regions of Europe and Americas are anticipated to show lower than average growth rates. www.unwto.org/facts/eng/vision.htm
24. Market for software as a service to rise	The web is quickly transforming from a collection of websites to a platform for business services. New developments in SaaS (software as a service) and "cloud utility" computing are set to solidify as a business model. This approach to "renting" and running software applications over the internet could support enterprise and association operations ranging from human resources and finance through to customer relationship management. SaaS is forecast to grow substantially over the next five years; by 2011, 25 percent of new business software could be delivered as SaaS. www.intelligententerprise.com/blog/archives/2007/08/
25. The rise of mobile payment industry	52 million consumers are forecast to adopt new mobile technologies such as NFC (near-field communication) and other physical mobile payment methods to pay for everyday goods and services by 2011. This could help drive the physical mobile payments market to $11.5 billion. By 2011, around 12 percent of the total mobile phones in circulation are expected to offer support for contactless payment—specifically, NFC—equating to nearly 470 million NFC-enabled handsets worldwide, creating a significant marketplace in which retailers will be able to offer goods via mPayment (mobile payment) applications. Pioneering "mobile-banking" projects are underway in the Philippines, Kenya, and South Africa and might grow quickly in regions that have traditionally lacked banking infrastructure and services. www.paymentsnews.com/mobile_commerce/ http://crmindustry.blogspot.com/2007/11/over-fifty-million-consumers-to-pay-for.html www.juniperresearch.com
26. Growth of infrastructure to support microfinance (microlending)	Microlending was initially introduced via the Grameen Bank as a finance strategy for small communities in developing economies. Today there are a growing number of microfinance providers emerging around the world and an increasingly sophisticated web-based infrastructure of applications such as www.kiva.org that support person-to-person lending for entrepreneurial efforts. Popularity is expected to continue to grow among global audiences who do not have access to banking services and among individuals seeking a lower-cost alternative to financing. www.marketwatch.com/news/story/demand-micro-financing-far-outstrips
27. Reverse brain drain	Companies will continue to struggle in attracting global talent into the United States. Tightened post-9/11 visa regulations have contributed to the reduced

Title	Description
	numbers of doctoral students from Europe and Asia entering the United States. In 2007 American colleges and universities received 27 percent fewer graduate applications from international students than in 2003. F-1 visas issued to international students fell 10 percent between 2001 and 2005. www.informationweek.com/story/showArticle.jhtml?articleID=205601557
28. Stagnant incomes	According to IRS data, Americans earned a smaller average income in 2005 than in 2000, the fifth consecutive year that they had to make ends meet with less money than at the peak of the last economic expansion. Although incomes have been on the rise since 2002, the average income in 2005 was $55,238, nearly 1 percent less than the 2000 figure of $55,714. http://bigpicture.typepad.com/comments/2007/08/real-income-fai.html www.commondreams.org/archive/wp-content/photos/0801_05.jpg
29. U.S. illicit trade grows unabated	Americans spend more on illegal drugs than on cigarettes. Although the nation's largest legal cash crop, corn (maize), produces about $19 billion in revenue, "plausible" estimates of the value of marijuana crops reach $25 billion. The total number of illegal immigrants is estimated at about 8 million, and many are being paid cash in the shadow economy that is estimated to be worth around 10 percent of the U.S. GDP. www.guardian.co.uk/usa/story/0,12271,947880,00.html
30. Market share in cross-border higher education declining	In 2000 the United States accounted for 26.1 percent of the higher education (degree-level and beyond) market, but by 2005 it had fallen to 21.6 percent. Other major countries were more or less stagnant— suggesting the U.S. fall has been due to tougher visa regulations and strengthening education systems in the traditional supplying countries, such as India and China. www.economist.com/world/international/displaystory.cfm?story_id=10143217
31. Growing popularity of "death bonds"	In the late 1980s and early 1990s, a market called "viatical settlements" appeared. This was essentially terminally ill people (largely AIDS patients) selling their long-term life insurance policies to pay for short-term medical procedures and treatments. The value of this "life settlement" market reached $10 billion by 2005 and was estimated at $30 billion for 2007. Projections expect that the industry could eventually be worth $160 billion. www.nowandnext.com/?action=sector/view&issueId=18&sectorId=9
32. Growing role for "creative class" workers in knowledge economy	Economists continue to monitor the rise of millions of "cultural creative" workers involved in higher-value aspects of the knowledge economy (e.g., design, gaming, entertainment). Creative economic strategies are starting to take root in places such as Korea, where leaders aim to make the creative economy at least 10 percent of GDP within the next two decades. www.culturalcreatives.org
33. Increasing numbers of innovation hotspots	The next decade is expected to see growth of geographically oriented industry clusters as knowledge workers gather to generate creativity and ensure an efficient labor market featuring collaboration, competition, and social networks. www.defra.gov.uk/science/ForwardLook/default.asp
34. Emerging standards and methods for full-cost accounting	Companies are responding to growing pressures for full transparency and accountability of business operations for their impact on society, politics, and the environment. New externalities such as carbon costs, water

Title	Description
	consumption, and energy usage are starting to be calculated in relation to product development and distribution. www.baylor.edu/bbr/index.php?id=10181
35. Continued long working hours among the global workforce	A study by the International Labor Office estimates that one in five workers around the world—or over 600 million persons—are still working more than 48 hours a week, often merely to make ends meet. An estimated 22 percent of the global workforce, or 614.2 million workers, are working "excessively" long hours. www.ilo.org/global/About_the_ILO/Media_and_public_information/Press_releases/lang—en/WCMS_082827
36. High-technology manufacturing industries continue to grow in Asia	The world share of value-added revenue of high-technology manufacturing industries for selected Asian countries grew from 35 percent in 1989 to 41 percent in 2005. During that same period, China's share increased from 2 to 16 percent, and Japan's share decreased from 29 percent to 16 percent. www.nsf.gov/statistics/seind08/c6/tt06-07.htm
37. Increase in importance of branding	Branding is increasingly a key element of "lifestyle" consumption patterns that reflect self-identity and aspirations, with fashion and style seen as critical components of any product. Producers will increasingly be "flexibly specialized" in order to meet fashion and style demands. Government agencies, nations, cities, and associations are increasingly focusing more attention on their branding strategies. www.wfs.org/next25/
38. Increased emphasis on "glocalization" for new product strategies	Organizations are paying heightened attention to local, national, and international contexts as the power of consumers increases and mass demand fragments into a focus on self-identity styling and branding. Local brands may become even more important, with small producers gaining cachet from localized branding. This may increase the vigor of rural and community economies. www.defra.gov.uk/science/ForwardLook/default.asp
39. Increasingly "smart" IDs and credit cards; evolution of digital cash	Smart cards will continue to evolve and replace IDs, cash and keys. People will increasingly carry their medical history and insurance information on smart cards. The range of security applications will grow: smart cards will remember computer passwords, store flight IDs for enhanced airport security, and be secured through retinal scan images and biometrics (e.g., fingerprints and DNA). The debate will continue as to whether it is more secure and efficient to store all data on a single master ID card or to maintain multiple cards. Vendors will push in the direction that best uses their offering in this growth market, particularly if they believe theirs could be the single card (e.g., major credit card companies). www.smartcardalliance.org www.gemplus.com www.smarttrust.com www.epic.org http://egov.gov

Socio-demographic Trends

Title	Description
40. Increasing migration	Global migration is on the rise; legal migrants alone may account for some 200 million people, or 3 percent of the world's population by the end of 2008. It is estimated that the West will receive an average of almost 1.6 million inward migrants from Asia and Africa every year from now until 2050. www.economist.com/theworldin/international/displayStory.cfm?story_id=10120091
41. Increasingly urban world	2007 was the first year during which more of the world's population (3.2 billion) lived in urban rather than rural areas. By 2030, over 4.6 billion people are expected to live in urban areas. Most of that growth is occurring in developing countries and in many other countries as well, primarily along coastal regions. By 2015 there will be 23 megacities with populations over 10 million. http://knowledge.allianz.com/en/globalissues/demographic_change/urbanization/urbanization_cities.html
42. City life is getting faster	City life is getting faster. Using residents' walking speed as an indicator of the pace of life, research has ranked Singapore, Copenhagen, and Madrid as the world's most frenetic cities. The study found that globally, people's walking speeds have increased by 10 percent over the last decade, with the biggest increases in the Far East. In Singapore, walking pace rose by 30 percent and in Guangzhou, China, the figure was 20 percent. http://news.bbc.co.uk/1/hi/world/asia-pacific/6614643.stm
43. Emergence of "slow" cultural movements	Leading cultural observers continue to see a spreading of aspects of the "slow movement" that seeks to counter the current day realities of a fast-paced, 24/7, always-on, always-connected society. The Slow Food movement promotes the enjoyment of more traditional, unprocessed, regionally produced foods. Other submovements include Slow Cities, Slow Travel, Slow Schools, and Slow Money. http://news.bbc.co.uk/1/hi/technology/4682123.stm www.slowmovement.com/ http://en.wikipedia.org/wiki/Slow_Movement
44. Ethical consumption	Consumers are increasingly applying ethical and moral filters in making purchasing decisions. Rather than focusing on traditional consumer variables such as price, quality, and convenience, buyers are considering ethical, religious, and political beliefs in their decisions. www.iconoculture.com
45. "Participatory panopticon"	Surveillance and privacy issues will continue to be front-and-center during the digital age. Individuals equipped with mobile network devices such as camera phones, webcams, and GPS-enabled cell phones are creating a "participatory panopticon" of self-surveillance that will redefine the parameters—and value—of personal privacy. www.openthefuture.com
46. Increasing corporate investment in the education system	The private sector is increasingly investing time and money in education in the United States and beyond. For example, Intel spends more than $100 million annually to educate more than 4 million teachers in 35 countries about how to incorporate technology into lesson plans. ExxonMobil sends current or retired employees into public schools via its

Title	Description
	Science Ambassadors program to serve as math and science teachers. In the company's Houston home base, more than 500 ambassadors volunteer in 22 schools.
	The Microsoft-designed "School of the Future" opened its doors in 2006. The school has a high-tech building and a learning process modeled on Microsoft's management techniques. The high school uses an "education competency wheel" patterned after a set of desirable traits Microsoft encourages among its employees. Officials, teachers, and students are trained in a range of skills, including organizing and planning, negotiating, dealing with ambiguity, and managing relationships. The project was paid for by the Philadelphia School District at a cost of $63 million. www.microsoft.com/education/schooloffuture.mspx
47. Reading on the retreat	The National Endowment for the Arts found that among 17-year-olds, the number of nonreaders went from 9 percent in 1984 to 19 percent in 2004. On average, Americans aged 15–24 spend only seven minutes of their daily leisure time on reading. www.writingthatworks.com
48. Increasing demand for university enrollment despite rising costs of tuition	The number of students in U.S. higher education institutions will continue to expand. By 2013, total university enrollment is expected to increase approximately 19 percent from that at the start of the century. This increased enrollment will continue despite the steady rise in tuition fees—an average rate of 10 percent yearly at public universities, far outstripping inflation. www.uri.edu/pspd/PP_Slides/Trends_and_Planning.ppt
49. Increasing expectations for higher education to contribute to workforce development for the knowledge economy	Demand will increase for "just in time" learning and customized "just for you" learning. Changing needs of the population will drive demand for more education for more people more often. Interdisciplinary learning is expected to become more widespread and essential. Experiential education will become increasingly important as a means to supplement both traditional classroom and online learning. www.uri.edu/pspd/PP_Slides/Trends_and_Planning.ppt
50. U.S. ranked last among industrial nations on preventing premature deaths	The United States ranks last among 19 industrialized nations in preventing deaths by assuring access to effective healthcare, according to researchers at the London School of Hygiene and Tropical Medicine. They estimate that more than 100,000 lives per year could be spared if U.S. performance equaled the top-ranked countries on effective healthcare measures: France, Japan, and Australia. All other nations showed significant improvements in preventing premature deaths, but progress in the United States slowed. Health Affairs (January–February 2008), The Commonwealth Fund
51. Number of disabled Americans to almost double by 2025	By the year 2025, the number of Americans aged 65 or older will expand from 35 million to more than 65 million, according to the U.S. Census Bureau. Individuals in that age group are more than twice as likely to have a disability as are those aged 16–65. If that figure remains unchanged, the number of disabled people living in the United States will grow to 24 million over the course of the next 20 years. www.wfs.org/next25/
52. Neurological disorders to rise steeply	Globally, neurological disorders such as dementia and Alzheimer's are on the rise: every year there are 4.6 million new cases of dementia, making it one of the leading health concerns of developed nations, with over 24 million sufferers worldwide. The number of cases is forecast to double every 20 years.

Title	Description
	By 2040, the world could have more than 81 million people suffering from dementia. www.alzheimers.org.uk/site/scripts/news_article.php?newsID=24
53. Happiness becomes an industry	A marked rise is expected in self-help and coaching services designed to improve individuals' senses of well-being. According to psychiatrists, 270 afflictions and 51 mood disorders can cause people "psychic distress" or similar discomfort. More than 35,000 books have been published on the topic of happiness. Harper's (U.S.), May 2007, "Manufacturing Depression," G. Greenberg. www.harpers.org
54. Life expectancy gap between U.S. and global average begins to close	In 1980 the average American could expect to live some 13 years longer than the global average. By 2020 the gap will be at or below 10 years. http://earthtrends.wri.org/pdf_library/country_profiles/Pop_cou_840.pdf
55. Coastal migration of U.S. population	In the United States, over 50 percent of Americans live in 772 coastal counties. By 2025, nearly 75 percent of Americans are projected to be living near a coast, with population density doubling in some areas, such as Florida and California. www.ruf.rice.edu/~soci/corrul/coastalcities.html www.economist.com/world/na/displaystory.cfm?story_id=10534077
56. Obesity epidemic	Between one-half and two-thirds of men and women in 63 countries across five continents—not including the United States—were overweight or obese in 2006. The World Health Organization forecast that by 2015, approximately 2.3 billion adults globally will be overweight—and more than 700 million obese.
	The cost of obesity to U.S. business is approximately $13 billion annually in direct health costs combined with the costs of disability, absenteeism, and lost productivity. U.S. companies today are paying about 8 percent more in health claims costs alone because of overweight and obesity. http://news.bbc.co.uk/1/hi/health/7057951.stm
57. Global impact of infectious diseases continues to pose high risks	About 30 percent of all deaths are caused by infectious diseases. The most common infectious disease in the world today is the hepatitis B virus, which affects 2 billion people. AIDS is the fourth leading cause of deaths in the world; 25 million people have died from AIDS, with 2.9 million deaths in 2006 alone. Globally, 34.1–47.1 million people have HIV, of whom 3.6–6.6 million were new cases during 2006. More than 30 new and highly infectious diseases have been identified in the last 20 years. Furthermore, 20 known strains of diseases have developed resistance to antibiotics, and old diseases have reappeared, including cholera, yellow fever, plague, dengue fever, meningitis, hemorrhagic fever, and diphtheria. www.millennium-project.org/millennium/Global_Challenges/Gc-08.html
58. Endemic surveillance society	Despite political shifts in the U.S. Congress, surveillance initiatives in the United States continue to expand, affecting visitors and citizens alike. In terms of statutory protections and privacy enforcement, the United States has the lowest ranking of any country in the democratic world. In terms of overall privacy protection the United States is out-ranked by both India and the Philippines and falls into the "black" category, denoting endemic surveillance. http://blog.wired.com/27bstroke6/2007/12/worlds-top-surv.html
59. Gated communities	About 40 percent of new homes in California are being built in some form of secured community. The analysis of the Census Bureau's 2001 American Housing Survey shows that more than 7 million households—about

Title	Description
	6 percent of the national total—are in developments behind walls and fences. About 4 million of these are in communities where access is controlled by gates, entry codes, keycards, or security guards. www.usatoday.com/news/nation/2002-12-15-gated-usat_x.htm
60. Increasing role of religion in public life	Globally religion is increasing its role in public life. The proportion of people attached to the world's four biggest religions (Christianity, Islam, Buddhism, and Hinduism) rose from 67 percent in 1900 to 73 percent in 2005 and may reach 80 percent by 2030. This growth and increasing influence is attributed to the "failure" of secular "isms" (i.e., communism and capitalism) to provide "solutions" and also a popular revolt against elitist secularism (i.e., courts legalizing abortion, homosexual marriage, etc.). Globalization is also considered a driver of this trend, for faith tends to act as a barrier against change (e.g., Turkey's political battle between secular and fundamentalist parties). *Economist*—"*The New Wars of Religion*" November 3, 2007
61. Rise of global media brands leads to greater scrutiny	Today's world of 24/7 news on politics and economics is leading to a rise of influential global media brands such as *AL-Jazeera English*, *BBC*, and the *New York Times*. The International Center for Media and the Public Agenda conducted a study to determine how transparent news outlets are based on correction of mistakes, editorial process, and news sourcing. Among those with global brand recognition, the *Guardian* (UK) and the *New York Times* were at the top of the list, with *Al-Jazeera* (English) and *Sky News* (UK) at the bottom of the rankings. www.icmpa.umd.edu/pages/studies/transparency/main.html
62. WHO reports "Global Tobacco Endemic"	The World Health Organization Report (2008) on the global tobacco epidemic warns of a possible 1 billion premature deaths related to smoking in the decades ahead. The recent study revealed that 5.4 million people die each year—one every six seconds—from lung cancer, heart disease, or other illness directly linked to tobacco use. Smoking killed 100 million people in the twentieth century, and the yearly death toll could pass 8 million by 2030—80 percent of those deaths in the developing world, where tobacco use is growing most rapidly.
	According to the report, nearly two-thirds of the world's smokers live in 10 countries—China, India, Japan, Indonesia, Bangladesh, the United States, Brazil, Germany, Russia, and Turkey. China alone accounts for nearly 30 percent of all smokers worldwide. Currently, only 5 percent of the world's population lives in countries that have any antismoking policies in place—predominately in Western Europe. www.who.int/tobacco/mpower/en/ www.time.com/time/health/article/0,8599,1711154,00.html
63. Advertising is becoming more pervasive, targeted, and immersive	The boundaries between advertisements and entertainment are blurring, leading, for example, to the growth of "contextual ads" specific to a location or activity and an individual, courtesy of personal GPS systems. Public service announcements (PSAs) will find it hard to compete for citizen attention in this new advertising environment. Because of this, PSAs could become much more expensive if they, too, have to follow the personalized, immersive route. On the positive side, contextual public service announcements, targeted at specific locales, activities, environments, and times of year, could be much more effective.

Title	Description
	Advertising will become increasingly selective and personal, offering unique individual choices not possible before immersive advertising. Manufacturing will become very personalized because of the increased amount of consumer feedback in response to personalized marketing messages. www.techtv.com/shopping/booksandvideos/story/0,23350,3393545,00.html
64. Depopulation trends challenge several nations	Despite rising inward migration from poor to rich countries, several industrial nations, including Germany, Japan, Austria, Spain, Italy, Sweden, and Greece, are experiencing a contraction of their working populations. Soon after 2010, the EU and Japan are expected to enter a period of population decline lasting for the foreseeable future. According to the U.S. Census Bureau, by 2030 the EU can expect to have 14 percent fewer workers and 7 percent fewer consumers than it does today. In Japan, over the same period, the numbers of workers and consumers are poised to decline by 18 percent and 8 percent, respectively. This will have an impact on economic growth and challenge secondary economic factors such as housing prices. It could put tremendous pressure on national governments to increase immigration. www.globalaging.org/health/world/depopulationeuropejapan.htm

Technological Trends

Title	Description
65. Anticipating the "Biotech Century"	Biology is expected to be a major driver of change across a number of major industries beyond those focused on human health. Biotechnology is being applied to things such as energy production (e.g., algae that produce biofuels or hydrogen, and in manufacturing to generate microorganisms that produce fibers and plastics). Although the last half of the twentieth century was shaped largely by information technology, the next fifty years might be defined by wider applications of biotechnology. Governments, researchers, and leaders are becoming more proactive in addressing the ethical and environmental implications of these disruptive technologies. www.foet.org/lectures/lecture-biotech-century.html
66. Genomic and proteomic sciences could transform the 21st century	Genetic advances could transform human, animal, and plant healthcare. All the genes in the human genome and the underlying protein structures are likely to be mapped, leading to new understandings of—and perhaps treatments for—human genetic diseases. Through genomics it becomes possible to evolve medical systems to a regime of "predict and prevent" from "diagnose and cure." Developments include gene replacement therapy, widespread genetic screening, the use of human tissue to grow replacement organs, and gene–gel stimulation for the regrowth of natural teeth on demand. An individual's genome may become part of his or her medical record. www.defra.gov.uk/science/ForwardLook/default.asp
67. Advances in health science—such as stem cell treatments—will raise new ethical debates	Technological advances such as gene manipulation and the use of human stem cells are fueling global debates about the religious, cultural, moral, and political implications of emerging health technologies. www.counterbalance.net/stemtp/index-frame.html

Title	Description
68. Personalized medicine	Breakthroughs in gene-based products and services are rapidly entering the market. Personalized mapping of an individual's genome is now commercially available for less than $1000. The correlation of specific genes and proteins with specific conditions, such as cancers, Alzheimer's, and heart disease will allow physicians and patients to anticipate and mitigate DNA-based health challenges. New "Web 2.0"–style peer health groups are also emerging in the consumer marketplace (e.g., patientslikeme.com, whoissick.org, and revolutionhealth.com). Their aim is to provide patients with far greater understanding of their conditions and with more detailed insights into alternative treatment regimes and their effectiveness. www.nature.com/embor/journal/v8/n10/full/7401070.html
69. Global AIDS epidemic might be leveling off	New data shows that the global percentage of people living with HIV has leveled off and that the number of new infections has fallen, in part as a result of anti-HIV programs. www.who.int/mediacentre/news/releases/2007/pr61/en/index.html
70. Growing acceptance of "functional foods"	Many consumers are turning to "functional foods" with added supplemental benefits to support healthier lifestyles. Functional foods include additives that claim to improve body performance or combat certain vitamin deficiencies (e.g., Vitamin C Orange Juice, Echinacea Tea, "smart" beer, and vitamin-enriched carrots). Californian market researcher Global Industry Analysts predicts that the functional food and beverage market will reach $109 billion by 2010. Today, the United States, Europe, and Japan account for approximately 90 percent of global consumption of functional food and beverages. www.foodnavigator-usa.com/news/
71. Web surfing speeds might begin to slow down	Although the internet is not about to grind to a halt, as more and more users sign up to download music, video clips, and games while communicating by email, chat, and instant messaging, the information superhighway may experience a dramatic slowing of access and surfing speeds. Spam accounts for 90 percent of traffic on the internet. www.economist.com/displaystory.cfm?story_id=10410912&fsrc=RSS
72. Narrowing global digital divide	The digital divide may be starting to narrow. PC ownership in the Middle East and Africa is forecast to rise to 17 percent of the population in 2008 from 7.2 percent in 2007, its biggest jump on record, because of lower taxes, falling prices, and government initiatives to get PCs into schools. www.economist.com/theworldin/forecasts/INDUSTRY_PAGES_2008.pdf
73. Visualization technology opens up new possibilities	3D visualization approaches are offering the potential to revolutionize a range of industries. For example, in medicine, comparing 3D images of an individual patient's heart against a database of other patients' images should enable far more precise diagnosis and treatment. www.ibm.com/ibm/ideasfromibm/us/five_in_five/12312007/index.shtml
74. IPTV challenges traditional broadcast television	Internet Protocol TV enables television and/or video signals to be distributed to subscribers or viewers using a broadband connection over Internet Protocol. This presents opportunities to make the TV viewing experience more interactive and personalized and to deliver highly interactive and personalized education content. The IPTV set-top box (STB) market in North America and Europe is expected to see strong growth up to the end of this decade with revenues for the two regions forecast at $765 million by 2010. www.iptv-news.com/content/view/1637/64/ http://en.wikipedia.org/wiki/IPTV

Title	Description
75. U.S. science and engineering PhD graduates are increasingly born outside of U.S.	In 1966, U.S.-born white males received 71 percent of science and engineering PhDs, U.S.-born females earned 6 percent of those degrees, and foreign-born students received 23 percent. By the year 2000, U.S.-born white males received just 35 percent of science and engineering PhDs; 25 percent of those doctorates were awarded to females and 39 percent to foreign-born students. In electrical engineering, 55 percent of master's and 67 percent of PhD graduates in 2005 were foreign students. www.nber.org/digest/jan05/w10554.html www.competeamerica.org/resource/h1b_glance/
76. U.S. maintains leading edge in engineering talent over China and India	Despite higher numbers of graduated "engineers" in China and India, a recent Duke University study found the results misleading when considering 4-year trained "employable" engineers. The graduate numbers are also not put into the larger context of each country's demographics, as *World Energy Monthly Review* noted. "China has roughly four times the population of the United States, and India is approximately three times as large. With those numbers factored in, the United States actually produces more bachelor-degreed engineers per million citizens (468.3) than do China (271.1) and India (103.7) combined." http://timesofindia.indiatimes.com/Number_of_engineers_in_India_inflated_says_study/articleshow/2841365.cms www.galeschools.com/article_archive/2007/01/engineers.htm
77. Shifts in engineering employment require new skills and knowledge base	The engineering industry is seeing a shift of employment from large companies to small and medium-sized companies and a growing emphasis on entrepreneurialism. Engineers are also being employed in nontraditional, less technical engineering work (e.g., management, finance, investment, patents, marketing, and policy). http://best.me.berkeley.edu/~aagogino/papers/NSB2005.pdf
78. Pervasive computing/ "Age of Sensor-based Computing"	Technologists are already designing products for the "post–personal computer" age. Using cheap sensors, almost every device or object in consumers' lives could be both smart and networked, giving rise to an "internet of things." Pervasive computing will drive the convergence of computing, the internet, voice communications, and television, ultimately blurring categories of infotech products and services. http://changewaves.socialtechnologies.com/home/2007/11/20/top-12-areas-for-technology-innovation-through-2025.html
79. Emergence of brain-to-machine interfaces	In the United States, clinical trials have begun on a new technology called the BrainGate Neural Interface System, which has been developed by Professor John Donoghue from the Department of Neuroscience at Brown University. The idea is to use the power of human thought to operate computers and other equipment. www.nowandnext.com/?action=sector/view&issueId=18&sectorId=3
80. Brain sciences become mainstream	Brain science is a rapidly growing discipline with an expanding knowledge base and increasing role in marketplace applications beyond traditional healthcare. The aim is to develop deeper understanding into the cognitive factors that drive our behaviors and decisions. Applied brain and cognitive research is used by a range of professions from marketers to workplace productivity consultants and transportation researchers. http://agelessmarketing.typepad.com/ageless_marketing/2005/03/brain_science_i.html

Title	Description
81. U.S. dropping further down rankings in global broadband league	The United States now ranks 15th out of 30 leading nations in per-capita broadband use—down from 12th place in 2007 and dropping from 4th in 2001. At the start of 2008, about 44.6 percent of U.S. households subscribed to a broadband service. Between June 2001 and June 2006, the number of homes with broadband in the United States increased by 599 percent from 9.2 million to 64.6 million. During the same period, the use of satellite and wireless broadband grew by 5,998 percent. www.freepress.net/press/release.php?id=226
82. Growth in use of Voice over Internet Protocol (VOIP) on mobile phones	The opportunity for VoIP in the United States on "dual-mode" mobile phones that can work over both the mobile network and Wi-Fi networks will increase as the number of units in use rises from 913,000 in 2006 to a forecast 22 million by 2011. www.allbusiness.com/services/business-services/4524783-1.html
83. TV programs migrating online	Forrester forecast that nearly half of all North American adults online—38 percent of the population—would watch at least some TV online in 2008, making online TV watching as common as online shopping. www.forrester.com/rb/research
84. Market for location-based mobile services to emerge	Morgan Stanley estimates that 20 percent of U.S. mobile phones currently include the satellite-based Global Positioning System (GPS) navigation aid—a number that is expected to grow to 50 percent within five years. This suggests that a critical mass of end users may have emerged to encourage the rise of location-based mobile services (LBS) that take advantage of GPS. http://venturebeat.com/2007/12/20/us-tech-trends-for-2008/
85. Rise of "embedded-expertise" software challenges professional services	Expert systems are goal-oriented software applications that use external knowledge to guide users through the stages of completing a task. The most common examples are QuickBooks and Turbo Tax, which in essence turn everyday users into bookkeepers and low-level accountants. Software developers are starting to embed expertise into programs and services across a range of industries. Airplane mechanics routinely use expert systems to diagnose and solve problems in real time. As software programs become "smarter," users may no longer feel the need to purchase professional services. http://edutechwiki.unige.ch/en/Expert_system
86. Growing economic value of personal metadata	Business futurists and technology pundits are now exploring potential business models and emerging issues around a plausible idea—individuals selling personal "metadata" to companies seeking insights into their own behavior, values, and consumer patterns. Metadata includes information related to personal profiles, web surfing behavior, purchases, hobbies, and activities. www.fastfuture.com
87. Emergence of new techno-logical disciplines and industries	Workers in the coming decades will respond to an emergence of unique professions based on innovations in nanoscale science and engineering and shifts in the global knowledge economy. New disciplines, including MEMS (microelectromechanical systems), mechatronics, biomechatronics, and organic electronics could become future growth industries. Major industries such as chemistry, energy, transportation, and medicine will see the emergence of new specialties that require new skills and knowledge bases. http://www.nap.edu/catalog/12055.html

Environmental Trends

Title	Description
88. Increasing species extinction	According to the World Resources Institute, the 21st century could witness a biodiversity collapse 100–1,000 times greater than any previous extinction since the dawn of humanity. www.wfs.org/Nov-Dec%20Files/TOPTEN.htm
89. Soil erosion limits food production	Although more than 99 percent of the world's food comes from its soil, experts estimate that each year more than 25 million acres of crop land are degraded or lost as rain and wind sweep away topsoil. UN figures suggest that an area big enough to feed Europe has been so severely degraded in its nutrient value that it cannot produce food. www.guardian.co.uk/conservation/story/0,13369,1148083,00.html
90. Overfishing	The diets of 2.6 billion people depend on fish as a source of animal protein. However, fish stocks are now declining, and some fish are even on the brink of extinction because of overfishing. It is estimated that more than 70 percent of the world's fisheries are overexploited, and several fisheries have already collapsed. www.globalvillage2006.org/en/find_out_about/sustainability/fisheries_and_overfishing
91. Climate change impact on infrastructure	A new report from the U.S. National Research Council explores the impact of climate change on domestic infrastructure. Every mode of transportation in the United States will be affected as the climate changes. The greatest impact on transportation systems may be the flooding of roads, railways, transit systems, and airport runways in coastal areas because of rising sea levels and surges brought on by more intense storms. www.sciencedaily.com/releases/2008/03/080311120617.htm
92. Energy-related carbon emission to grow by 25 percent to 2030	U.S. energy-related emissions of carbon dioxide (CO_2) are forecast to increase by 25 percent over the period 2006–2030. www.eia.doe.gov/oiaf/aeo/trends.html#growth
93. The rise of carbon markets	The World Bank reported that the carbon market more than doubled in value in 2007 to $64 billion from $31 billion in 2006. Credits representing some three billion tons of CO_2 emissions traded hands, mainly involving European Union Allowances (EUAs) or CERs. Carbon "cap and trade" markets exist in Europe and are likely to be established within the United States within the next few years. Beyond utility-scale carbon trading markets, organizations and individuals are increasingly participating in markets such as TerraPass and Carbon Fund as a way to demonstrate their ecoawareness. www.theglobeandmail.com/servlet/story/RTGAM.20080514.wrcarbon14/BNStory/energy/home
94. Policy makers continue to push new carbon technologies	The world currently produces about 22.3 gigatons of CO_2; this is projected to reach 38 gigatons by 2030. To help address this growth and the associated risks to the planet, large-scale carbon capture systems and next-generation "zero-emissions" coal plants are being explored, but they are still in the early stages of development and investment with all the inherent risks of unproven technologies. Future costs will come not only from the development and adoption of alternative power solutions (e.g., coal gasification, fuel cells, synthetic fuels) and CO_2-capture technology development but also from additional investments in power plants, CO_2 pipelines, and injection wells.

Title	Description
	A recent estimate suggests that compared to power plants without carbon capture systems, investment costs for those adopting such measures can increase by 28–78 percent for coal plants and 75–118 percent for gas plants. www.iea.org/textbase/speech/2004/haug/vancouver.pdf
95. Energy imports still key to the U.S. economy	Net imports of energy are expected to continue to meet a major share of total U.S. energy demand through 2030. Rising fuel prices over the projection period are expected to spur increases in domestic energy production and to moderate the growth in demand, tempering the projected growth in imports. www.eia.doe.gov/oiaf/aeo/production.html
96. Peak oil scenarios are explored	The phrase "peak oil" is used to describe a condition such that the amount of oil that can be extracted from Earth in a given year begins to decline as geological or production capacity limitations are reached. In a post–peak oil world, the costs of oil will rise sharply as supply rates diminish. There are several peak oil scenarios. The most optimistic is a "managing peak plateau" in which global production peaks and is sustained along a plateau, then declining gradually thanks to technology advances enabling greater efficiencies and conservation. The most negative scenarios involve a "peak and crash" outcome in which the world economy is crippled by rapidly falling reserves, resulting in increasingly high energy costs. www.theoildrum.com/node/2693
97. Personalization of energy solutions	Consumers are starting to take more personal steps toward environmental change by buying retail-level energy solutions. New software programs help homeowners manage their electricity and power consumption to avoid waste. Clean energy startups are developing decentralized power generation technologies such as thin-film solar roof panels, home natural gas generators and stationary fuels cells. Individuals can purchase "green" energy alternatives through most major utility providers or purchase their own carbon offsets. www.fastfuture.com
98. Emergence of bioenergy solutions	Researchers and entrepreneurs are in a race to make "next-generation biofuels" a reality. Companies such as GreenFuel Technologies, Solazyme, and PetroSun are using algae to produce energy. These carbon-eating algae absorb carbon from the air or from waste streams from local coal plants or industry centers, converting the energy into fatty acids that are converted into biodiesel. These bioreactors are a more economical alternative to biofuel feedstocks derived from food supplies such as corn, soybeans, and palm oil. http://news.cnet.com/8301-11128_3-9933355-54.html
99. Electric vehicles close to commercialization	In May 2008, Nissan stated its intention to commercialize an all-electric, zero-emissions vehicle for U.S. markets by 2010 and globally by 2012. General Motors and Toyota have stated similar plans with their Volt electric vehicles and Plug-in hybrids. New startups in the electric vehicle landscape include Tesla Motors, Gordon Murray Design, Fisker Automotive, and Zap. www.forbes.com/business/2008/05/19/nissan-nec-batteries-markets-equity-cx_jc_0519markets1.html
100. Floods to increase in African countries	The rapid urbanization taking place throughout much of Africa makes flooding particularly dangerous, altering the natural flow of water and cutting off escape routes. If global sea levels rise by their predicted 38 cm by 2080, the number of Africans affected by floods could grow from 1 million to 70 million. www.wfs.org/Nov-Dec%20Files/TOPTEN.htm

Appendix 3
The Strategic Choice Framework

1. Purpose, Strategic Direction, and Vision

Focus Area and Key Questions	Key Trends	Implications and Opportunities	Key Issues, Decisions, and Choices
1. **Current Context** *What is the current health and capability of the association?* *What are our strengths, weaknesses, opportunities, and threats?*	8. Funding and chronic diseases shaping healthcare challenges 13. Increasing interest in philanthropy and volunteer work 20. Energy: increasing demand and rising cost accelerate the search for alternative sources 23. Growing financial market risks and uncertainty 33. Education falling behind employers' expectations 41. Changing patterns of U.S. income, wealth, and savings	Associations may seek to test the viability of using their aggregated buying power to provide group membership plans for supplemental healthcare insurance or alternative coverage. Associations could promote their own volunteer leadership roles as an opportunity for individuals and employers looking for opportunities that combine service with personal development. Encourages associations to ask whether they are adopting best practices in energy efficiency and advanced energy-management solutions across all association activities, such as group buying, green fuels, eliminating the use of paper, ecolighting, carpooling, and selection of green venues. Faced with domestic uncertainty, associations may choose to innovate, explore new geographic and service markets, and experiment with new revenue and business models. Could open up opportunities to help close the gap between the capabilities of high school and college graduates and employers' expectations.	**Membership** • What does our membership profile look like? • How well we are serving current members—how do staff views compare to members surveys and perceptions? • What is the profile of members who are joining and leaving our association? • What kinds of people are stepping forward for volunteer roles—how representative are they of the membership demographics? **Strategy** • What are our emerging opportunities, risks, and liabilities (strategic, operational, HR, financial)? • What new market opportunities and potential sponsors are presenting themselves? How are these possibilities being perceived internally? • What does the emerging "competitive landscape" look like (e.g., online services, overseas associations developing a global reach, academic institutions and for-profit organizations extending existing offerings or entering our market niches)? • Where do we see ourselves on the spectrum of service provision in terms of target audience, price, added value, and channels? • Where do we see ourselves on the spectrum from personalized offerings to "one size fits all" solutions?

1. Purpose, Strategic Direction, and Vision (Continued)

Focus Area and Key Questions	Key Trends	Implications and Opportunities	Key Issues, Decisions, and Choices
		Opportunities to provide advice on confronting a wide range of emerging financial situations for U.S. workers (e.g., facing retirement with no savings).	**Operations** · What are the true costs, revenues, levels of cross-subsidy, and profitability of our various activities? What do the trend lines look like? · To what extent are we using reserves to finance current activity? How long could this continue? · What are staff perceptions of what's working and what's not? Where are the key tension points in our organization? Which services and activities are at breaking point? · What's the profile of forthcoming major-expenditure items (e.g., IT infrastructure and software, office premises, satellite offices, marketing campaigns, publications)? · What are our HR strengths and challenges—capability of current leadership and staff, areas of weakness, ease of recruitment, healthcare costs, age profile, suitability and sustainability of compensation and benefits structures, readiness for change? · How well is the current governance model working?
2. **Future Landscape** *How can we factor regular "environmental scanning" into our strategic and operational decision making?*	16. Social media explosion creating new approaches for engagement, communication, publishing, and marketing 38. Evolution of tomorrow's company	Social web tools could build stronger relationships and facilitate deeper information exchange about the future among association staff and with members, particularly those involving a large body of knowledge, a broad web of moderators/facilitators, "expert" contributors, and highly decentralized participants. Potential leadership role for associations in facilitating strategic conversations and	**Environmental Scanning of Issues and Trends** · What formal or informal mechanisms do we have in place to scan for and evaluate the drivers of strategic and operational change for our members? · How can we encourage and institutionalize the processes for staff, volunteers, and members to identify trends, ideas, and developments in the environment that suggest endings, new beginnings, or uncertain outcomes

1. Purpose, Strategic Direction, and Vision (Continued)

Focus Area and Key Questions	Key Trends	Implications and Opportunities	Key Issues, Decisions, and Choices
		leading collaborative research to ensure that associations understand the forces and factors shaping the future, the impact on members, and the implications on members' needs of the associations that serve them.	for the professions or sectors we serve? **Applying Knowledge and Foresight** · What changes in the environment will have the greatest impact on members, their needs, and our ability to serve them? · Should we create a core set of alternative "scenarios" or "future landscapes" to support our environmental scanning efforts and strategic conversations?
3. **Purpose** *What role should our association play for citizens, society, business, and the nation in the 21st century?*	14. Deepening personalization of products, services, communications, and experiences 46. Diminishing U.S. political influence internationally	Personalization places major pressures on an organization's business models, product costing, and pricing strategies; can be highly labor intensive; and does not eliminate the need to provide quality service. Associations with international aspirations may have to accelerate their global development plans if they are to meet members' needs and achieve their ambitions for international service delivery, reach, and influence.	**Exploring Value-Added Roles for Associations** · What is the primary purpose of this association? · What are the key ways in which we want to add value? · What role should we be playing in helping to drive innovation and renewal in existing professions and industries? · Do we have a role in helping facilitate or incubate the creation of new professions, new industries, or new ventures in existing sectors?
4. **Members** *Do our members see the association as a vital partner in their personal and strategic development? Which other target segments in society do we want to attract?*	3. Rising life expectancy, aging global populations 26. Future U.S. growth fueled by rising immigration 47. Emergence of India and China as global powers and "spokesnations" of the developing world	Challenge of shaping membership strategies (e.g., communication, retention, recruitment, programs, and services), leadership development, and workforce strategies to cater to potentially increasingly wide variation in the age and geographic origin/base of members and association staff. Associations may want to collaborate on researching the tendency of immigrants to join associations, what their prime needs are, and	**Whom to Serve** · Should we only focus on those who are currently members and seem to find value in our offerings? · Should the membership mix reflect the changing ethnic makeup of the United States? If so, what are the needs of those segments that have proved harder to attract? · Should we aim to serve the increasingly diverse needs of a multigenerational society, from Millennials seeking full self-expression and engagement through retiring Baby Boomers to those working past retirement age because of economic necessity?

1. Purpose, Strategic Direction, and Vision (Continued)

Focus Area and Key Questions	Key Trends	Implications and Opportunities	Key Issues, Decisions, and Choices
		their interest in volunteering and taking on leadership roles. How do we best meet the needs of the non-U.S. constituency through service offerings, membership categories, chapter structures, policy positions, and communication strategies? For example, should membership be a single rate globally, or priced in local currencies at the same proportion of member income throughout the world?	**Understanding and Serving Member Needs** · How can we get beyond surface stereotypes and access research that helps us understand how our membership needs may segment and the shifts taking place in attitudes, expectations, work styles, professional development needs, and attitudes to volunteerism and association membership? · With rising life expectancy, what services should we offer to the retired and semiretired, and what are the long-term cost implications of lifetime membership? · Should we be developing services targeted at the needs of entrepreneurs in our profession or sector? · How can we manage member expectations about what can be delivered for their membership dues while still retaining their interest and support? **Recruiting New Members** · To what extent do we need to reinvent ourselves to reach those who have been reluctant joiners? · Given rapid changes in communications preferences and technology usage, what strategies and tactics will associations need to adopt to recruit new members? · How can we learn from those who've proved effective at running "word of mouth" campaigns via the internet and social networks to recruit customers?
5. **Serving other Stakeholders** *With which other stakeholder groups in society do we wish to*	6. Increasing political and economic impact of diversity—minorities one third	Rising diversity will continue to shape old and new traditions and test the attitudes and tolerance of individuals and communities for absorbing new	**Expanding our Base of Stakeholders and Social Policy Positions** · Who are our most important stakeholders—for example, are education associations there to serve education professionals,

1. Purpose, Strategic Direction, and Vision (Continued)

Focus Area and Key Questions	Key Trends	Implications and Opportunities	Key Issues, Decisions, and Choices
connect, and what impact are we aiming to have?	of the U.S. population 10. Increasing economic power of women 36. Global rise in entrepreneurship 50. Changing patterns of global governance—growing influence of non-state actors	populations into neighborhoods, schools, and work environments. It is imperative that associations ensure that they understand and adopt emerging best practices in terms of ensuring full and equal participation, opportunity, and reward for women in the workplace. How might global entrepreneurs and influential non-state actors change the landscape for businesses and non-governmental associations operating on the global stage? Greater demand from members seeking to understand and monitor the influence of non-state actors in key industry sectors and global markets.	students, or the wider society, and to whom do we have the greatest responsibility? · What are the pressures and expectations emerging from society, government, and other stakeholders as to what responsible associations should be doing for "the greater good"? · What is our social responsibility policy? To what extent should we be trying to address broader issues and needs in society—at a local, national, or international level?
6. **Global Ambitions** *What is our strategy for serving international markets?*	24. Rising economic strength of China and India, representing an increasing share of global GDP 25. Rise of the "Next 11" nations on the global stage 35. Global outsourcing market could hit $1.43 trillion: U.S. outsourcing deepens 40. Shifting patterns of global inequality and unmet needs 49. Increasing global role for single-party states	There is a large emerging market opportunity for associations to support their members—and the broader market—with training, advice, and guidance on how to do business and succeed in China, India, and other markets and for businesses from those markets looking to expand into the United States and Europe. The emergence of the N-11 nations creates an opportunity to provide guides and specific materials covering key economic, political, social, and cultural factors for members thinking of entering these markets.	**Global Agenda** · Do we have to look at international expansion, or is there a viable model for our association to stay domestically focused? · What do we want to achieve by going international? Where do we see ourselves on the spectrum from becoming a truly global association to staying as a U.S. association while tapping into profitable opportunities as they arise in international markets? · Can we serve international markets without changing our core offerings? · What assessment have we done of global markets? What do we need to know? Do we need to update our assumptions about threats and opportunities? Where can we access appropriate expertise?

1. Purpose, Strategic Direction, and Vision (Continued)

Focus Area and Key Questions	Key Trends	Implications and Opportunities	Key Issues, Decisions, and Choices
		Global integration requires changes in the paradigms and thinking of associations as many U.S.-based industries and companies enter an era in which sector leadership is not guaranteed and best practices, innovation, and winning business models could come from a range of geographic markets. Associations may increasingly be called upon to consider their social responsibility and to provide tangible solutions and support for global goals to address unmet need—possibly through initiatives such as the UN Global Compact. Operating or investing in a single-party state requires sophisticated analysis and good internal connections. The association community may want to undertake a community-wide evaluation on behalf of it is members.	**Aligning Global Operations & Business Models** · How are foreign membership rates and enquiries growing? What needs are those members expressing? · What could it cost, and how long might it take, to see a return on investment? How much are we prepared to invest to develop our international presence? · What are the opportunities to help countries looking for assistance from associations in providing content, conferences, and training and in helping build up industries and the professional skill base? · What are the support needs of U.S. individuals and organizations going overseas and foreign individual and organizational members coming to the United States? · What is the potential for providing content to—and partnering with—associations in more developed markets?
7. Culture *What kind of organization do we want to be?*	4. Widening generational gap: values, attitudes, behaviors, technoliteracy 12. Evolving trust: declining trust in government and media	A culture that supports a multigenerational environment holds potential for providing programs and services to help organizations handle intergenerational differences through best-practices guidance, education, and training focused on mentoring, succession planning, communication styles and media, negotiation, managing cross-generational employees and teams, conflict resolution,	**The Foundations of Organizational Culture** · What kind of culture are we trying to build? · What kind of culture, decision making approach, empowerment model, and staff development would be required to become the kind of organization we want to be (e.g., member-focused, growing, forward-thinking, entrepreneurial, agile, responsive)?

1. Purpose, Strategic Direction, and Vision (Continued)

Focus Area and Key Questions	Key Trends	Implications and Opportunities	Key Issues, Decisions, and Choices
		financial planning, and healthcare. Associations will face the constant challenge of remaining trusted and relevant in a world of changing values and attitudes.	
8. **Vision and Direction** *Where are we trying to take the association over the next 5–10 years?* *What would success look and feel like for our members and staff?*	26. Future U.S. growth fueled by rising immigration 39. Continued shift in global wealth and spending power 46. Diminishing U.S. political influence internationally	This domestic and global power realignment represents an opportunity for U.S. associations to explore previously unconsidered demographics and markets, developing new partnerships, expanding membership and operations, and providing and acquiring content and services from peer global organizations.	**Testing Vision & Strategic Direction against Changing Global Dynamics** · If we were successful in delivering on our purpose, what could that look like? · What difference would we be making for members and the communities and constituencies they serve? · Can our members and partners see what we can make possible for them? **Aligning the Organization with New Challenges and Opportunities** · What would be different from the way we operate today? What might stay the same? · Do our staff and board understand the kind of organization we need to be if we are to be successful in delivering our vision? · Are the decisions we are making creating or taking away future options?

2. Core Products and Service Offerings

Focus Area and Key Questions	Key Trends	Implications and Opportunities	Critical Issues, Decisions, and Choices
1. **Core Products and Services** *What is the core set of products and services that will add the greatest value for current and potential members?*	14. Deepening personalization of products, services, communications, and experiences 1. Generation Y (Millennials): digital, "civic," and connected 5. Baby Boomer retirement and unretirement; talent shortages	A fundamental rethink may be required of internal structures, budgeting, funding sources, and delivery models in order to provide personalized products and services. Personalization and market-driven solutions also require associations to take a fresh look at the biggest shifts in human talent and the policies for addressing recruitment, event design, development and retention, conflict resolution, attitudes toward work, mentoring, collaboration, and support for innovation.	**Assessing Strategic Needs** · What are the future strategic needs of the profession or sector we serve and of the economy and society as a whole (which individual members may not recognize as emerging needs)? · How are member needs evolving in terms of requirements for information, education, credentialing, networking, support, and preferred delivery channels and communication styles? · What are the offerings required by members entering retirement or partial retirement? **Competition** · What does the competitor landscape look like—do we understand how their offerings are evolving and why members choose them over us? · How can we differentiate our offerings from the competition? **Extending New Forms of Value to Members** · How can we extend the reach of our current product and service portfolio, both within the current membership base and to a wider audience? · What new offerings could become critical? Can they help us change the market perception of the association's positioning in the marketplace? · What value is placed on our current credentialing offering by individuals and employers? How could current offerings be extended to reflect changing marketplace needs? What new credentialing opportunities are emerging? · How can we develop cost-effective offerings for target market

Focus Area and Key Questions	Key Trends	Implications and Opportunities	Critical Issues, Decisions, and Choices
			segments that have limited financial resources or are harder to reach? · What are the criteria for withdrawing offerings from the portfolio? · How important will "green" considerations be in the choice and design of offerings?
2. **Global Offerings** *What is the core of offerings required to fulfill our international ambitions?*	2. Millennials increasingly seeking overseas experience 24. Rising economic strength of China and India, representing an increasing share of global GDP 25. Rise of the "Next 11" nations on the global stage 38. Global rise in entrepreneurship	Proactive associations may seek to create programs that generate overseas opportunities for their members and encourage overseas members to gain experience working in the United States. New opportunities may open up around the creation of associations serving different emerging markets and global entrepreneurial sectors and entrepreneurs from groups not currently served or considering joining an association.	**Determining Scope of Global Products and Services** · Which of the needs of customers in international markets can be met through existing products? What new product development is required? · How much tailoring is required of current products and services? What will it cost? How can we ensure the quality of adaptation or translation? · How do we price for customers in international markets—will cost models have to change to reflect local income and buying power? · What product development lessons can be learned from other associations that have "gone international"?
3. **Representation** *What distinctive and value adding representation role can associations play on behalf of members?*	4. Widening generational gap: values, attitudes, behaviors, technoliteracy 12. Evolving trust: declining trust in government and media 37. Rise in U.S. corporate and individual social responsibility 45. Rises in ecoliteracy, "green"	Representation on social, environmental, and industry issues will be shaped largely by a multigenerational and global stakeholder base, placing more pressure on associations to be a conduit to satisfy individual and corporate members' desire to "do good" and respond to expectations to meet changing societal demands for corporate responsibility. Creates the potential for monitoring and sharing best	**Assessing Needs and Association Capabilities** · What do members want and expect? What are the key topics on which we want to be a trusted voice, "taking a position" or exerting influence on behalf of our members? · Have we identified emerging issues that might soon arise as relevant to our members? · What are the areas in which we need to stimulate new thinking to challenge and develop our members' current perspectives?

2. Core Products and Service Offerings (Continued)

Focus Area and Key Questions	Key Trends	Implications and Opportunities	Critical Issues, Decisions, and Choices
	practices, and ethical consumption	practices, emerging issues, compliance strategies, reporting, assurance, and peer indexes, as well as facilitating debate and expertise sharing among members.	• What dialogue forums do we need to create to develop a consensus perspective among our membership? • How effective are the current lobbying techniques we and other associations use? What new channels and approaches are emerging? • How can we lobby in an increasingly complex environment full of competing pressures on public funding and regulatory authorities, well-funded professional lobbyists, and the growing role of the internet as a tool for corralling opinion and campaigning? • How do we get on the right "radar screens" and build a reputation as a "trusted brand" in the marketplace (e.g., well-researched and supported positions, clear and coherent arguments, balanced perspectives, long-term thinking and broader societal focus)?
4. **Sharing Foresight and Best Practice** *How can we help members prepare for the future through the provision of best-practice guidance and foresight materials?*	16. Social media explosion creating new approaches for engagement, communication, publishing, and marketing 19. Nanotechnology: the next trillion-dollar market? 21. Evolving personal technology "ecosystem": intuitive, visual, and smart	Social web tools offer a platform on which to reinforce foresight efforts by building stronger relationships and enabling deeper information exchanges among association staff and with members. Topics that drive conversations on the future will emerge from a range of new industries such as nanoscale science and engineering, biotechnology, and new information technology systems. Associations may seek to be central to and even facilitate the ethical,	**Evaluating Best Practices** • Is there a member need or requirement for providing guidance on best current practices and foresight on emerging trends, issues, and developments that could have a significant bearing on their profession or sector? • How do we help our members stay ahead of the curve and navigate the complexity of becoming more globally focused and market-oriented in their service offerings? **Expanding Association Roles in Strategic Conversations** • Should we become a research portal gathering a range of relevant information into a single location for members?

Focus Area and Key Questions	Key Trends	Implications and Opportunities	Critical Issues, Decisions, and Choices
		scientific, and commercial debates about new science and technology developments in their sectors and professions.	• How frequently do members need and want updating? Would a monthly insights newsletter be read and valued? • Is there a role in pooling member funding to finance collaborative precompetitive research and state-of-the-art studies? • What is the potential role of the member community in sharing best practices, environmental scanning, and the transfer of institutional knowledge? • Should we be trying to use social networks to build up communities of interest around best practices and foresight? • Could we bring nonmember experts into our member communities to share their insights?
5. **Community and Networking** *How do we want to develop the face-to-face, virtual community, and networking elements of our association?*	16. Social media explosion creating new approaches for engagement, communication, publishing, and marketing 21. Evolving personal technology "ecosystem": intuitive, visual, and smart 38. Evolution of tomorrow's company	In the years ahead, hundreds of millions of new users will come online and connect with each other using personal technologies that look very different from the ones we know today. "Smart applications" and more intuitive electronic hardware will change how we live and work in the world. Community building around this rapidly changing ecosystem raises the challenge of ensuring that staff stay up to date with the technology being used by members and society at large, as well as evaluating the resulting return on investment in hardware, software, and staff training.	**Expanding the Value of Communities** • How important will face-to-face and virtual community engagement, events, collaboration, and networking be to our members in future? What will they be willing to pay for? • As society changes, our community could become more diverse, dynamic, and possibly temporary; how best can we support the networking needs of members? • How will our notions and definitions of community change in the face of a growing range of segments we could serve based on gender, interest, geography, outlook, age, preferred communications and learning styles, and ethnicity? • How do we access expertise in new approaches to community building—recruit, build it up in-house, partner, or outsource entirely? • Given the rise in energy prices and time pressures, can we establish

2. Core Products and Service Offerings (Continued)

Focus Area and Key Questions	Key Trends	Implications and Opportunities	Critical Issues, Decisions, and Choices
			sustainable ultralocal chapters that fulfill both professional and personal networking needs? What support might they need from the center? Is there potential for collaboration across associations on this? **Exploring Roles and Protocols** · What role should associations play in the management of internal social networks? Should we define and manage the forums, or should we allow members to create and run them according to their own needs and interests? · Should we allow social networks and conversations to expand beyond core member circles? · How do we handle issues of honesty, decency, and privacy in a world of self-managing forums?
6. **Learning and Development** *How will we support the lifelong learning needs of members?*	9. Growing popularity of online education relative to that of classroom-based courses 29. Nations competing in science investment to drive economic performance 30. Growing economic importance of global knowledge economy—50 percent of U.S. GDP by 2010	Creates opportunities for associations to expand their role in delivering "just in time" educational and training services to members and major industry sectors. Could supplement (or replace) physical classroom–based courses delivered in traditional settings. Associations may seek to play an active role in tracking science and technology investment as R&D continues to drive long-term value creation and industry competitiveness. Challenge of ensuring association services and content are current and updated at the same pace industry knowledge and best practices are. Keeping up with societal expectations of what it	**Association Roles** · What role should we play in addressing the perceived shortfall in basic educational standards of high school and college graduates? · What research should we be doing on new models of skills development—from accelerated learning solutions through to complex problem-solving approaches for those at the top of their discipline? · Should we partner with industry to develop sector-level skills roadmaps? · How will the growth in telecommuting, freelancing, and collaborative ventures impact the vision and missions of associations? **Needs Assessment** · How are the core professional skill sets and soft skills requirements evolving for our target members?

2. Core Products and Service Offerings (Continued)

Focus Area and Key Questions	Key Trends	Implications and Opportunities	Critical Issues, Decisions, and Choices
		means to be a professional could create new training and development opportunities for associations.	• What new skills requirements are emerging, and how can we track them? • What particular learning needs emerge for firms wanting to compete in global markets? • How do we address the learning needs of those who are running organizations? **Delivery Models** • What business models and capabilities are required to support just-in-time learning? • Could we provide a platform through which members could define new requirements, evolve the course outline, aggregate their demand, invite providers to bid, and then select their preferred supplier? • How can we test performance and certify for new learning requirements? • What new delivery models and partners are required? Could we adopt the business-school model of lifelong learning for alumni? • How do we deliver on emerging requirements for interdisciplinary learning and experiential education?
7. **One Stop Shop** *Can we become an effective portal for third-party solutions to the information, education, and support resources our members need?*	14. Deepening personalization of products, services, communications, and experiences	Associations may see an opportunity in becoming a "one-stop shop" for a range of approved vendors who can provide personalized services to members. A new revenue stream could emerge from aggregating, interpreting, and reselling the data gathered regarding member's personalized choices.	**Needs Assessment** • How can we engage members in defining their current requirements and anticipating future needs? • What are the critical member needs that we cannot, or should try to, deliver in-house? **Partnerships** • Which third-party resources do members clearly value? • What is the right menu of third-party products and services to offer?

2. Core Products and Service Offerings (Continued)

Focus Area and Key Questions	Key Trends	Implications and Opportunities	Critical Issues, Decisions, and Choices
			• How do we evaluate potential third-party suppliers?
			• What should the business model be—should we charge a listing fee, transactional fee, commission, profit share or some combination of all of these?
			• What are the legal liability issues of presenting or endorsing third-party offerings?
			• To what extent could this cannibalize our own offerings?
			• Will members still make use of third-party offerings if we don't offer a consolidation function?
			• What value would members place on this consolidation role?
			Online Components
			• What are the implications for the design and maintenance of our website?
			• Where are these services emerging online? Are the providers competitors or potential partners? How might we form partnerships to leverage the opportunities?
			• Will personalization of services be inevitable if we go down the portal route?
8. **Markets of One** *What are members' expectations when it comes to the personalization of services? What new membership segments and market opportunities could we open up through the provision of*	14. Deepening personalization of products, services, communications, and experiences 21. Evolving personal technology "ecosystem": intuitive, visual, and smart	Personalization will establish a level of expectation among members. Associations must think through the longer-term implications of the choices they make today around offering the personalization of services.	**Changing Relationships between Associations and Members** • Personalization implies developing different kinds of relationships with members, adopting new methods for sharing information and continuously responding to changing members' needs. This requires different training for staff, an increased investment in technology, and dedication of research resources to track continuously evolving requirements. Are we prepared to go down this route?

2. Core Products and Service Offerings (Continued)

Focus Area and Key Questions	Key Trends	Implications and Opportunities	Critical Issues, Decisions, and Choices
personalization facilities?			· What do members want? What kinds of personalization of services will we need to deliver? Will this change our mission, or just our delivery strategy?

Supporting Personalization

· How can we engage members in selecting and defining the services that they would like to see personalized and the way in which it should be done?

· What does personalization mean in our context? How would or could we do it?

· What kinds of systems will we need to adopt to allow for complete customer relationship management, including an easy way to track key information on member needs and interests? What are the IT infrastructure and skills implications? Would such solutions have to be outsourced?

Assessing Effectiveness

· What could happen to membership numbers if we do—or do not—pursue personalization?

· What are the most effective examples of personalization we have witnessed?

· What level of support would we have to provide on an ongoing basis?

· What content would we provide? Would any of this need to come from third-party providers?

· How frequently should we update the content offered?

· Does personalization go hand in hand with offering a one-stop shop?

Focus Area and Key Questions	Key Trends	Implications and Opportunities	Critical Issues, Decisions, and Choices
9. **Life Solutions** *What role should we play for individual members beyond the information,*	7. Work–life balance 5. Baby Boomer retirement and unretirement; talent shortages	Associations may be expected to provide programs, services, and coaching solutions that translate the vision of "work–life" balance into a	**Assessing Life Solution Demands and Expectations** · What are the areas of greatest individual need with which members would or could trust us to help? What are the key areas in

2. Core Products and Service Offerings (Continued)

Focus Area and Key Questions	Key Trends	Implications and Opportunities	Critical Issues, Decisions, and Choices
networking, and professional development services we have traditionally offered?		reality. Given the range of life stages between younger Millennial generation and aging Baby Boomers, these solutions may require a higher level of personalization and interactivity.	which we could provide information, education, and mentoring that would be of genuine value to individual members (e.g., financial planning, debt management, preparation for retirement/unretirement, family issues, career coaching)? · Millennials emerging into the workforce already have far less distinct "work–life" boundaries; will this generation have a natural expectation for life solution services from associations? **Exploring New Services Models** · Could we leverage the aggregated buying power of our membership to secure deals on purchases such as energy, communications, healthcare/supplemental coverage, and insurance that would help bring down members' living costs? · How could we manage and deliver such services in a cost-effective manner? Would we seek to do it in-house or via third-party partners? · How would we address service failure and liability issues?

3. Delivery Model

Focus Area and Key Questions	Key Trends	Implications and Opportunities	Critical Issues, Decisions, and Choices
1. Channels *What is the right economically sustainable mix of delivery channels with which to serve current and target members in light of the growing multigenerational mix and its increasingly broad range of communication and technology preferences?*	15. Internet continues transforming government, governance, and business 16. Social media explosion creating new approaches for engagement, communication, publishing, and marketing 17. Rise in mobile and location-based web services as "smart" phones displace laptops	There is a growing expectation that association services should be delivered seamlessly via the web, evolving in a more personalized and social manner to incorporate member input and facilitate two-way engagement in the creation and distribution of content. Mobile platforms could become a new delivery channel for associations, attracting younger members (e.g., member alerts via text messages) and enabling personalized event experiences.	**Scoping Channel Benefits and Feasibility** · Do we want to service a full range of channels that could include print, online, mobile, live (local, regional, and national), virtual, 3D, video, and audio? · Given concerns about cost and the environment, how long will paper be a viable delivery channel? · How important will "green" considerations be in the choice of delivery channels? **Aligning Channels with Multiple Audience Groups** · If we are going to make increasing use of electronic delivery channels, how will we explain our reasoning to members and help the "unwired" members make the transition? · What delivery channels are appropriate for each of the different international markets we are targeting?
2. Technology *What are the key technological capabilities required to serve an increasingly diverse multigenerational membership?*	4. Widening generational gap: values, attitudes, behaviors, technoliteracy 15. Internet continues transforming government, governance, and business 21. Evolving personal technology "ecosystem": intuitive, visual, and smart	Potential to provide programs and services to help organizations handle intergenerational differences through best-practices guidance, education, and training focused on mentoring, succession planning, communication styles, and media; negotiation; managing cross-generational employees and teams; conflict resolution; financial planning; and healthcare. Growing expectation that association services should be delivered seamlessly via the web, evolving in a more personalized manner. There will also be increasing demand for web services to	**Evaluation** · What current technologies are critical for evolving our association and member services? · What developments should we expect to cater for in the next five years? · How do we engage members in defining our future technology offerings without skewing the solutions too much in favor of those who contribute most? · What capabilities will we require in-house to ensure effective evolution of our technology offering that supports our members' preferred way of living and working (e.g., collaborative work styles, increasingly mobile lifestyles, smart phones as "remote controls for life")?

Focus Area and Key Questions	Key Trends	Implications and Opportunities	Critical Issues, Decisions, and Choices
		be more open to member input and facilitate two-way engagement in the creation and distribution of content. Raises the challenge of ensuring that staff stay up to date with the technology being used by members and society at large, as well as evaluating the resulting return on investment in hardware, software, and staff training.	**Cost Considerations** · What level of cost should we expect to incur, whether we stay in-house or outsource? · If we go down the outsourcing route, what benefits could we gain in terms of speed of delivery, range of functionality, reliability, and cost?
3. **Social Networks** *How can we get the maximum benefit for members as a return on our investment in social networking?*	16. Social media explosion creating new approaches for engagement, communication, publishing, and marketing 4. Widening generational gap: values, attitudes, behaviors, technoliteracy	Offers the potential for associations to create new products and services born out of engagement with social media. Tools could be used to facilitate collaborative, team-oriented activities and projects and experiential learning activities—particularly those involving a large body of knowledge, a broad web of facilitators, "expert" contributors and moderators, and highly decentralized participants.	**Assessing the Range of Member Expectations and IT Capabilities** · What are the expectations of different member segments? · Have we researched the adoption patterns, usage, and preferences of the current membership segments? · What does third-party research tell us about how these patterns change over time? · How is the technology evolving? What will be the impact of developments such as the forthcoming incorporation of social network functionality into email programs and web browsers? **Application Considerations** · What are the opportunities? How can we use social networks for communication, engagement, education, cocreation, and member recruitment? · How can we use social networks internally and with volunteers to enhance product delivery, productivity, decision making, and team building and to bridge geographically separate teams and members? · Could effective engagement through social networks encourage people to participate in live events?

3. Delivery Model (Continued)

Focus Area and Key Questions	Key Trends	Implications and Opportunities	Critical Issues, Decisions, and Choices
			• How can we use social networks before during and after conventions, exhibitions, meetings, and educational and social gatherings to enhance the value of events? • How can we ensure that staff stay up to date with the technology being used by members and society at large? • What are the costs and benefits of developing in-house solutions rather than developing a presence on a range of third-party networks? • What are the low-cost approaches to experimenting with how such networks could be of benefit to our members? • Should we start with exploring third-party networks and building a presence in key ones to learn about their functionality and see who uses them?
4. **Responsibility** *How do we ensure that our association and its members conduct activities in a transparent, ethically sound, and environmentally sustainable manner?* *What is our broader societal responsibility?*	11. Growing role for "social entrepreneurship" 37. Rise in U.S. corporate and individual social responsibility 48. Increasing political and economic transparency	Creates the opportunity to positively promote social entrepreneurship and provide solutions that help members establish social ventures. Associations could evaluate best practices, risk assessments, and operational knowledge exchange as expectations for transparency and accountability spread beyond governments to private sector businesses and nongovernmental organizations.	**Determining the Scope of "Responsibility"** • How will common-use definitions of responsibility, transparency, and ethical practices evolve? • What is, and what will be, expected of associations from members and the broader community? • What standards and practices does society expect from members of professional associations? • What is the "brand value" of a clearly articulated and enacted stance on responsibility and transparency? • How will the notion of responsibility play out in the different international markets we are targeting? **Internal Policies** • What should our environmental goals be? How do we deliver these across our activities?

3. Delivery Model (Continued)

Focus Area and Key Questions	Key Trends	Implications and Opportunities	Critical Issues, Decisions, and Choices
			• Should we be signing up to public commitments and indices such as the UN Compact and the Transparency Index?
			• Where are we currently falling short of our own or society's expectations and needs?
			• How can we reflect and embed the desired standards in all our activities?
			• Should we be defining codes of responsible, transparent, environmentally sound, and ethical conduct with our members?
5. **Business Model** *What are the right models with which to support our association's progress over the next five years in a changing environment?*	34. Pay-as-you-go and "freemium" services becoming more prevalent business models 15. Internet continues transforming government, governance, and business	Associations could become more market-driven and explore the potential for pay-as-you-go and "freemium" approaches to expand the reach and sales of core services and third-party offerings.	**Reevaluating Current Business Models** • Do we, our board, and our members understand our current cost base, revenues, and cross-subsidies and the long- and short-run trends in these key figures? • Which aspects of our budget are under most pressure to date, or could be if current trends continue or accelerate? • If current member services are already highly subsidized by nonmember dues, then should we open up the potential market for additional services through lower dues and other classes of membership? • Should we abandon membership fees and move to a menu selection of pay-per-use services? How would we cover overheads? • What steps can we take to protect against the impact of an economic downturn or recession? **Exploring Alternatives** • What is the preferred mix of dues/nondues income to support our future plans? • Should all of our activities be economically self-sufficient?

3. Delivery Model (Continued)

Focus Area and Key Questions	Key Trends	Implications and Opportunities	Critical Issues, Decisions, and Choices
			• What are our strategies for locking in future revenues? Should we discount multiyear membership?
			• What are the right business models for the international markets we want to serve? Should we protect against possible currency fluctuations?
			• How can we monetize our content (e.g., selling videos of conference sessions after the event)?
			• Where could we start to experiment with alternative models?
			• What are the risks and benefits of staying with our current pricing structures and business models?

4. Organization Model

Focus Area and Key Questions	Key Trends	Implications and Opportunities	Critical Issues, Decisions, and Choices
1. **Resilience** *How do we ensure that our organization can withstand potential shocks in the system such as an economic downturn, rapid rises and falls in membership numbers, dramatic increases in travel costs, or the loss of key sponsors?*	18. Cybercrime, cyberwar, and cyberterrorism 23. Growing financial market risks and uncertainty 28. Growing challenge of maintaining physical infrastructure 22. Uneven economic growth 27. Rising U.S. personal and federal indebtedness	Faced with the growing risk of cybercrimes and domestic financial uncertainty, associations may choose to innovate, explore new strategies and new geographic and service markets, and experiment with new revenue and business models; others may become more risk-averse and less entrepreneurial. Creates the opportunity for associations to develop guides and "roadmaps" for global markets to identify opportunities around rising income groups—both for their members and for their own marketing efforts. Financially stressed members may question the return on their investment in membership dues with increasing vigor.	**Evaluating Risks** • What range of critical shocks and "wildcard" (low-probability, high-impact) events we should prepare for? • How can we formalize systems to monitor changes and anticipate potential disruptions? Can we engage members, volunteer leaders, and our board? • Is there potential for coordination across associations? **Anticipating and Preparing for Change** • What are our contingency plans for different types of risk? • What are the key early warning signals we should be monitoring? • How can we help members adopt the same kind of thinking to increase their resilience?
2. **Responsiveness and Agility** *How quickly can we respond to external changes and new member requirements?*	21. Evolving personal technology "ecosystem": intuitive, visual, and smart 32. Attractiveness of U.S. business environment weakens relative to that of other countries	Associations must respond to changes across a range of areas, ranging from information technology to generational shifts and a decline in U.S. competitiveness alongside the rise of other emerging economies, that could change the potential make up of membership demographics over a 10-year timeframe.	**Assessing Needs and Competitive Alternatives** • What can and should members expect in terms of responding to new and changing requirements? • Who in the marketplace are we being compared to? • How can we use third-party relationships—formal and informal—to give us greater flexibility and agility? • How will internal structures and decision making processes need to change to enable faster responses to changing member needs? • If we don't or can't respond at the speed members are demanding, what could the implications be? • What level of spare capacity/contingency do we need to build into our organization to

4. Organization Model (Continued)

Focus Area and Key Questions	Key Trends	Implications and Opportunities	Critical Issues, Decisions, and Choices
			ensure that we have the resources to respond quickly to evolving member needs? · Are we always looking for ideas and developments that could affect members, as well as for ways in which we could deliver current and new services and products to them?
3. **Sustainability** *Are we operationally, financially, and environmentally sustainable?*	42. U.S. organizations and investors focusing on green issues 43. Global consumption patterns challenge Earth's resource capacity 44. Climate change a growing political and economic priority globally 45. Rises in ecoliteracy, "green" practices, and ethical consumption	Opportunity for associations to provide environment-related products, services, and discussion forums for members, acting as a clearing house for the latest research and best practices. Opportunity also exists for helping to establish industry sector certifications, standards, and measurement strategies that can be tested by third parties who compare claims against actual environmental footprints.	**Defining Sustainability** · In practical terms, what does it mean to be economically, socially, and environmentally sustainable? · What do members expect, and which aspects of sustainability do they care about most in relation to our association? · What would a truly sustainable association look like? **Measuring Sustainability** · What key measures should we apply to tell us how sustainable we are and whether we are moving toward or away from our goals? · What are the aspects of our operation that are most sustainable or trending that way? Which are most in need of attention?
4. **Talent** *What critical capabilities do we require?* *How will we recruit, retain, and develop a staff that can serve the needs of a multigenerational and potentially international membership?*	1. Generation Y (Millennials): digital, "civic," and connected 5. Baby Boomer retirement and unretirement; talent shortages 31. Global talent shortages increasing with economic growth	The scale of the challenge creates an opportunity to develop and test a range of imaginative new solutions, such as improved event design, accelerated learning, improving worker knowledge and volunteer productivity, and facilitating improved knowledge management and exchange within and across industries and professions. Associations could take on the role of retraining their older members to reenter or remain in the workforce	**Assessing Talent Base and Gaps** · How does our current staffing profile fit the talent we need to deliver on our plans? · Where are the biggest gaps—and what are the priorities and possible solutions—in terms of gap closure? **Professional Development Strategies** · Could secondments be an option? Can we demonstrate that working on important roles in an association is an excellent contribution to an individual's personal and leadership development?

4. Organization Model (Continued)

Focus Area and Key Questions	Key Trends	Implications and Opportunities	Critical Issues, Decisions, and Choices
		(e.g., increased focus on lifelong learning, reward systems, compensation packages, volunteerism, performance reviews, securing knowledge transfer, and reaffirming personal relationships with partners and clients).	• How will our reward structure need to evolve to capture and retain the right talent? • What are our succession plans for key roles in the organization? • What will we do if we cannot recruit or retain the right level of talent? • What are the implications for the kind of HR function we require? Should we be trying to build it up in-house, or considering outsourced services?
5. **Partnerships** *What are the critical partnerships we will need to deliver our range of member offerings in the most effective and cost-efficient manner?*	6. Increasing political and economic impact of diversity—minorities one third of the U.S. population 13. Increasing interest in philanthropy and volunteer work 37. Emergence of India and China as global powers and "spokesnations" of the developing world	How reflective is association membership of the broader population mix in U.S. society? What strategies are required to address any perceived gaps? The rise in social volunteerism (and required community service) could change both the landscape of issues considered important on the national political scene and expectations for institutional support to assist this new level of civic engagement. Both India and China see the value of associations in building up civil society infrastructure, cocoordinating the voice of industries and professional groups, and driving up professional standards.	**Strategic Partnerships** • What current and future activities could and should we consider outsourcing (domestically and internationally) to give us the greatest flexibility, responsiveness, quality, and cost benefits? • How can we keep our partners involved and contributing to our strategic thinking? • What new delivery partnerships will we need to enable our goals as regards to flexibility, resilience, just-in-time on-demand solutions, one-stop-shop provision, and personalization? • What are the cost savings or increases that come with going down the partnership route? • What management model is required to support increasing use of third-party relationships? • What new service providers will we need as partners who can deliver additional and/or lower-cost services to association members in diverse global markets?
6. **Measurement** *What is the right set of performance measures with which to manage the association?*	37. Rise in U.S. corporate and individual social responsibility 44. Climate change a growing political and	Creates the potential to monitor and share best practices, emerging issues, compliance strategies, reporting, assurance, and peer indexes, facilitating	**Operations: Transparent and Accountable** • What are our critical success factors? What do we absolutely have to get right, and what are the critical measures of performance that would tell us how we are doing?

4. Organization Model (Continued)

Focus Area and Key Questions	Key Trends	Implications and Opportunities	Critical Issues, Decisions, and Choices
	economic priority globally 45. Rises in ecoliteracy, "green" practices, and ethical consumption	debate and expertise sharing among members. To be credible, associations may have to increasingly demonstrate their own dedication to responsible and sustainable business practices and take care of their own "triple bottom line"—member value (profit), staff and community (people), and the environment (the planet).	• What are the key early warning indicators that all staff should be tracking? • How do we know whether we are moving in the right direction on longer-term plans and projects? • How can we ensure that measures track outcomes, impact, and results and not just inputs, such as hours worked and costs? • Would ASAE & The Center's 7 Measures model help us establish the right measurement framework for where we are taking the association?
7. **Legal Structure** *What is the right legal structure to support what we want to do for our members, in the way we want to do it?*	18. Cybercrime, cyberwar, and cyberterrorism 48. Increasing political and economic transparency	Associations will need to plan for higher IT security costs as the range of cyberrisks grows alongside the increasing amount of personal data stored online. Associations could evaluate best practices (e.g., reporting standards) and model guidelines for operating inside nations with high corruption and poor transparency ratings. Transparency in how governments operate, set standards, and enact laws can only benefit American organizations seeking to expand into new markets. Creates the opportunity to provide country guides and risk assessments and facilitate knowledge exchange on international economies.	**Evaluating Legal Structures for the 21st Century** • What are the benefits and downsides of our current legal status? • What do members think about our legal structure, and do many of them care, so long as they are getting the services they want? • Could an alternative legal structure make it easier to achieve our goals? **Cost and Global implications** • What are the costs and servicing requirements for the alternative legal structures we might consider? • If we changed our legal status, what are the implications for how we would be perceived in the United States and in the key international markets we wish to serve? • What process would we need to go through to bring about the change in legal status?
8. **Organization** *What is the right managerial structure going forward to fulfill*	38. Evolution of tomorrow's company	Will encourage associations to look outside the sector at a range of alternative models.	**Assessing Organizational Capacities and Potential Partnerships** • What are the critical capabilities we need in-house and through third parties?

4. Organization Model (Continued)

Focus Area and Key Questions	Key Trends	Implications and Opportunities	Critical Issues, Decisions, and Choices
our purpose and deliver on our vision?			· What new capabilities do we need to recruit and/or develop to support changing requirements around community building, international expansion, technology development, and managing a portfolio of third-party relationships?
			Effectiveness and Implementation
			· How can we ensure efficiency and effectiveness? What can we stop doing in order to free time and resources for new requirements?
			· How can we adapt our working patterns to reflect different work styles and preferences of a multigenerational workforce (e.g., home working, working hours, communications styles, technology preferences)?
			· What is the right management structure to put around those resources to enable them to perform to full effect?
			· What kind of support infrastructure do we need in order to enable our governance structures to work effectively?
9. **Governance, Effective Strategic Boards, and Volunteer Leadership** *What is the right governance model and structure to drive the association forward?*	4. Widening generational gap: values, attitudes, behaviors, technoliteracy 38. Evolution of tomorrow's company	The presence of four generations in one work environment presents opportunities to blend the experience, knowledge, and social relationships of older staff, the innovative energy of youth, evolving business policies, and practices, and changing communication styles to work in a multigenerational environment. Creates an imperative for collaborative research to ensure that associations understand the forces and factors shaping the future,	**Governance** · What are the risks and benefits of adopting "off the shelf" governance practices and models? · How much effort should serving the board and governance matters consume? · What do members want and care about in relation to governance— how much of their dues are they prepared to spend on governance issues? · What is the right composition of the board in terms of size, experience, capability, and representation of the membership?

4. Organization Model (Continued)

Focus Area and Key Questions	Key Trends	Implications and Opportunities	Critical Issues, Decisions, and Choices
		the impact on members, and the implications on members' needs of the associations that serve them. Potential leadership role for associations in facilitating strategic conversations about the future of their sector or profession that addresses the opportunities and challenges associated with a changing environment and workforce dynamics.	• How should we be appointing, preparing, and assessing the performance of board members? How can we get boards to adopt a strategic focus when it may not be something they have experience of or know how to do? • What are the best practices in establishing lean and effective governance models? • How should we handle nonperforming board members? • What are the governance implications, and what new models do we require for serving international markets? • If we change our legal structure, what are the governance implications? **Strategic Planning** • What are the critical issues we want the board to focus on? • What time horizon should the board be looking at and planning for? • What is the right balance between a strategic and operational focus for the board? **Volunteer Engagement** • How do we encourage and support volunteering from all segments of membership? • Do we need a formal volunteer development structure that enables people to progress from chapter leadership to board participation?

Appendix 4
What You Can Do Tomorrow Morning

Immediate Actions—A Checklist

We recognize that some readers may want to step straight in and focus on immediate actions to address specific trends and challenges. Others who feel they do not have the time to work through the strategic choice framework may still want to take action where they can. In this appendix, we have presented a set of short summaries of actions you can initiate immediately in three areas:

- Identifying additional trends and drivers of change;
- Determining the implications; and
- Creating solutions.

Identify Additional Trends and Drivers of Change

- *Identify critical trends and assess their impact.* Start a process of regular scanning. **Pick out what stands out:** what trends will have the biggest potential impact on your members and what they need from your association? Discuss them internally and with staff and boards.
- *Encourage "environmental scanning"* by all management and staff. Have a prominently placed **"future wall"** for people to put up articles and ideas that could be of relevance; use them to facilitate discussion.
- *Encourage a culture of foresight.* Encourage all staff to focus on **what's coming next for members** and how you can help them prepare for it—don't wait for members to raise an issue before you start thinking about it.
- *Leverage what exists.* Use the internet to seek out scans at the profession/sector-level. Add these to the trends presented here and use the combined set as a **rapid start point for your own scanning and analysis,** adding to what those trends tell you rather than replicating what's already being done.
- *Ask the member.* Ask your members what the **5–10 top issues** are on their personal or business priority list. What are the **big trends** they see coming toward them? Brainstorm how you can help address those issues through your **member services and products.**
- *Develop member insight.* How can you identify the **"unarticulated needs"** that the trends may create, which members may not yet be aware of, or have not expressed? Don't rely on market research. **Simulations** and experiential learning activities can help provide insight into how members will react to new trends, and what they truly think and need help with.
- *Formalize foresight.* Set up regular **member foresight panels** to discuss the **future of their industries** and **cross-industry issues** such as leadership development, globalization, technology, and corporate social responsibility.
- *Scan for new sources of funding.* The rise in the **super-wealthy** has created a new breed of **philanthropists.** How can we identify these people and understand the issues on their priority list?

Determine the Implications

- *Look for the drivers of action*—In analyzing the trends, look for the biggest emerging **opportunities and threats**—how do your current **strengths and weaknesses** compare against those challenges?
- *Engage members in analysis.* Create forums where members can come and discuss the trends, helping you assess the impact on them, as well as the implications on their needs of the associations that serve them.
- *Timeline.* Develop a **timeline map** of the critical external trends and developments that will affect your sector and members over the **next 5, 10, and 20 years.** Use it to help determine the implications for members and their requirements of your association. It can also help in defining the services and delivery approaches you will need to offer in the future. Help your members develop similar maps for their industries.

Create Solutions

- *Map your personal future.* Use the exercise in Appendix 7 to think about your own future. If you can't see your own personal future, it is hard to work on defining a future for the organization.
- *Focus on the vital few.* Pick **1 or 2 key areas** that you want to focus your efforts on first—experimenting with the social networks, reducing costs, finding talent, using new technology, or developing member insight. Allocate some dedicated time to investigation—don't rush to action. Focus on understanding the issues first, and consider a range of alternatives.

- *Focus on members.* Put the **member** at the heart of your association. Involve members in the design of all new services and products.
- *Challenge your assumptions and practices.* Do a **"what if" session**—what if you had to run the association at half the current cost, with half the resource consumption, using half the energy? Force yourselves to look for **out of the box solutions.**
- *Think laterally.* Do you have capabilities or contacts that could help other organizations test new market needs and ideas or launch new products, which in turn would provide you with new insights and revenue opportunities?
- *Become an "idea magnet."* Look at your association through the eyes of outsiders with new ideas: **how easy is it for them to bring new ideas to you?**
- *Encourage "outside in" thinking.* Involve people from outside your sector when doing environmental scanning and designing your next proposition. Invite students from art and design colleges to share how they might design products or services to reach the younger generation and encourage networking.
- *Create "markets of one."* Members want more **personalization** from their suppliers. How can you build this into your propositions for members before, during, and after they engage with you?
- *Be responsive.* If people enjoy more **spontaneity,** how can you build it into your offerings? How quickly can you **develop new propositions** that respond to market moods and changes of priority?
- *Identify technological best practices.* Do some **research using the internet** to find examples of how others are using technology to reach new and existing markets (e.g., social networks, online exhibitions, virtual worlds, podcasts, webcasts, etc.). Share the insights with members to test their interest.
- *Integrate technology.* If people want to lead increasingly **mobile lifestyles,** how will that impact your offerings? Can you integrate their laptops, PDAs, iPods, and Blackberrys into your product or service offering? Go and look at others who are already doing this—see how it's working.
- *Join social networks.* Register on forums such as www.linkedin.com and www.xing.com and start learning how they are being used across a range of industries. Join in the discussions—ask network members around the world to tell you about the best services and products offered by the associations in their local markets.
- *Look for environmental savings.* Investigate how you can **reduce costs** for you and your members by reducing waste, energy use, and carbon emissions. Look for initiatives already underway in your members' industries. For ideas, go to websites such as www.greenbiz.com.
- *Encourage sharing of best practices.* Create online forums that enable your members to **share their expertise** with each other. Do it across the different types of roles and industries represented in your membership base.
- *Adapt to changing lifestyles.* If **people are living longer** and there are increasing numbers of **older people** in society, what special **needs might they have? How can you accommodate them?**

Appendix 5
Scenario Analysis Workshop

Objectives

This workshop process is designed to be used with any group that wants to think about how the emerging economic scenarios could affect its association and the resulting choices and challenges that would be created.

Approach

The workshop can run as a two-hour, half-day, or full-day session—with time allocations being adjusted accordingly. The framework shown below assumes a half-day discussion.

1. Plenary Group Activity—Framing the Exercise

- Be clear at the outset what the objectives are—you are using predefined scenarios that help you assess the implications for the association. The aim is not to challenge the scenarios or to write new ones. (5 minutes)
- Ideally, have the group read all four scenarios before they arrive. If this is not possible, allow them to review the scenario outlines at the start. (15 minutes)
- Have a brief group brainstorming session to identify any additional descriptive criteria that need to be covered for each of the scenarios (e.g., inflation figures, unemployment levels, number of new jobs being created, etc.). Agree upon the list of additional criteria—try to keep this to a maximum of five. (10 minutes)
- As a group, agree upon the list of impact questions you want to cover. (A number of example questions are included below.) Brainstorm any additional ones, and agree upon those that must be covered for all scenarios. Aim for a maximum of 10–12 impact questions. (15 minutes)

2. Breakout Group Activity—Scenario Analysis

- Break the participants into four breakout groups and have each of them take one of the scenarios and discuss it, adding their views of what would be happening to each of the additional criteria under this scenario (e.g., unemployment levels). (30 minutes)
- Within the breakout groups, work through the list of impact questions, capturing how you think they would be answered under that group's allocated scenario. (60 minutes)

- Break after one hour to let the teams go around and read each others' answers. This can help the facilitator ensure that the questions are being answered with the same clarity and to the same level of detail in each breakout group. (30 minutes)

- Return to the breakout groups and have them finish off the review of impact questions, documenting all their answers as they go. The breakout groups should then select the following to share with the entire group: (15 minutes)
  - Two to three key implications for the association's strategy
  - Two critical actions that emerge from their analysis of the scenario that they think should be pursued no matter which scenario might transpire.
  - Two actions that should be pursued under their particular scenario.

3. Plenary Group Activity—Feedback and Prioritization

- Each breakout group would then be given a maximum of five minutes to share its feedback. (20 minutes)
- Working as a plenary group, review the list of strategic implications and action recommendations. Either through discussion or voting, prioritize the list of implications and critical actions and agree what the next steps will be in taking these forward. (30 minutes)
- A group discussion could then be used to assess the value of the day and how best to institutionalize such a process.

4. Close the Workshop

Some may want to use the exercise to drive specific action, and others may want to use it as part of a broader strategic planning process. This will determine the extent to which specific actions can or should be committed to in closing the workshop.

Scenario Impact Analysis Questions

Select from this list those questions that will add the most value in developing your future strategy. Ask these questions for each of the scenarios you are looking at.

Impact on Members

- What would be the impact on economic prospects and levels of confidence in the economy?
- What will the impact be on the professions or sectors we serve?
- Which segments could grow or decline under this scenario?
- What kinds of new competitors could emerge for our members domestically and internationally? What would be the implications for our members?
- What will it take for our members to stay in demand and remain competitive?
- What impact would it have on their requirements of the associations that serve them?

Impact on the Association

- What critical roles could associations play in society and the economy?
- What new membership segments could open up? Which could become difficult or impossible to serve?
- What products and services could be required? Which could be in decline?
- What could be the preferred delivery channels?
- Where could new opportunities open up for associations? Where might doors be closing?

- What would the implications be for costs, revenues, and profitability?
- What new competitors could emerge to our association? Which existing players may want to move into our niche?
- What will it take to stay competitive?
- Which new skills and capabilities will we require? Which might become less relevant?
- What critical delivery partnerships will be required?
- What will be the implications for volunteer leadership and boards?
- What will be our critical success factors?

Scenarios for 2013

These are four scenarios or "stories about the future." They are not forecasts or predictions. They are outlines of ways in which the key parameters shaping the global economic environment *might* play out in the period to 2013. The aim is to help the reader test the strategies of his or her association, nonprofit, or organization to see how robust those strategies might be under each scenario, identifying opportunities and risks that we should be addressing today.

Parameter	Scenario 1 "Love is in the Air"	Scenario 2 "Suspicious Minds"	Scenario 3 "Dancing in the Dark"	Scenario 4 "Highway to Hell"
Political Outlook	Global tensions kept in check. New U.S. president in 2008 seeks to reestablish relations with international partners.	Political and economic tensions increase with China's rise and growing Russian reluctance to follow the U.S. and European line on key issues. Developing nations look increasingly to China to argue their case on major issues. Europe and U.S. become closer after new president elected.	Increasing isolationist pressures in U.S. results in gradual withdrawal from multilateral institutions while reserving the right to defend its security abroad. Strengthening of ties between increasingly assertive China, India, ASEAN, Middle East, Africa, and Latin America.	U.S.—European splits are found to be more deep-seated than just disagreements over foreign policy. Resurgent Russia and assertive China result in multipoles of power.

Parameter	Scenario 1 "Love is in the Air"	Scenario 2 "Suspicious Minds"	Scenario 3 "Dancing in the Dark"	Scenario 4 "Highway to Hell"
Average Global Economic Growth to 2013	Global Growth averages 4–5 percent through 2013.	Global growth stalls at 4 percent over the period, sustained by rapid rises in Asia	Global growth declines to 2 percent because of increasing inflation, short recessions in key markets, and increasing conflicts over trade barriers.	Global growth rate falls to 0 percent because of deepening recession in Western economies, sharp declines in Asia, and rising energy and food prices.
Global Economic Outlook	After major problems in 2008 and early 2009, strong global confidence returns. Asian and African markets continue to develop, and the United States, Japan, and Europe return to stable growth of 2–3 percent per annum by 2013.	Global growth increasingly fuelled by China's and India's growth—at over 8 percent—pulling other developing countries along with them. Competition from emerging economies drives down margins, profits, and growth in Europe, Japan, and the United States. Constant concerns about recession throughout the period.	Virtually zero average growth in U.S., Japan, and Europe; China and India slow to 6–7 percent and most developing economies see declining growth. Some collapses among the poorest and fastest-growing economies.	Recession and stagnation in the United States, Japan, and Europe challenges China's largely export-based economy. China's slowing growth has a significant recessionary impact on many of its supplier nations in Asia and Africa.
Emerging Markets Outlook	Chinese and Indian growth continues at over 8 percent. India addresses infrastructure concerns. Strong growth across Asia at over 5 percent. Increasing signs of economic progress and optimism in Africa.	Domestic market development and increasing internal consumption in China in particular, combined with continued external market development leads to strong growth for most developing economies. Emerging markets play increasingly important role on the world stage. Concerns increase over overheating, inflation, and poor	Global economic slowdown causes recession in some emerging markets. Disparities across regions and classes maintained. Increasing concerns over rising unemployment in China and India as both fail to create sufficient jobs for their growing labor markets (20–25 million new jobs required each year).	Global recession affects emerging market's exports to Europe and North America. Most emerging markets stagnate or go into recession. Some of the weakest or most unstable economies collapse.

Parameter	Scenario 1 "Love is in the Air"	Scenario 2 "Suspicious Minds"	Scenario 3 "Dancing in the Dark"	Scenario 4 "Highway to Hell"
		credit in several fast growth economies.		
International Trade	Basic agreement on current round of WTO talks.	The United States and China fail to resolve most differences on trade and tariffs. China's trade surplus widens with U.S. and Europe. Russia begins process of joining WTO, but no agreement on DOHA round and a new "clean sheet" round of talks is initiated.	The world becomes increasingly split into primary resource economies and consumer societies, exacerbated by China's resource consumption. U.S. punitive tariffs toward China seen to be hurting U.S. as much as China. WTO process sidestepped by bilateral agreements between nations.	Open trade war between more isolationist U.S. and China. WTO collapses, global institutions such as IMF and World Bank largely ignored by developing nations who look to strengthen local institutions such as Asian and African development banks. Middle East states step in to bolster finances of these institutions.
Energy Outlook	Concerns about peak oil recede as new fields identified. Oil prices stabilize at $80–100 per barrel. Increasing use of alternative fuels.	Increased global growth drives oil price and demand. Severe weather causes regular disruption to U.S. refining, causing short-term spikes in prices. European nations accelerate switch to alternative sources and construction of nuclear facilities.	Energy demand stabilizes as a result of zero or declining growth in many key markets. Short-term economic concerns slow progress on alternative energy and construction of new energy infrastructure.	Tensions in Iraq, Iran and Nigeria, plus increasing impact of severe weather on U.S. oil facilities, lead to global oil price instability and rising prices. Little progress on alternative technologies or construction of new energy infrastructure.
Business Outlook	Confidence in Western markets returns toward the end of 2009, particularly among firms with a solid long-term foothold in Asian markets.	Clear divides begin to emerge. Strong performance achieved by many of the businesses that have developed effective globalization models and	Declining global business confidence. International firms with high levels of economic and environmental efficiency considered best positioned to	A decline in consumer spending in a U.S. beset by subprime woes and the resulting foreclosures, negative savings,

Parameter	Scenario 1 "Love is in the Air"	Scenario 2 "Suspicious Minds"	Scenario 3 "Dancing in the Dark"	Scenario 4 "Highway to Hell"
		penetrated multiple emerging markets. Those that focus purely on the domestic United States, Japan, and Europe face increasing price and cost pressures and falling demand in key markets. Increasing number of globally strong competitors emerge, from Asian markets in particular.	withstand market volatility. China and India, in particular, increasingly favor local firms and joint ventures with local partners over wholly owned foreign enterprises. To stem short term losses, many major firms withdraw from all but the most profitable emerging markets and consolidate footholds in domestic markets.	high levels of consumer debt, and declining spending tilts the world into recession, taking the rest of the world with it in a "domino effect."
Shareholder Drivers	Although earnings per share (EPS) and share price growth remain key priorities, shareholders start placing greater emphasis on global footprint, environmental performance, employee retention, innovation, and R&D expenditure	Shareholders struggling with tensions over maintaining financial returns in the face of market uncertainty while meeting increasingly demanding ethical and environmental expectations. Shareholders increasingly wary of investing in firms with any environmental issues.	Short-term concerns predominate over environmental and ethical factors. The talk of "soft economics," trust, and other factors that cannot be easily monetized diminishes, leading to a refocus on solid numbers and a reversion to EPS and share price growth.	Shareholders increasingly focused on costs, EPS, dividends, and firms' ability to withstand recession.
Incomes	Dramatic Y-on-Y increases in incomes in high-growth economies. The United States, Europe, and Japan see real term income growth of 2–3 percent over the period.	Dramatic Y-on-Y increases in incomes in high-growth economies U.S. and Europe see zero or small real terms gains	Average U.S., Japanese, and European incomes stagnate or decline. Emerging market income growth slows with economic growth. Some economies in recession experience major falls in average income.	The spreading of debt by investment banks across the financial markets creates a bubble of debt that, when burst, severely reduces expenditure. Average incomes slashed as companies shed workers to stay afloat.

Parameter	Scenario 1 "Love is in the Air"	Scenario 2 "Suspicious Minds"	Scenario 3 "Dancing in the Dark"	Scenario 4 "Highway to Hell"
Customer Expectations	Customers increasingly placing ethical factors, environmental concerns, and CSR in their top three purchasing criteria across purchase categories. Consumers increasingly willing to pay premium prices for brand, quality, and environmental performance in most geographic and product markets.	Customers increasingly expect higher standards of ethical and environmental performance in all markets but show an increasing reluctance to pay a premium for these benefits. Concerns over recession in the United States, Japan, and Europe lead to some softening in demand for premium products.	Customer expectations in the emerging markets focus on performance, price, and usability, rather than ethics or the environment. Although environmental and ethical concerns remain strong in Western markets, few customers show a willingness to pay for these.	Low cost becomes the order of the day. Customers only remain committed to ethics and the environment so long as their wallets support it. Rhetoric is not matched by action.
Socio-demographic Forces	Continued population growth across the globe. Rising aging population, particularly in Europe, Japan, and the United States, increased longevity forcing lifestyle changes.	Aging becomes a worldwide issue after breakthroughs on the prevention and treatment of malaria and AIDS, raising the issue of elder-care costs for economies everywhere.	Populations in Europe, Japan, and the United States continue to age, and birth rates decline in the face of economic concerns. Progress on tackling major diseases in developing markets slow as economic issues force a resource shift.	Poorly enforced monitoring systems lead to a worldwide pandemic that decreases life expectancy and population levels for a decade.
Public Attitudes to Environmental Issues	Increasing pressure on governments to regulate poor performers. Customers increasingly boycott firms with weak environmental records and poor brand image.	High-profile "single environmental issue" campaigns proliferate, with big business the prime target.	Stagnation in the Western world, coupled with more pressing concerns about poverty and other such issues in other countries, ensures environment remains a concern but not a priority.	Awareness of environmental issues, but short-term concern over personal incomes, recession, and education dominate the public's attention.

Parameter	Scenario 1 "Love is in the Air"	Scenario 2 "Suspicious Minds"	Scenario 3 "Dancing in the Dark"	Scenario 4 "Highway to Hell"
Progress on Climate Change	Kyoto signatories all making progress against climate change targets. Increasing number of signatories. U.S. signs up to principles but not the convention.	The United States creates its own internal process but refuses to sign Kyoto. Progress in some parts of the world countered by increasing impact of rapid industrialization in others. Europe introduces increasingly broad legislation, incentives, widening of carbon-trading schemes, and punitive tax measures to encourage reduction of emissions and a switch to alternative energy.	Kyoto is reworked, reworded, and watered down in an effort to sign up the world's most polluting economies. Progress of implementing legislation slows in most economies in the face of economic concerns.	Increasing numbers of climate-related disasters, coupled with limited public funds to address them, lead to a growing sense of inevitable crisis.

Appendix 6
Trend Analysis Workshop

Objectives

This exercise is designed to help participants identify key trends that could have the greatest impact on the association and to explore the critical implications, determining any resulting actions to pursue.

Approach

This workshop has been designed to run as a half-day event, although the length and scope could be extended or shortened as appropriate.

Preparation

Prior to the event, send all participants the set of trends included with this report and add to it any additional trends that you think are of importance.

Ask the participants to review the document as pre-reading, afterward identifying and describing any additional trends that should be considered; have them select the top five that they think could have the greatest impact on the association.

Workshop Structure

1. Plenary Group Activity—Framing the Day

- Remind participants of the objectives for the day. (5 minutes)
- Ask participants to select the sheets containing their top five trends from those distributed and from those they identified themselves, posting them on flipcharts carrying the relevant STEEP headings. (10 minutes)
- Divide the participants into five breakout groups: one per STEEP category. (5 minutes)

2. Breakout Group Activity—Trend Review

- Working in their breakout groups, have the participants review the list of trends on their flipchart and prioritize them according to their assessment of the likely scale of impact and importance for the association. For each of the top three prioritized trends, discuss how it is already being felt, and assess the impact it will have on the following: (60 minutes)

  - Members and their expectations of the associations that serve them
  - The association's purpose, strategic direction, and vision

- Core products and service offerings
- The service delivery model
- The organization model

- Additional questions syndicates could explore include

- How might competitors respond?
- How should we track the evolution of this trend?

- For each trend, determine whether it can be addressed through existing activity or whether a separate initiative is required to research it further to explore member impacts or to design and implement specific association responses.
- Where a specific response is required, define each action using the following framework: (30 minutes)

  - Trend being addressed
  - Why we need to address it (e.g., creates new opportunity to attract members)
  - Brief description of the task (e.g., scope of research)
  - Objectives
  - Key steps
  - Timescales
  - Expected benefits if we get an effective solution

3. Plenary Group Activity—Feedback and Prioritization

- Each breakout group should have a maximum of five minutes to share the list of trends evaluated with a brief assessment of the impact each would have. For those where actions were defined, a short overview should be given of the proposed actions. (30 minutes)
- The participants should then walk around and review the detailed action briefs and vote for the top three they think should be carried forward. The votes would then be counted and a prioritized list of actions produced. (20 minutes)
- A group discussion could then be used to assess the value of the day and how best to institutionalize such a process.

4. Close the Workshop

Some may want to use the exercise to drive specific action; others may want to use it as part of a broader strategic planning process. This will determine the extent to which specific actions can or should be committed to in closing the workshop.

Appendix 7
Mapping Your Personal Future

Objectives

This exercise is designed to help you think through your own personal future before going on to map the future of your association.

Approach

This exercise outlines a set of nine questions designed to help you think through and map out your preferred future. The exercise can be done in one sitting and revisited regularly or conducted over a period of days, weeks, or months as you explore the changes taking place in your world and start to evolve a vision of what you want to achieve.

1. *What is my "probable almost-certain future"?* If you continue on your current career path, what will your professional, personal, and family life look like in 5 to 10 years?

2. *What is my "preferred future"?* What are your true goals? What would happen if you could maximize or go beyond your probable almost-certain future and have what you really desire? What would success look like for you in 5 to 10 years? If you succeed, what will be happening in your organizational, professional, personal, and family life?

3. *What assumptions am I making?* What assumptions are you making about the world around you, the trends that will shape it, and the factors that will be important? What key changes do you assume will occur? What do you assume will not change about your external environment, work, family, and friends? How do the assumptions in your preferred future differ from those in your probable almost-certain future? Which negative assumptions start to disappear?

4. *Who are my future role models?* Who best display the key aspects of the future you want? Who's doing what you want to do? Who's displaying the behaviors you want to exhibit? There may be many—each doing parts well. The key is studying and practicing their behaviors.

5. *How do I make it happen?* What key steps will take you in the desired direction? What will you do in the next year, the next 6 months, the next 3 months, the next 30 days, next week, tomorrow? What comes first? Remember the vision; focus on those vital few tasks.

6. *What/who would be with me?* Which organizations, personal resources, and individuals are essential to your success? How many are already there? How can you bring in those elements that are missing in your life?

7. *What/who wouldn't be there?* What or who currently holds you back? What must you let go of? For example, which people drag you down, make you lose self-respect, or generally stop you believing in yourself and fulfilling your potential? How can you change your relationship with them in a sensitive manner or distance yourself from them?

8. *How do I make it sustainable?* How do you avoid trying to do too much too quickly, then losing momentum because you can't sustain it? How can you make the choices and changes stick? What lessons can you learn from your past successes?

9. *Who do I want as my future coach/conscience?*— Who could you ask to help you do regular progress reviews against your future roadmap? Choose people who will ask questions about what you are doing to achieve the vision without judging you, exploring what is and isn't working and helping you see what you can learn from both.